AF400569

For Uwe

And to my father

I have stated that Che Guevara did not die; that his death was a planed even, a screen script. To answer why, I had to ask other questions.
Why did you need a Hero?
Why start a revolution under the North America's nose?
Why did you need to plunder Angola of its resources?
Who did you need to create to produce such a spectral?
The little man standing on the corner had all the resources he needed to create 'Another New World Order.' That man was Gabriel Garcia Marquez.
As some of the statements are surprising; the facts with their relevant address are enclosed in the text.

Evelyn Guevara Lohmann

Gabriel Garcia Marquez
the creator of Che Guevara

Bibliografische Information der Deutschen Nationalbibliothek:
Die Deutsche Nationalbibliothek verzeichnet diese Publikation in der Deutschen Nationalbibliografie; detaillierte bibliografische Daten sind im Internet über http://dnb.dnb.de abrufbar.

Illustration: Evelyn Lohmann

Herstellung und Verlag: BOD – Books on Demand, Norderstedt

ISBN: 9783744894968

Gabriel Garcia Marquez the creator of Che Guevara

This book is to explain, how and who, were involved in the making of a propaganda hero Che Guevara. It is safe to say the Guevara family, were not the parental family of this hero, the Jurado family were; among them were international lawyers, film stars, Mexican statesmen.
Mexico City was Gabriel Garcia Marquez's home; his friends were statesmen from around the world. In Mexico he had the elate of show business, international lawyers, film stars, film producers to offer support, he connect the CIA and the drug world's Mafia.

They used the same script repeatedly; gave their actors different names; built a spy network around the globe.

Gabriel Garcia Marquez owned and ran large newspapers groups, owned and organized collages for journalist and producers of film, owned television and radio stations.

Gabriel Garcia Marquez was adviser to political leaders from Panama and the South Americas; presidents, Fidel Castro and Bill Clinton.

Gabriel Garcia Marquez was the man on the corner.

I apologize for using a computer translation program. A fantasy script for a film should not be thought of as true history.
'Spies-CIA-Lies-Terrorist-Che Guevara' explains why I was looking.

Chapter list
Gabriel Garcia Marquez the creator of Che Guevara.

Chapter one.
Another New World Order?

Questions I was beginning to ask.
Why place a revolution under the United States
nose? Cuba is around 80 kilometers away.
Why does Gabriel Garcia Marquez name pop up no
matter where I am investigating?
-He was Fidel Castro's best friend.
Ciro Bustos adviser in Bolivia as stated in his book-
'Che Wants To See You.'.
-Was he Ciro/Che Guevara's stage manager?
Did Gabriel Garcia Marquez want a new world
order?

Fidel and Gabo. A portrait of the legendary
friendship between Fidel Castro and Gabriel Garcia
Marquez. The book written by Angel Esteban and
Stephanie Panichelli has given me some of the
answers I have been looking for.

In their introduction they ask was it really Cuba's
revolution? The next thing they say is Gabriel
Garcia Marquez moved in political circles, referring
proposals from country to country, as Fidel Castro's
ambassador!

Gabriel Garcia Marquez association with Fidel
Castro started in 1948 in Bogota, as did the
association with Alfredo Guevara, who would
become the head of ICAIC. 'Insitituto Cubano del
Art e Industria Cinematograficos.' He was also there

with the rioting students, when Jorge Eliecer Gaitan the liberal leader of the opposition in Colombia was shot.

There are three of my actors in the rioting streets of Bogota, when a political leader in gunned down. That the group had to go the Cuban embassy, as it was said Cuban communists were behind the insurrection. They were not ordinary men having a day out!

Alfredo Guevara spends the early fifties in Mexico with the producer Manuel Barbachano Ponce who, not forgetting produced a regular film magazine in Cuba; at the same time.

Gabriel Garcia Marquez with Alfredo Guevara, Santiago Alvarez and Tomas Gutierrez Ale along with Julio Garcia Espinosa were involved in the political news paper, 'Nuestro Tiempo' during the fifties.

Julio Garcia Espinosa and Tomas Gutierrez Ale went to Rome to study film at the Central Sperimentale- Neorealism, where we find Gabriel Garcia Marquez as an assistant and script writer.

Angel Esteban and Stephanie Panichelli state that Jon Lee Anderson interviewed Gabriel Garcia Marquez in 1958. 1958. (Jon Lee Anderson he was the one that wrote the Che Guevara, a Revolutionary life- an absorbing and convincing book of fiction.)

Jon Lee Anderson was invited to write this book and spent three years with Che's second wife Aleida March Torres. Not forgetting he also spent one year in Malmo. He lived in the flat above Che/Ciro Bustos while constructing the said book.

In the Jon Lee Anderson's interview with Gabriel Garcia Marquez. Gabriel Garcia Marquez stated he was a close friend of dictator General Omar Torrijos of Panama, and he had traveled in the Soviet Union. In his articles of 1957/1958 he writes he had visited another dictator's tomb in Red Square, Stalin. (Was he collecting dictators?)

Gabriel Garcia Marquez had in the 18th of April 1958 published 'My Brother Fidel.' This was the year he met Elisabeth Burgos-Debray. (Another actress in the play, at this time she was not married to Regis Debray. They were married in Camiri, to brighten up his prison stay, or add romance to the prison scene.)

Gabriel Garcia Marquez was to ask her get him into the inner circle of the Revolutionary elite; she was a member of the Venezuelan Communist Party in 1958. You can also see her sitting with Fidel Castro when she was very young.

Interviews Document Long but Largely Ignored
anti-Castro Guerrilla War from ...
hoover.org

This lady invented the Biography of Ribogerta
Menchu with the idea of coursing unrest in
Guatemala. She and Regis Debray made the
arrangements for Che's Bolivian adventure. She
moved on to Chile to support Salvador Allende. As
for Regis Debray he was involved in the Cuban
Revolution at its start.

Friends are beginning to emerge on this page,
Regis Debray's books were being printed by
Giangiacomo Feltrinelli, who could be found in
Bolivia at the same time as the Che Guevara death

part; he had with him $50,000,000 to ease the planning.

If there was a hero he could have been Jorge Ricardo Masitti. He was given the news paper Prensa Latina to run; it is said by Che Guevara. Gabriel Garcia Marquez also wrote for this news paper. He had started with Apuleyo Mendoza the Magazine, 'Accion Liberal.'

Rodolfo Walsh was responsible for Prensa Latina's special services. Gabriel Garcia Marquez, Jorge Ricardo Masitti and Rodolfo Walsh!

The three mentioned were said to be close friends; Jorge Ricardo Masitti just happens to intercept a CIA massage which he is able to decode. The three make a counter plan for the CIA's preparations for the intended Bay of Pigs invasion. Gabriel Garcia Marquez immortalized this incident in his 'Recuerdos de periodista.' published in 1981.

Gabriel Garcia Marquez, Jorge Ricardo Masitti and Rodolfo Walsh must have been close to the Cuban government to offer them a counter plan.

Gabriel Garcia Marquez says he sat out the Bay of Pigs invasion in New York. He was intending to open a Prensa Latina office in Canada. Instead he was held up in the Latin Press office. Why would Gabriel Garcia Marquez feel under pressure in the safety of the New York office, if he was not involved in the Cuban Revolution!?

Gabriel Garcia Marquez seems to lose control of Prensa Latina as director of the news paper, Rodolfo Walsh, Jorge Ricardo Masitti were taken off stage,

the first one was assassinated the other walks off
into the jungle, his remains were not found.
There could be another reason why his remains
could not be found-

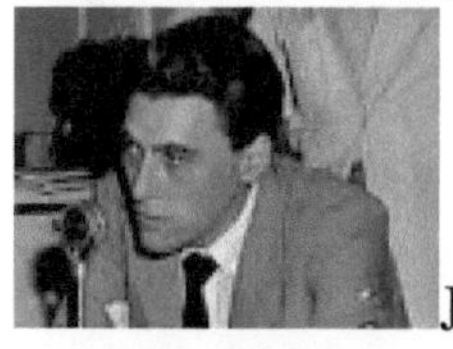Jorge Masetti.
En la semana del 21 al 25 de este mes, a 50 años de
su desaparición en la ...
anred.org

THE MAN WHO LIES, (L'Homme qui ment), Jean-Louis Trintignant, 1968

But Jorge Masetti died in 1964 or at best never seen again according to-
Wikipedia-

"Jorge Josè Ricardo Masetti Blanco (31 May 1929 – ?), also known as "Commander Segundo", was an Argentinean journalist and guerrilla. Born in <u>Avellaneda</u>, Masetti entered the jungle at <u>Salta</u> and after 21 April 1964 was not heard from again. He was the founder and the first director of the Cuban news agency <u>Prensa Latina</u>, and became the leader of one of Argentina's first guerrilla organizations, the <u>Guevarist</u> People's Guerrilla Army.

The reason Jorge Masetti is important is becouse we are told he played such a big part in the plans they were making for the South Amriecrs.

The Salta adventure I had thought had some truth in it even when I read Jounal Pampero Cordubensis. The editor is a Gabriel Pautasso's acount in. Ciro Bustos's repeated the acount in his book 'Che wants to see you.' The same story Jon Lee Anderson repeats in his book 'Che Guevara A Revolutiony Life.' But the same story is to be seen in the Bolivian Diaries! And now Jean-Louis Trintignant is the voice of Che in The Bolivian Diary, documentary Richard Dindo, Arte video."
Jon Lee Anderson gives credit to Richard Dingo for information, pictures in his book.
Lenardo Werthein name lead me to a program titled, 'Jounal Pampero Cordubensis. The editor is a Gabriel Pautasso.

Three things came out of this that surprised me. (Point A I have not found much to confirm this.)

A) *My grandmother was from a Russian Jewish family.*

B) *That Mario Vargas Llosa says that the bones in Cuba's mausoleum are not Che Guevara's.*

   Mario Vargas Llosa newspaper account from 10/3/2007 is the ‚Bones of Che'

C) *The account Ciro tells about building a guerrilla arm matches nearly word for word an account in, 'Journal Pampero Cordubensis. By Masetti.*

I had asked the editor of the journal who had written the report about the Salta Guerrillas as I was not sure the computer translation had not muddled up the author.

If Masetti was the author why is the account so near, word for word to the account I have read in Ciro Bustos book? As nothing before seems to match between one author to another is strange.

A revolutionary should be a solitary soul, but history shows they had lots of children, as if the starting point for revolution is love-Che want to see you. Stuck in my mind as both men used it. Masetti to make a revolution there must be love. - in Pampero Journal.

To talk about men dying of starvation, having to cook roots herbs is one thing but to use the same references is another!

The account written by Jon Lee Anderson of the time before the death party is also to liken to Ciro Bustos and Masetti's account of Salt. If you think I am thinking rubbish can you answer one question? Why make the same mistake twice?

From- "Richard Dindo's documentary, Arte video.

Based on the eponymous story of Ernesto Guevara on his Bolivian journey (ed. Arabian Nights or Maspero, exhausted). For those who do not speak or read Spanish or English, or who appreciate the talents of Christine readers and Jean-Louis Trintignant.

"Taking it as a starting point for the death of "Che" Guevara and thread notes for his diary of Bolivia, this documentary comes 27 years after the time of what was the last fight of the commander. In 1966, "Che" had mysteriously leafed Cuba. He actually headed to La Paz to swarm the revolution across South America from Bolivia. Size of the project, weakness means. Follow eleven months marked by simmering fighting between reduced troop of guerrillas in the Bolivian army supported by the CIA, and repeated failures to win the peasants to revolution. The words of "Che" and the voice of Jean-Louis Trintignant guide this journey who's outcome will die the commander and his myth born. The interviews collected over the course and the bias of achieving reposition the figure in the field of living memory."

Richard Dindo was the person who gave Jon Lee Anderson the Bolivian dairy and photos for him to use for his book.

Infact I found the simalarty of the adventures in Salta and Bolivia alarming but now Jean-Louis Trintignant photo likeness to Jorge Masetti make me feel sad; was that story faked as well?

Who are Jean-Louis Trintignant connections? Feltrinelli Giangiacomo

 Libri da Babuino ilfoglio.it
Libri da BabuinoEpitaffio per la Feltrinelli romana dove si poteva rubare rischiando alla peggio d'imbattersi in Günter Grass di <u>Redazione</u> |04 Agosto 2013
This article is in fact announcing the closing of the Feltrinelli's book shop.
Look who were at its opening-----
Gabriel García Márquez, Jean-Louis Trintignant, Gunter Grass.
(I will leave the computer English Translation as it is. It is to prove their connections.)

'From next January, it's official, will close the Feltrinelli bookshop in Via del Babuino. The first opened in Rome in 1964: half a century round and many stories to tell, and has already begun the race to "I remember, yes, I remember", with the corollary of the "inevitable it was that, there was that." It was all there, indeed: there were Elsa Morante and the '63 Group, Marcello Mastroianni and *Gabriel García Márquez*, Monica Vitti and Federico Fellini, De Martiis Pliny and Mario Schifano, Gian Maria Volonte and Mary McCarthy, *Jean-Louis Trintignant* and Simone Signoret ... All of the house, in the house of the books he wanted to be different, most modernizing, politician, electrifying, militant. There they could buy the first poster of Che Guevara and well Carnaby Street ties, in the year (1969) in which the British street fashion is its twin via the Baboon. In step with the times and new rhythms: so he had thought Giangiacomo Feltrinelli, who had personally chosen the local one step away from Piazza del Popolo, in the years when a lot of cultural-social life - Roman, national and even international - was gathering around there.

But we do not we will join a little 'cloying chorus that everything turns into the dusty Grandma Hope seating, including (not ever) that world that you wanted and imagined "non-conformist, counter, irreverent, provocative, transgressive, merciless and uncomfortable, discordant, anti-here and there-against. Among general consensus ", one might Alberto Arbasino. We do not, if only because we feel we appreciate more the stuffed parrot quoted seating compared to Günter Grass, another regular at the Baboon. Our real, deep regret about something and someone with that unrepeatable Feltrinelli had a lot to do in Rome between the Sixties, Seventies and even a little 'of the eighties. We are talking about an anonymous hero, the now extinct thief of books (common books, sold in bookstores, not those of the precious historical libraries: there the thieves still raging). Noble and daring figure who lived in that place, favored by the atmosphere uninhibited and compagnarda, lush season. If not encouraged at least not enough dissuaded, young and old leftists tried, in the pews of the Feltrinelli Via del Babuino, the thrill of expropriation kind and culturally authorized, in the natural order of things. The books were still - today it seems incredible - the subject of real yearning, while budgets were often empty, and, above all, it had not yet invented the anti shoplifting alarm system. But having read or not some novel or some pamphlet yet made the difference, and that was enough to transform poor young intellectuals thieves deftly. Even the chief librarian, the mustachioed Carlo Conticelli, educated man, affectionately gruff, always open to tips, represented an effective deterrent. If you pecked - happened - did not call the swift, it is obvious. The same Inge Feltrinelli, recalling long ago years sumptuous and festive the Baboon, told that only Fellini, among the many celebrity clients of the bookstore, bought and paid immediately in cash, in times "in which no one had any money." He stole everything: Sartre and Lin Piao, Fachinelli and Pasternak, Bulgakov and Borges, London and Mayakovsky. Someone also reminds vocabularies disappeared beneath able coats and / or eskimo. Today, we should find the desire to steal Saviano or Labor. But then what about the wound to legality?

(In Senior Service there are interesting references- One states that Gabriel García Márquez, was often marked in Giangiacomo Feltrinelli's dairy for various meeting.)

Look at what *INGE FELTRINELLI has to say- and who were connected to the book shop and the Cinema.*
"In 1960 via the Baboon was a dusty road and died, except for a few d 'antique shop. The moment took shape the artistic avant-garde, the 'opening of the Libreria Feltrinelli was throughout the neighborhood as the' arrival of a locomotive: immediately became the reference point for those who worked at Cinecitta. C 'were Jean-Louis Trintignant, Simone Signoret, and c' was naturally Federico Fellini, who had a house nearby, in via Margutta. He never slept the night and arrived in bookstores in the morning early, virtually opened along with the cleaning ladies. He was one of the very few who bought and paid cash, an amazing thing for those times when no one had any money. Thanks to him, who always

paid much attention to the literary innovations of young people, the authors have also been discovered as Pino Cacucci. In addition to books, the Feltrinelli bookshop in via del Babuino surged through the shelves of the first gadgets: the first poster of Che Guevara was sold by us, c 'were the ties coming from Carnaby Street, the first jukebox. Home to many literary and artistic events, the Feltrinelli the Baboon had become a true cultural center. Of course in those years came and went all the international artists, actors, writers, many beautiful women, but no one who ever would pay a book! It was a world of penniless, people with empty pockets. But 1 'in compensation atmosphere was always extraordinary. Among the sensational episodes of that season, there was a representation of the show The Deputy by Rolf Hochhuth, with Gian Maria Volonte, who had been considered blasphemous by the Vatican. It was decided to do it to represent in the warehouse, in that space where today you do the book launches. That day, after the performance, the police arrived. With us he c 'was also the writer Mary McCarthy, and then Giangiacomo Feltrinelli told the agents "do not happen by chance, c' is an internationally renowned writer." C 'were then the young painters of the Roman School: Giosetta Fioroni, Tano Festa, Mario Schifano, Franco Angeli. And again, the young literary vanguard of Group 63: Angelo Guglielmi, Nanni Balestrini, Alberto Arbasino, Alfredo Giuliani, Elio Pagliarini ~ I remember so many people around this movement. For example, Luisa

Spagnoli, a true patron of 'art, which always opened his big house for meals and parties. I remember Alberto Moravia, sniffing books, always come to us after being at the Rose Bar. I remember Monica Vitti, beautiful. And the old Carlo Emilio Gadda, with a large and serious cold face, from Lombard. All they considered him a master and greeted him saying "Good morning, engineer." All this happened until the end of the seventies: then, as the years of lead, even go to the bookstore had become dangerous. C 'was less political activity but more afraid, people were tapped home. However, in that 'time, but basically since the Sixties, the books had a much stronger value today, mainly because there' was less television. The reference to that 'time writers were masters such as Gabriel Garcia Marquez, Manuel Puig, Manuel Scorza, Ingeborg Bachman, Gunter Grass, all arrived in Italy thanks to our publishing house and the Feltrinelli Library. In particular Moravia had contacts with foreign writers: it was a very generous man, gave advice to young writers, the afternoon was always the movies, then went to the library and tried "the most beautiful lady of the house" to get invited to dinner. I was already at that time I was a close friend, among others, Alberto Arbasino. Many meetings were happening even in the small Amerigo piano-bar near the Feltrinelli, where Eugenio Scalfari I remember playing the piano singing La Vie en Rose. It was a season in which he always held great feasts in Rome because l 'avant-garde art was more alive than ever.

Some ladies willingly opened their homes to see
them full of artists and writers, people from film and
books. Besides Luisa Spagnoli, as I said, c 'was also
the Countess beans Brandolini and then the
superintendent of the d' modern art gallery, Palma
Bucarelli, beautiful and elegant, he always had with
him at least three admirers. Behold, the library was
the real star of Via del Babuino: happenings,
meetings, going all there, in a truly magical moment
for Rome that has not repeated that 'intensity and
that' happiness. "

INGE FELTRINELLI <u>June 28, 2003</u> **sez.**
This is an interesting connection to find- El Che –
In this one film you can bring together Regis
Debray- Richard Dindo- Pierre Kalflon- Jean-Louis
Trintignant. Connects you to Jon Lee Anderson---.
<u>El Che - Enquête sur un homme de légende:</u>
<u>Amazon.fr: Maurice ...</u>
https://www.amazon.fr/El-Che-Enquête-
homme.../B004CG2IH6
... sur un homme de légende. *Maurice Dugowson*
(Réalisateur) Classé: Tous publics Format : DVD ...
Interview de *Régis Debray* (10' - VF) Interview de
Carmen ...
<u>El Che - Chro</u>
www.chronicart.com › Cinéma
24.04.2000 - Le premier, El Che,, de Maurice
Dugowson, est co-scénarisé par *Pierre Kalfon,*
l'auteur d'un Che aux Éditions du Seuil. ... La
démarche du film de Richard Dindon, Le journal de
Bolivie, une reprise de 1994, ... *Richard Dindo*

"It was thirty years ago, on 9 October 1967, the guerrilla Ernesto Che Guevara fell under the bullets of the Bolivian army. This anniversary has already resulted in the publication of several provided biographies. Both documentaries are now showing. The first, *El Che,* Mauritius Dugowson, is co-scripted by Pierre Kalfon, author of *Che* Editions du Seuil. His producer, namely Fabienne Servan-Schreiber, discount get a hit in theaters. Twelve copies of the film are being distributed -including four in the Parisienne- region; an output of this magnitude is extremely rare in the documentary field. The bet is bold, but, given the media coverage it receives, it should bring a lot. It is feared that the film Maurice Dugowson do not really have other ambitions. Merely a linear development of the life of Che and a paraphrase of the book of Kalfon, pouring too often in the story, the documentary can never maintain the necessary distance from the images he offers. So it cannot get rid of the age-old question which is that of the construction of the myth révolutionnaire.La approach Film Richard Turkey, *The Bolivian Diary,* a recovery in 1994 is itself much more interesting. The narrative is based on the book drive has held Che during his year of Bolivian guerrillas. The camera simply follows the route of the troop and simply accompanies the words from beyond the grave came from the newspaper scroll leaving a desperately empty landscape. Here Ernesto Guevara traveled to himself, debunked, almost human. It seems possible that the wandering soul of Che can finally find a decent burial.

Regis Debray- Interview is to be seen in **El Che**.
                His work was printed by
                Feltrinelli Giangiacomo.
(Most people's work was printed by
                Feltrinelli Giangiacomo.)
Regis Debray was in prison with Ciro Bustos.
Richard Dindo- gave Jon Lee Anderson a copy of the Bolivian Diary;
                Jon Lee Anderson wrote the book
'Che Guevara a revolutionary life,'
                using this information.
Richard Dindo produced the Film **El Che**.
Pierre Kalflon- co-scripted **El Che** and has written a
        book about Che and Fidel Castors' man in Chili-
                Salvador Allende.
Jean-Louis Trintignant- is the commentator in the film- El Che.

    The next step I took was to compare wives of Jean-Louis Trintignant and Jorge Masetti; each had more than one wife.
Jean-Louis Trintignant=Nadine Marquand and Stephane Audran, Marianne Hoepfner.

Jorge Masetti= Dora Clelia Jury and Conchita Dumios.

I could not find any photos of Dora Clelia Jury, she is said to be the mother of Garciela and Jorge Masetti jr. Who was an agent for Fidel Castro.

Jorge Maseitti jr

(Jorge Masetti jr was born in 1955 in Argentina, but grew up in Cuba. In 1974 he starts as agent of their services of espionage Cuban, its activity in several fronts of Latin America that continued uninterruptedly until the sadly famous «process Ochoa». That was started in 1989 by Fidel Castro who feared the United States would reveal their evidence of the involvement of Cuba in the traffic of drugs and of ivory. This process culminates with the condemns to death of the general Arnaldo Ochoa hero of war in Africa, and Antonio de la Guardia and Patrick, his twin brother.

Jorge Masetti Jr was Antonio de la Guardia's son-in-law-

Illeana de la Guardia- Who in turn **godfather was Gabriel García Márquez**.

Jorge Masetti wrote down his experiences they were published in 1993 'El Furor y el delirio.'

Conchita Dumois proved to be most interesting!
It is said she had a draught with Jorge Masetti-Laura.
She just happened to have written Jorge Massetti's memories.

She had close associations with Alieda March- Che 2nd wife.

She was one of Gabriel García Márquez writers. Her closest friends were Mercedes García Márquez and Gabriel García Márquez.

De izquierda a derecha, Ricardo Sáenz, Gabriel Molina, Conchita Dumois, Gabo, Marta Rojas, Juan Marrero y Joaquín Oramas.

"And I insist that after 1964 was so faithful to Masetti as it had been before when he participated in project momentum agency Prensa Latina to oxygenate the world with truth and not lies, distortions and manipulations of agencies and media serving hegemonic forces, particularly the United States. Each time the Gabo came to Cuba, and whenever he could, made contact with Conchita Dumois, widow of Masetti (now deceased), and had enjoyable encounters with some of the founders of the agency and other figures of Cuban journalism. Central themes of these meetings: journalism in Cuba and, of course, the important role of Prensa Latina, that next June 16 celebrates 55 years of life, although the imperial forces gave most a month of life."

In 'La Policia Secreta Mexicana Espioa Gabo Imagenes) Eipionero.com. Conchita Dumois.
 This program states that the Mexican Secret Police observed in 1981 Regis Debray and a member of the Cuban Communist Party Conchita Dumois, were gusts in his house; she was present at his funeral. Mercedes García Márquez.
 Interesting to find such a close relationship; which would have meant nothing had Jean-Louis Trintignant not so closely resemble Jorge Masetti.

 UNEAC- Union of writers and artists of Cuba
 Follow the twist and turns with the UNEAC- Union of writers and artists of Cuba with Alfredo Guevara and with the ICAIC Insitituto Cubano del Art e Industria Cinematograficos- to find most of the names mentioned in chapter- 'Interesting People' connected to the world of poetry and or as a writer, their names appear again in Angel Esteban and Stephanie Panichelli's book.

Fidel Castro and Gabriel Garcia Marquez, Alfredo Guevara along with others had planned a Latin American Revolution as far back as 1948. No one wanted to be blatant about it then, but slowly and systematic they have built the means to do so. Gabriel Garcia Marquez builds relationships with those that can support this idea. Gabriel Garcia Marquez states he is a defender of the Latin American revolution movement. He defends Salvador Allende for sending the Chilean president Pinochet a telegram! Pinochet must have been upset at some stage with Gabriel Garcia Marquez as he had his books burnt publicly.

Did Gabriel Garcia Marquez with Fidel Castro really express the desire to unite the Latin American world? Both have at one time or another! Was it just an observation Gabriel Garcia Marquez notes in his novel, 'The General and His Labyrinth' "Simon Bolivar's wish to create the largest country from Mexico to Cape Horn?"

If Fidel Castro was in the habit of reading Gabriel Garcia Marquez's texts for his novels, he must also have read his articles about Cuba in Angola. 1977 Gabriel Garcia Marquez published an article 'Operation Carlota: Cuba in Angola.' it was first published in the Colombian news paper El Espectador. Cuba sent 50,000 men to support MPLA and 300,000 Cubans fought under the name of international solidarity. It is Gabriel Garcia Marquez who tells us that Cuba gave aid to Algeria in the early years of Cuba's Revolution. Aid was extended

to Mozambique, to Guinea-Bissau and the
Cameroon as well as Sierra Leone. Aid had been
provided since the sixties.

*I had read the Soviet Union used Cuban men as if
they were their own.*

Pierre Kalfon

Pierre Kalfon- he was a rock idle, a university
professor. Salvador Allende's adviser, Che
Guevara's biographer and a film actor, he fits into
the packet with Lean luc Godard and the lady that
played Che's sister. I wonder if Angel Esteban and
Stephanie Panichelli know he may have stood in as a
double for Che?

Carmen Belcells- she was Gabriel Garcia
Marquez's literary agent. She was supposed to have
made contact with Danilo Bartulin, he had been the
chief of security under Salvador Allende. Was it
from him Gabriel Garcia Marquez heard that
Salvador Allende wanted to be left alone to die?

The conservative Colombian president Belisario
Betancur Cuatas offered Gabriel Garcia Marquez
various government posts and an ambassador ship
for both Madrid and Paris! He was twice invited to
run for Colombia as president. The then Nobel Prize
winner turned the offers down. But this man is at his
own admission was present at Paraiso on Contadora
Island. Where he says, three people were involved in
the recuperation of the Panama Canal.They were,
Carlos Andres Perez-Venezuela and Alfonso Lopez

Michelsen- Colombia, Omar Torrijos- Panamanian leader. Each one was presidents of their countries.

Gabriel Garcia Marquez says Felipe Gonzalez was his disciple, who would become the president of Spain.

Gabriel Garcia Marquez wrote articles about Omar Torrijos and talks about the CIA infiltrating the radical groups of 'The Left' in exile in Panama. It has been recorded that he remarked to Jimmy Carter's negotiator that the best thing they could do was give back the Panama Canal. If they did not they would be screwed around for many years till they said take back it back your goddamn canal.

Gabriel Garcia Marquez is diplomat at large! Sregio Ramirez was a Nicaraguan writer and politician, Gabriel Garcia Marquez and he met in RIT studios. Sregio Ramirez asked Gabriel Garcia Marquez go to Caracas to suggest to Carlos Andres Perez president of Venezuela that the triumph for the Sandinista revolution was imminent; would he recognize the new government of Felipe Mantica? Felipe Mantica's secret government were living in exile in Costa Rica.

Did Gabriel Garcia Marquez really say in El Nacional, Alternativa 1978, that it was Jimmy Carter's view that Somoza could not fall as long as the Sandinista Front existed, because they wanted to establish a regime like Cuba's in Nicaragua? (Anastasio Somoza Debayle was a dictator/president of Nicaragua from 1967 to 1972 and from 1974 to

1979. He used the interim years as head of the
National Guard, when others exercised the
presidency. Wikipedia.)

Cuba was supplying large amounts of ammunition
and men to aid the conflict. The men from Chili and
Uruguay all trained in Cuba. There was an aerial
corridor between Havana, Panama and Liberia.
Carlos Andres Perez- Venezuela also sent arms.

Jorge Masetti jr not to be confused with his father,
in his book 'El Furor y el delirio' tell us he
witnessed the happenings, states that Gabriel Garcia
Marquez buried the information not wanting to harm
the image of the revolution. Just to note, Elisabeth
Burgos-Debray wrote the foreword to Jorge Masitti
son of Jorge Ricardo Masetti, book. 'El Furor y el
delirio'

Gabriel Garcia Marquez before winning the
Nobel Prize, he had to get himself and his wife out
of Colombia. To have heard that there was a military
plot against him must have been hard.

President Belisario Betancur asked his old friend to return from exile with honor. Before he had received the Nobel Prize he was honored with awards from France, Mexico and Cuba.

Colombia's next president Virgilio Barco called Gabriel Garcia Marquez Colombia's great ambassador.

Cesar Gaviria the president after Virgilio Barco also a close friend of Gabriel Garcia Marquez, as a close friend he took the role of mediator and counselor to Cesar Gaviria on various national and international matters.

Cesar Gaviria gave a birthday party for Gabriel Garcia Marquez, where they had the idea to fix a meeting with Bill Clinton. The idea was mentioned to William Styron, he in turn passed the request on to his friend.

Gabriel Garcia Marquez's friend was Ernesto Samper, he was Gabriel Garcia Marquez's guest when they visited Cuba and met Fidel Castro, before he became Colombia's president, it was reported in **the Magazine 'Semana'.**

Moving onto the next president! Andries Pastrana he relied on Gabriel Garcia Marquez as his personal adviser- So much so they went together to the United States to met Bill Clinton.

Alvaro Uribe the next in line continued the growing tradition of becoming close friends with Gabriel Garcia Marquez.

If every Colombian president had to be close friends with Gabriel Garcia Marquez it is not surprising he did not need to be president himself.

Gabriel Garcia Marquez stared a new independent newspaper in Colombia the same year as his Nobel Prize. There is truth in the words, 'the pen is mightier than the sword.'

This fact comes over clearly in Angel Esteban and Stephanie Panichelli's book.

Did Pablo Neruda- supposed to be Che's favored poet and Chili's ambassador in Paris 1971, did he really lobby Jake Mitterrand and the Nobel Prize committee on Gabriel Garcia Marquez's behalf? I bet Mario Vargas Llosa was lobbying as well. Regis Debray was reportedly at the diner when Gabriel Garcia Marquez was told he had the prize. His friendship with Jake Mitterrand brought him in contact with Olof Palme, the Swedish prime minister. Who was interested in Latin American issues. (This would explain why Che/Ciro Bustos lived in Sweden.)

Who is was Gerardo Molina Ramirez? He is according to Wikipedia he was an intellectual writer and Colombian Politician. It was three times member of Congress (1933-1935, 1939-1941, 1962-1964), a columnist for the daily El Espectador, senator (1935-1939 and 1982), ombudsman of Bogota (1942-1943) Rector of the National University of Colombia (1944-1948), rector of the Free University (1955 and 1960-1962), a candidate for the Presidency of the Republic (1982), member of the Committee for the Defense of Human Rights during the administration of Belisario Betancur Cuatas, and member of the Peace Commissions named during the administrations of Presidents Julio Cesar Tubay Ayala and Belisario Betancur Cuatas.

Why is Gerardo Molina Ramirez interesting, because he wrote in El Espectador on February 13, 1980. "Gabriel Garcia Marquez the novelist has become identified with the revolutionary experiment."

Revolutionary experiment! Did Gerardo Molina Ramirez really write Gabriel Garcia Marquez could pass for a leader of the Cuban revolution?!

(On every crossroad, every junction I have found Gabriel Garcia Marquez standing, whether it is with films or books or plain politics. There stands this man; this small man takes Fidel Castro in his arms, puts him in front to a revolutionary experiment so others can copy, and sets the blue print right under the noses of the North Americans.

Did Gabriel Garcia Marquez really dream of making a country: one nation, free and unified, from Mexico to Cape Horn?

He would not be the only man to have written his intentions in a novel. He had the means, he had the connections, and he held the power in his hands.)

Gabriel Garcia Marquez dinned with the president of Sweden, Olof Pame, when he was in Sweden to receive the Nobel Prize. It is stated in Angel Esteban and Stephanie Panichelli's book, after a detailed analysis the decision was made to contact the six presidents of Central America to urge them to undertake peace talks. 'Never had Central America been so close to al out war; 1981'

There is another close friend of Gabriel Garcia Marquez the Spanish politician Carlos Fuentes; Carlos Fuentes was also a close friend of Fidel Castro!

(Anthony Quinn was in the film 'Man from Del Rio, 1956 with Katy Jurado.

Anthony Quinn repeated the experience in 1957 with Anna Magnani in the film 'Wild is the word.' This would not be interesting if Gabriel Garcia Marquez had not been offered one million dollars for the dramatic writs to 'One Hundred Years of Solitude, by Anthony Quinn. The condition was another million dollars be given to the revolution in Cuba and Latin America. If Gabriel Garcia Marquez was not happy with the aid received by his friend the French President Jake Mitterrand; other means had to be explored.)

Gabriel Garcia Marquez was the man that pointed out there is the United States of Mexico and the United States of Brazil. But the United States, United States of what? While I was enthralled with the last sentence I nearly missed the relevance of what Angel Esteban and Stephanie Panichelli were telling me!

Gabriel Garcia Marquez acted as an intermediary-between Cuba, Colombia and the United States.

Gabriel Garcia Marquez worked with the President of Colombia Andrés Pastrana Arango, from 1998 to 2002. He brought Andrés Pastrana Arango into contact with Fidel Castro, with the intention that Fidel Castro would insure a dialogue with the active guerrillas.

Gabriel Garcia Marquez- helped restore relations between Bogota and Washington
Gabriel Garcia Marquez met with President Bill Clinton to mediate on subjects concerning-

The lifting of the embargo.

The Cuban raft crisis.

Report on the results of decisions between the Colombian government and the Guerrillas.
Gabriel Garcia Marquez pointed out that the Cuban government had the closest contacts with the Guerrillas. Therefore Cuba was an important in the necessary negotiations.

As Andrés Pastrana Arango could travel to Cuba under two hours to attend necessary meetings, Gabriel Garcia Marquez pointed out again the important position of Cuba.

Monica Lewinsky's name has come up before; before I saw her name in Angel Esteban and Stephanie Panichelli's book; it can be found in Juan F Benemelis book 'Las Guerras Secetas de Fidel Castro.' Juan F Benemelis says Monica Lewinsky was accused of spying for Moscow.

(As Gabriel Garcia Marquez wrote about Bill Clinton, he was sympathetic about the lady in the broom cupboard. Maybe it was one of his or Fidel Castro's little tricks!? Don't quote me on this it is just one of my gut feelings.)

Again and again Alfredo Guevara's name comes up he is described a powerful man in the Cuban Government. He was also the director of the ICACI. The Cuban Institute of the Cinematic Arts and Industry.

(Fidel Castro and Gabriel Garcia Marquez, Alfredo Guevara's association began in 1948 at the time of turmoil in Bogota. Alfredo Guevara was considered one of the most important men in Cuba.)

Gabriel Garcia Marquez calls on his help in 1980, at the time intellectuals were are being persecuted for being homosexual and counterrevolutionary; they were trying to leave Cuba. The situation became so intense with those wishing to leave Cuban resorted to rafts!

<u>Mariel boatlift - Wikipedia, the free encyclopedia</u>

*https://en.wikipedia.org/wiki/**Mariel_boatlift***
The *Mariel boatlift* was a mass emigration of Cubans who departed from Cuba's Mariel Harbor for the United States between April 15 and October 31, 1980.
<u>Background</u> - <u>Prelude</u> - <u>Exodus</u> - <u>United States Naval and Marine</u> ...

Wikipedia describes it adequately, but I will add Fidel Castro's regime added a few spies for good luck to those wishing to leave!

Among others that wished to leave were Juan F Benemelis- 'Las Guerras Secetas de Fidel Castro.' He left in 1980.

Angel Esteban and Stephanie Panichelli tells us that Norberto Fuentes was among those that are named in bring Gabriel Garcia Marquez into Cuba's high society and therefore to Fidel Castro notice. What does make this remark interesting is the connection to Colonel Tony De la Guardia and General Arnaldo Ochoa.

Why are they interesting? As they were executed by firing squad in 1989 for their connections to the world of trafficking arms and drugs! (Which is a joke as Fidel Castro was deeply involved in trafficking arms and drugs.)

Gabriel Garcia Marquez name in connection with Alfredo Guevara-

I point out Alfredo Guevara was the director to the ICIAIC. **The Cuban Institute of the Cinematic Arts and Industry**. The fantasy film world! The foundation of the New Latin American Cinema was established in 1985 by the committee of Latin American Film Producers. Its headquarters was located close to Gabriel Garcia Marquez and Fidel Castro's mansions in the outskirts of Havana.

New Latin American Cinema has its origins further back in time, between 1952 and 1955 four of the fonder members were studying at the Center of Experimental Cinematography in Rome with Gabriel Garcia Marquez were Julio Garcia Espinosa and the Vice-Minister of Culture of films; Fernando Birri and Tomas Gutierrez.

It is important to mention that in 1954, Gabriel Garcia Marquez wrote a weekly column in the news paper El Espectador; on which films were opening in Bogota. It must have been an exciting experience discovering the Olympia Theater and the traveling school of Alvaro Cepeda. Before he went to Rome! Álvaro Cepeda Samudio - Wikipedia, the free encyclopedia
https://en.wikipedia.org/.../Álvaro_Cepeda_Samudio
Álvaro Cepeda Samudio (March 30, 1926 – October 12, 1972) was a .... not have been possible had he not partaken in "*the traveling school of Álvaro Cepeda*".

The Center of Experimental Cinematography in Rome is where Gabriel Garcia Marquez met and assisted Alessando Blasetti; his name did not make a direct connation to any of names in, 'The four in one lady.' The name that did appear was Cesare Zavattini his name connects to Katy Jurado and Anna Magnani. In the Children of Sanchez he must have met Katy Jurado; he was the scriptwriter, as he was for Anna Magnani, 'Soggetto' and 'Bellissima.'

The foundation of the New Latin American Cinema also has an exchange program with the 'Sundance Institute in Utah, run by the actor and director Robert Redford.

What is important is the founding of the International School of film and Television in San Antonio de los Banos; where Gabriel Garcia Marquez, Anna Magnani- Pier Paolo Pasolini and others have come together. The columniation of ideas they had been using as early as 1952! Gabriel Garcia Marquez, Fidel Castro, Raul Castro, Alfredo Guevara were ready to make 'Che Guevara'!

Max Marambio, a Chilean with many talents, he was sponsored by Fidel Castro when he was in Cuba in 1966 to train in the 'Special Troops' in the early seventies. He returned to Chile to lead the 'Group of friends of the President- GAP.' He was in charge of security for Salvador Allende.

Joel *Max Marambio* Rodríguez (n. Santa Cruz, 1947) es un empresario, productor cinematográfico y político chileno. En Cuba desarrolló una exitosa carrera ...
Estudios - Carrera empresarial - Productor de cine - El hermano

The Spanish Wikipedia is more helpful than the English! Max Marambio provided financial services to both Cuba and Chile. A personal friend to Fidel Castro, he involved in the Cuban intelligence for many years.   Max Marambio was able to amass a huge personal fortune; he was director of CIMEX-Corporation for Importation and Exportation, from 1978 to 1993.

Max Marambio's name is linked to the revelations regarding Fidel Castro's private bank account.

In 1983 Max Marambio formed a film production company, which was a holding company for 'International Network Group' to bring together other companies from Chile, Ecuador, Mexico, Cuba, and Spain.

To come back to Gabriel Garcia Marquez, Max Marambio was personally involved in the founding of the Foundation of New Latin American Cinema. With his financial activities he supported the administration of International School of film and Television in San Antonio de los Banos.

Susan Sontag name also come up at the end of 'Fidel & Gabo.' She was the lady that translated Che Guevara's work and she is connected to the ICAIC Insitituto Cubano del Art e Industria Cinematograficos and the UNEAC- Union of writers and artist of Cuba.

She is the lady I feel plaid the part of Tamara Haydee Bunke 'Tania'. It is not a surprise to see her defined Gabriel Garcia Marquez when he was called on to speak out against the planed executions of General Tony De la Guardia and General Arnaldo Ocha. Who were supposedly tried and executed for drug-trafficking. (Colombian cocaine was exchanged for arms for the Guerrillas.1988.)

Tony De la Guardia was the father of Ileana De la Guardia, she married Jorge Masitti the son of Jorge Ricardo Masetti, and Gabriel Garcia Marquez acted as godfather for Jorge Masitti's stepsister, at her wedding. He hung paintings by Tony De la Guardia and his twin brother Patricio De la Guardia in his house, he attend their family events.

Gabriel Garcia Marquez did not support his friends, he supported a dictator and their planed intentions- he chose another World Order.

Chapter two.
Hotel Nacional De Cuba. Italian
Neorealism Instituto Cubano del Art e Industria
Cinematograficos. ICAIC

The History of the HOTEL NACIONAL DE CUBA - Among its ...

www.hotelnacionaldecuba.com/en/history.asp
In the same month, Commander-In-Chief *Fidel Castro* founded the Ana Betancourt .... the Mafia bosses, Bola de Nieve, Tyron Power, Gary Cooper, *Agustín Lara*, Jorge Negrete.

I put in Fidel Castro's name along with that of Agustin Lara to find the history of Hotel Nacional De Cuba. Ironic to think that this hotel was built by American film moguls in the late twenties. Anyone that was anyone has passed through it doors, even when Castro took it over; it was used by him and 'Che Guevara' as their head quarters.

It was the center where many paths crossed, every actor and actress of the time, every writer producer and camera man-woman, every politician and political mined person met there. A place to stimulate any revolution!

In fact all the names I have come across, in the time span I have been looking at, have passed through its doors. Names from the Mafia and film moguls will appear many times as they are twisted in the allusion of 'Che Guevara.'

Gabriel Garcia Marques lived in this hotel when he was staying in Cuba, before Fidel Castro gave him a villa next to his.

Italian Neorealism

The Italian Neorealism provides many of the contacts and links, just to list them would be boring but it might help us to understand how Gabriel Garcia Marquez was involved. He started to learn his trade with their principles.

Italian Neorealism *'The rejection of reconstruction and rhetoric meant by implication creating a "true" and near-reality film, which is more political action as a cinematic narrative (every film is always part of a dramaturgical rules). Unlike Nazism in Germany so Italian fascism permits certain pluralism in the art. Against this background, unfolds with the Neorealism already during, and vehemently after the end of World War II, the second flowering of Italian cinema.'*

'As the context of artistic achievement in the New Cinema unfolded, tended to the forefront and experimentation. Boom literature, which has the Colombian writer Gabriel García Márquez as one of its main exponents, built new types of fiction and magical realism and magical realism, based on the identification of own cultural dynamics. As for the European influences are felt Italian Neorealism, French New Wave cinema and free English.' Is how a Wikipedia explains it.

<u>The Untold Story | Havana Streetview</u>
<u>www.havanastreetview.com/hmotiv/untold-story</u>
03.08.2014 - Pre-revolutionary cinema *radio* and *television* in *Cuba*: the untold story ... after the *Cuban* Revolution in January 1959 was the *Cuban* Film *Institute*. ... García Espinosa, Tomás Gutiérrez Alea, *Alfredo Guevara* and José Massip.

A team of four film activists of the post-revolutionary cinema collaborated in 1955 to produce the documentary *El Mégano* (1955). They were Julio García Espinosa, Tomás Gutiérrez Alea, Alfredo Guevara and José Massip. Two of them had studied with Nobel Prize and founder of the International of Film and Television School of San Antonio de los Baños, Gabriel García Márquez at the Institute of Cinematography in Rome. Hence the remarkable influence of Italian Neorealism in Cuban cinema in the early sixties. *El Mégano* is perhaps the boldest criticism of its time to the plight of the Cuban working class as it portrays the harsh working conditions of charcoal makers in the 'Zapata Swamp'.

Instituto Cubano del Art e Industria
Cinematograficos
ICAIC

Alfredo Guevara- became director of ICAIC in 1959

The history of ICAIC is an interesting subject on its own; it gave them the tools to create a hero like Che Guevara.

The Club of Havana was founded in 1948, to become the film club in 1953 and at Fidel Castro's request Alfredo Guevara became director of ICAIC in 1959 two months after Fidel Castro had his hand over Cuba.

Alfredo Guevara first became friends with Fidel Castro when they went together to Colombia in 1948 for an international student conference, and found themselves caught up in the riots, known as the Bogotazo, sparked off by the assassination of the popular presidential candidate Jorge Gaitán, whom they were supposed to be meeting.

Alfredo Guevara stated, Fidel was not a communist, and it was Alfredo Guevara who first introduced him to the writings of Marx. Alfredo Guevara could combine cinema with a political commitment to the leader of a popular revolution.

Alfredo Guevara was said to have been born in 1925. His father was a railway engineer who was one of the founders of the railway workers union. He was a member of the cultural society, Nuestro Tiempo-Our Times. It is said he was not a member of the 'Che Guevara' family.

Alfredo Guevara belonged to an extraordinary generation of filmmakers with Santiago Alvarez (1919-1998), Tomas Gutierrez Alea (1928-1996) and Julio Garcia Espinosa (b.1926). All of them were members of Nuestro Tiempo during the 1950s. This group was close to the Young Communists to which Alfredo also belonged.

Tomas Gutierrez Alea and Julio Garcia Espinosa went to Rome to study film at the Centro Sperimentale; the hotbed of Neorealism.

Alfredo Guevara had to flee to Mexico after entering the urban underground, narrowly escaping with his life.

Mexico is where he learned the trade of the producer with Manuel Barbachano Ponce, including a stint as an assistant on Buñuel's *Nazarín*, whose spirit of anti-clericalism he shared. Barbachano Ponce also produced a regular ten-minute film magazine in Cuba on which the group served their apprenticeships, sometimes contributing comic sketches.

Tomas Gutierrez Alea and Julio Garcia Espinosa were seated in Italy, Rome and its cinema center, into the circles where Pier Palo Pasolini and Feltrinelli were-

Manuel Barbachano Ponce (April 4, 1925 – October 29, 1994) was a Mexican film producer, director, and screenwriter. A great-grandson of Miguel Barachano y Tarraso, a five-time governor of Yucatan, he was born in Mérida, Yucatán, Mexico.

(He produced a film with Katy Jurado, 'Torerro'.

Alfredo Guevara worked with Luis Bunuel on the film, 'Nazarin.'

Katy Jurado acted in Luis Bunuel's film, El Bruto.)

In <u>Joaquín Ordoqui and the "greatness of the revolution"</u> you can find a small remark confirming Alfredo Guevara's political involvement. And, if show how to connect him to Colonel Nicolai Leonov and the Eusebio Lopez Azcue, who really were Victor Pina Cardoso, Consul of Cuba in Mexico at the time of the assassinate of John F. Kennedy.

El blog de Tania Quintero: Joaquín Ordoqui y la "grandeza de la ...
taniaquintero.blogspot.com/.../joaquin-ordoqui-y-la-grandeza-de... ▾ Diese Seite übersetzen
01.02.2016 - Joaquín Ordoqui y la "grandeza de la revolución" ... Mesa, que Roberto Fandiño tecleó para dar copias a Chomón, Alfredo Guevara y el G-2.

El blog de Tania Quintero: febrero 2016
taniaquintero.blogspot.com/2016_02_01_archive.html ▾ Diese Seite übersetzen
29.02.2016 - Web, taniaquintero.blogspot.com ...... Joaquín Ordoqui y la "grandeza de la revolución". El miércoles 24 de septiembre de 2014, el periódico ...

(The connection to events in Mexico will become clear.)

In the next stage of ICAIC's development. 'When the rebels seized power on 1st January 1959, it was Che Guevara who almost immediately got them started making films on behalf of the Revolution, by setting up a unit in the fortress of La Cabana that until a fortnight earlier was used to hold political prisoners. This was the core group of the film institute created by the Revolutionary Government's first decree about cultural matters, which started by taking over the film businesses (including a studio) owned by one of Batista's henchmen who'd fled the country. Later it would acquire the local distributors, being mainly the subsidiaries of the Hollywood majors, and some cinemas.'

G. Cabrera Infante- was a Cuban novelist, essayist, translator screenwriter. His parents were founding members of the Cuban Communist Party.

As the author of the article, 'Cuba's Shadow' G. Cabrera Infante says he is indebted to Alfredo Guevara's account of the political history of the early sixties. Confirming he was one of a small group around Fidel Castro in the early months of the Revolution. G. Cabrera Infante also confirms that the young filmmakers were eager to participate in film institute's program.

Alfredo Guevara struck G. Cabrera Infante as a man of deep political intelligence, a Marxist intellectual who had a strong commitment to the defense of artistic freedom within the Revolution; his detractors saw him as Fidel Castro's minion, charged with keeping the filmmakers in line. This can be seen within the Institute and the Party Ideological Committee, which always had more direct control over broadcasting and the press.

(The number of Cuban films which didn't reach the screens is far fewer than those made by the BBC about the Troubles in Northern Ireland which were stopped or shelved.)

The problem the Institute had to face was what to put in place of the 266 Hollywood films out of a total of 484 films exhibited in Cuba in 1959, since the supply was cut off by Washington's declaration of economic blockade. The answer was more films from everywhere else. G. Cabrera Infante says when Che Guevara visited Tokyo in 1959 in search of new foreign trade agreements, he inquired on Alfredo Guevara's behalf about the possibilities for the ICAIC distributing Japanese films as well as purchasing equipment. The result was that Cuban filmgoers soon became exposed to a wider variety of world cinema than anywhere else in Latin America at the time, and this, in turn, encouraged the exciting effervescence of Cuban cinema in the 60s, ICAIC quickly started garnering prizes at films festival in every continent.

They had the means to make a myth.

Instituto Cubano del Arte e Industria Cinematográficos ...

*de.wikipedia.org/.../Instituto_**Cubano**_del_Arte_e_I ndustria_Cinematogr...*
Die ersten Mitarbeiter des *ICAIC* waren meist Mitglieder der von Fidel Castro ...
Gründungsdirektor *Alfredo Guevara* war seit gemeinsamen Studienzeiten an der ...
Bekannte kubanische Regisseure ... - Bekannte kubanische Filme ...

Cuba's Shadow - ProQuest

search.proquest.com/openview/.../1?pq-origsite... – Guevara became the head of a monopoly, for that's what the *ICAIC* was - and still is. ... the members of the Communist cultural apparat, *Alfredo Guevara* and Carlos ... or threatening, to buy out the numbers sung by the film's star *Ruben Blades*, ...

In Cuba's Shadow, G. Cabreara Infante informs us that everything from the buildings films were shown in- to pirated American movies- every foot of positive and negative film- even for a box camera, including instamatics was bought abroad by ICAIC from the Soviet Union and Japan. The Institute in the only producer and Sole distribute of Cuban and foreign movies.
The IACIA exported Cuban films it owned every Cuban co-production. ICACI was in controlled the censorship of any film made. They were an all powerful instrument of propaganda.

Varias veces, Alfredo Guevara se mostró harto de que siempre le estuvieran ...
cubanet.org

German Puig-

To get to the point I want to make, Fidel Castro appointed Alfredo Guevara the as the head of Cuban Film Institute two months after taking over Cuba. This cannot have pleased German Puig or Nestor Almendros and G. Cabrera Infante much as they founded ICAIC in 1950.
The interesting point about German Puig is he taught Alfredo Guevara in Mexico the film and Cinema trade; where he met all relevant producers and actors.

Notas para una prehistoria: antes de llegar al baile… - La …

www.lajiribilla.cu/2011/n541_09/541_03.html Por esa fecha el yucateco Manuel *Barbachano Ponce* (1924-1994), productor ..... *Aníbal* de Mar, Leopoldo Fernández y Mimí Cal en sus creaciones de Pototo,

This program tells me that Manuel Barbachano Ponce signed the contract to make the film 'Cuba Dance' when he stopover in Havana en route to Mexico; ready to produce with Luis Brunel. In this brief stay he met with Guillermo Cabrera Infant, Tomas Gutierrez, Paco Rabal, Alfredo Guevara the filmmaking team of *Cine-Magazine*.

Alfredo Guevara, who then travel with them to Mexico, officially to work in the film, but was

actually on a mission related to the supply of arms to the insurgents.
Alfredo Guevara had control of the film busyness; he controlled not only the making of films but also the martial such as the film, the cameras. No one could make a film without his permission.

(I just want to say, Alfredo Guevara was in the game of arms and propaganda.)

Escuela Internacional de Cine y TV de San Antonio de los Banos, Cuba
Founded in 1986 by the late "100 Years of Solitude" writer Gabriel Garcia Marquez, Argentine poet and filmmaker Fernando Birri and Cuban filmmaker Julio Garcia Espinosa, the school draws students from over 50 countries. After completing one year of general study, students can focus on such tracks as writing, directing, editing, production and sound and also participate in international workshops.

I noticed in the book 'La viuda de Montiel, Mexico, Venezuela, Colombia and Cuba, 1979 the name of Katy Jurado and her connection to ICACI.
Below this paragraph I have entered address showing the working relationships between some of those involved in the making of the Che Guevara myth. Names like Mario Vargas Llosa and Jean-Luc Godard, Regis Debray, Giangiacomo Feltrinelli.

Anna Magnani-Katy Jurado names also appear along with Gabriel Garcia Marquez,
(Mario Vargas Llosa has stated that Che's Mother stayed in his Paris flat after she had to leave Argentina.)

La viuda de Montiel, **Mexico, Venezuela, Colombia and Cuba, 1979**

Production:	Cooperativa Río Mixcoac, Universidad Veracruzana, Macuto Films, ICAIC, Macondo Filmes, Marusia Filmes.
Director:	Miguel Littín
Writing Credits:	Gabriel Garcia Márquez (short story), José Agustín, Miguel Littín (screenplay)
Cinematography:	Patricio Castillo
Music:	Leo Brower
Film Editing:	Nelson Rodríguez
Cast:	Geraldine Chaplin, Nelson Villagra, Katy Jurado, Ernesto Gómez Cruz, Pilar Romero, Reynaldo Miravalles, Alejandro Parodi, Ignacio Retes, Jorge Fegan, Emilia Rojas, Eduardo Gil

Gabriel García Márquez and the Cinema: Life and Works

https://books.google.de/books?isbn=1855662833 - Alessandro Rocco - 2014 - Performing Arts
... Universidad Veracruzana, Macuto Films, *ICAIC*, Macondo Filmes, Marusia ... Nelson Villagra, *Katy Jurado*, Ernesto Gómez Cruz, Pilar Romero, Reynaldo ...

Katy Jurado filmography - Wikipedia, the free encyclopedia

en.wikipedia.org/wiki/Katy_Jurado_filmography
This is a complete filmography of *Katy Jurado*.
Jurado .... 1976, Pantaleón y las visitadoras, "La Chuchupe", *Mario Vargas Llosa* · José Sacristán, Rosa Carmina.

<u>Germán Puig | кино-глаз</u>

https://manuelzayas.wordpress.com/tag/german-puig/

Posts about *Germán Puig* written by Manuel Zayas. ... Mentor político de Fidel y Raúl Castro, *Alfredo Guevara* (1925-2013) ejerció algún ... de Arte e Industria Cinematográficos (ICAIC), fundado por él en *1959*, era una institución obsoleta. ..... que regresaba muy enfermo desde *México* después de trabajar con Luis Buñuel, ...

Luis Bunuel Portes moved to Mexico after his involvement in politics and the ideas that were everywhere in pre-Spanish Civil War. He joined the Communist Part of Spain (PCE) in 1931.
Luis Bunuel made the film 'El Bruto' with Katy Jurado.

Goffredo Alesandrini was another husband attributed to Anna Magnani; he has worked very closely with Gabriel Garcia Marquez. They made the film 'The Wild Bunch' 1969 with Jean luc Godard.

Ayn Rand author scriptwriter and atheist philosopher was an associate of Gabriel Garcia Marquez and Giangiacomo Feltrinelli. Giangiacomo Feltrinelli was in the habit of publishing their books.

Giangiacomo Feltrinelli was considered almost a member of the Russian communist party till there was controversy over Boris Pasternak (Doctor Zhivago) (he was also a poet.)

(Mario Llosa and Gabriel Garcia Marquez both point out the Nobel Prize for Literature was wrapped up in politics. Boris Pasternak did not accept the prize in 1958, due to his fear he would not be allowed to return to his home country.) 'Senior Service' by Carlo Feltrinelli informs you about the importance of Giangiacomo Feltrinelli's communist contacts with the Russians.

Roberto Rossellini founded the Italian Film Company 'TEVERE' in 1947.
The fact is you can go round and round in circles with authors and poets film stars with political points of view, one thing you notice is on every corner, at every cross road Gabriel Garcia Marquez is standing.

<u>Regis Debray's MEDIA MANIFESTOS - Cultural Logic</u>
clogic.eserver.org/2-1/szeman.html von R Debray - *Media Manifestos* is a *book* that is fundamentally about materialism rather than the ... manifestos for "mediology," a practice that explores "the *Technological* ...
Regis Debray attended Giangiacomo Feltrinelli's funeral. Regis Debray's book 'Media Manifestos' on technological traismmissions, *he is interested in gullible TV watchers.*

EICTV

Escuela Internacional de Cine y Televisión: Inicio
www.eictv.org/
Atrás. Estudio de sonido · Consultoría y asesoría de
guiones · *EICTV* Producciones · Publicaciones ....
GALERIA | Igor Martinovic en la *EICTV*.
igor_martinovic_1 ...
Have schools in Cuba and Brazil.

 Fidel and Gabo. A portrait of the Legendary
friendship between Fidel Castro and Gabriel Garcia
Marquez. A book written by Angel Esteban and
Stephanie Panichelli names others that I could
include in this chapter. The thoughts of The Italian
Neorealism has reached out to other lands films,
become universal. Some films were made in Chili,
the other place popular to make films was Cuba.
UNEAC the union of writers and Artist of Cuba.

FNP- **Fundación Nuevo Periodismo Iberoamericano: La ...**

*www.**fnpi**.org/*
Organización sin ánimo de lucro creada y presidida
por el periodista y escritor *Gabriel García Márquez*,
Premio Nobel de Literatura. Su misión es promover
la ...
Roberto Rossellini founded the Italian Film
Company 'TEVERE' in 1947.

'Wege Der Revolution Che Guevara. 9 783940 415516

This film can be found in most languages. I could not have known how important it was, till I had studded the inner workings of the ICAIC. It had fallen into my hand as I wandered through the film department of a well known store!

What make this film so important is it shows Ciro Bustos as an American adviser getting out of a jeep, under the name of Felix Ramon. The same code name as Felix Rodriguez, Oliver North used.

The film shows two men that played the part of Che Guevara's brothers. We are told that they are military advisers and interrogators.

The same two men are to be seen as lawyers for Ciro Bustos and Riges Debray in Camiri; down the road from Che Guevara's death party in La Higuera. (Spies-CIA-Lies-Terrorist-Che Guevara. ISBN 9783738674453. Explains in more detail.)

The film also shows Salvador Allende greeting the said survivors from the death part. One of whom looks like good old Che! And if that is not enough there is the seine where Che's death party companions are filmed returning to Cuba, Jubilant! In the back ground you can see a man bouncing with glee- Che Guevara.
But! That is not why I have mentioned this film at this point.

It is an ICAIC film.

Who were the ICAIC= Alferdo Guevara and Gabriel Garcia Marquez.
And, other members of the ICAIC such as Manuel Perez and Tomas Gutierez, Rebeca Charvez, Pedro Chaskel. All have Wikipedia's explaining their connection to the ICAIC.
In the leaflet with the film it says Pedro Chaskel was known for his documentaries, leader of the Cineteca Univircitaria de Cile. He worked with Miguel Littin amongst others. (Miguel Littin worked with Katy Jurado.)
Rebeca Chavez She worked eight years with renowned Cuban documentary maker Santiago Alvarez, she was his researcher, scriptwriter and directors assistant.
Santiago Alvarez a Cuban born Film maker. He directed the second chapter of French Director Jean-Luc Godard film 'Historie (S) du Cinema.'
Who were the ICAIC ? Alferdo Guevara and Gabriel Garcia Marquez.

Chapter three.

Interconnecting people and places.

Che Guevara had to be created, come from somewhere! I want to point out that their names interconnect with each other, I don't wanting to set long lists of their connections, but I feel a short list with information will helpful when seeing how the plan was woven.

Jean-Luc Godard-
Jean Luc-Godard made the film- 'Far From Vietnam' 1968. Fidel Castro was in this film.

Regis Debray-
   Regis Debray, to point out that he was in Bolivia at the same time as Che/Bustos is not what I want to say hear. He met Fidel Castro when he was nineteen; that was in 1959. At twenty two he held a professors' potion at the Havana University. (The ICAIC's building backs on the university's buildings.) (As do the International of Film and

Television School of San Antonio de los BañoS.

Run by Gabriel García Márquez.) – EICTV.
Regis Debray- was only twenty-seven when he was present in Bolivia.-young impressionable!
He has written a script for Katy Jurado- The use of the Method.

El recurso del método - Watch Full Movie Online FREE ...

*anontv.com/.../449754-the-recourse-to-the-**method***
Alejo Carpentier; *Régis Debray*. Stars: *Katy Jurado* · Nelson Villagra · Ernesto Gómez Cruz ... Cast; Reviews; Comments; Images. *Katy Jurado*. La Mayorala ...
He is known to be a film citric. In an article- Against Venice, 'he writes'- 'Don't tell me it is possible to like Anna Magnani.'

El rescate de lo popular en forma de cine revolucionario ...

reflexionesmarginales.com/.../el-rescate-de-lo-popul...
01.04.2014 - ... publicó en la Isla el ensayo de *Regis Debray* ¿Revolución en la revolución? ... Entre los errores que Debray detecta en la lucha por la liberación ..... en http://www.*eictv*.co.cu/miradas/index.php?option=com_content&task= ...

Cinema Verite is a style of documentary film making (he played himself in Chnonique.) This form Regis Debray studded in Paris before he went to Cuba. In Regis Debray's book –
Media Manifestotos, on the Teemdgical Transmissions of Cultural Forms. On page 144 he talks about the gullibility of the TV watcher. *He has written the book to the film about Monika Ertl. His books have passed through the hands of the*

Feltrinelli publishing houses. He liked to quote Fidel Castro, as did Claire Sterling.

Katy Jurado and **Mario Vargos Llosa**- Pantaleony Las Visitadoras.
Luis Brunel, Carlos Funta-Divine.
Gabriel García Márquez- The Widow of Montret.
Anna Magnai with Luis Brunel in Mexico- La Rosa Tatuada.

Gabriel García Márquez. Owns the schools-started the schools of cinema and film journalist. International of Film and Television School of San Antonio de los Baños. This concern has a branch in Rome, Santa Fe.
Central University Comombia. Depending on which Wikipedia you read tells you it has Worldwide branches.
Katy Jurado's Wikipedia tells us she was training as a journalist and Claire Sterling trained at the for mentioned university. Che's Father that stated that his wife, (he states she was Che's mother.) was a correspondent in the Spanish Civil War.!?

Fernando Birri-
The EICTV were selling the idea of Guevara romantic, he as one of the founder members of the EICTV came out of retirement to make the film- Che muerte de una Utopia?= Che, death of utopia?

Fernando Birri a close friend Gabriel García Márquez, Birri was the man behind the film awards and for all connecting arties. One of his assistance was Pier Pablo Pasolini. (Who directed Anna Magnani.)
The other film of interest Fernando Birri made after his retirement was 'Mi Hijoel Che.= my son Che. **Surprise! This film is contains an interview with Ciro Bustos and Regis Debray.**
Francisco Rabal-Paco is an actor. He worked with-Pier Paolo Pasolini= Hexer Von Heute.

Luis Brunel= Caster.

Katy Jurado= Diven
        Francisco Rabal-Paco is the actor who took the part of Che in the 1968 film, directed by Fernando Birri. The film about Che has been given many names but the cast is the same. Bloody Che Contra is just one way to find it!

<u>Bloody Che Contra (1968) - IMDb</u>
www.imdb.com/title/tt0064157/
Bewertung: 5,6/10 - 68 Abstimmungsergebnisse
With *Francisco Rabal*, John Ireland, Susanna Martinková, Howard Ross. ... or the like, they don't even name *Regis Debray*, instead they just call him the 'French ...

Mario Vargas Llosa was a member of the Peruvian parliament. Charger de Affairs to Chili. Writer and a

Poet with a Nobel Prize and had the Venezuelan Romulo Gallegos Prize. As will as writing the script for Katy Jurado. *There is evidence that Peruvian men were additional solders in Sera Master: luzpensamientoylibertad.blogspot.com/…/libro-hilda Written by Ricardo Gadea Acosta. Ricardo Gudea Acosta was Hilda Gadea's Brother! Che Guevara's first wife!*

Mario Vargas Llosa was a member of the Peruvian parliament. Charger de Affairs to Chili. Writer and a Poet with a Nobel Prize and had the Venezuelan Romulo Gallegos Prize.
In the open letter- 'Peru 21' it states that Mario Vargas Llosa was hospitable to- *Celia de la Serna Llosa. Che's mother.* The lady that asked him to assist Celia was- *Hilda Gadea- Che's first wife.*
Mario Vargas Llosa states that Celia de la Serna Llosa was a close friend of Mario Vargas Llosa's family. He and his first wife Julia Urqnidi was a Scriptwriter as it so happens, they were married in 1955. Julia Urqnidi tells me in her interview that their relationship was a close one; they live together, she and Celia went to the theater together and when Hilda Gadea needed help, she was there to support her.
(Mario Vargas Llosa remarks, 'Celia de la Serna Llosa did not have any money to pay for a hotel. She was in his house before returning to Buenos Aires where she was put in jail and would soon after her release, died.)

I am told by Froilan Gonzalez- a world renowned racing car driver, who travelled the word freely; about an Argentinean publisher Adys M Cupull. Adys M Cupull- is an author for a political publisher. In 'Unfinished Song.' For which they won literary awards for in Cuba in 1998. (I found out that they are part of the propaganda machine. Nice that they could have prizes for their efforts.)
Political publisher- 'Unfinished Song.' States that Celia travelled from Salto, Uruguay with abundant material proclaiming Fidel Castro's brand of communist propaganda; where she was arrested. They tell me it was the twenty third of April; she was registered as dangerous.

Alego Carpentier was in charge of Cuban state publishing and enjoyed a friendship with **Jouis Jorvet** a French theatrical director and was Cuba's ambassador to France 1975 and won the Cervantes Prize in 1977. This gave me the idea that 'Poets and their prizes could be a very useful way of transferring money and information. Alego Carpentier's name is connected to public money being hand over to the guerrilla Che Guevara there are many rumors floating on the internet about this.
   Julio Cortazar- translator/poet/ UNESCO translator. actor/writer.
 He connects to Jean Luc Godard and can be seen in Pier Paolo Pasolini's films.
As will as simpering with Fidel Castor and Salvador Allende.

Just out of interest the Wikipedia tells me he spent his childhood just outside of Buenos Aires, he was a teacher in a high school in Buenos Aires Chivilcoy and later in Bolivia. Interesting to read that he was a professor in French in the National University of Cuyo Mondoza. One of the Wikipedia's tells me he was Chili's ambassador in France. He died in Paris 1984.

writers/poets/journalists!

Peru-

Lucho Loayza= writer/poet/journalist.
(Is in many photos with Mario Vargas Llosa.)
Raul Porras Barrenehea = writer/poet. Literary prize winner. Peruvian Canceller in Salvador Allande's government. Believed to have been murdered shortly after Allande's demise,

Hilda Gadea's brother was Castro's contact to Esterban Colomban's drug barron, Claire Sterling can explain the Mafia connection!

Ricardo Gadea Acosta- is an author, a journalist who wrote a lament at the death of Javier Herard. One of the poets-Guerrillas lost in the Salsa campaign.

As an author Ricardo Gadea Acosta has spoken over the revolution and is influence in the Southern Americas. Many of his remarks are in a philosophy program on Cuban net.

I had read in Ricardo Gadea Acosta 2013, May 15 "Javier in the memory." That he had been in Cuba to share their defense in April 61 at the Bay of Pigs.

http://nuestrabandera.lamule.pe/2013/05/18/javier-en-el-recuerdo

As a Peruvian he had received military training, under Fidel Castro's instructions. He is Peruvian!? *Ricardo Gadea Acosta is Hilda Gadea Acosta's brother. Hilda Gadea Acosta was Che's first wife.* And Fidel Castro's contact to Pablo Escobar.

Hilda Gadea Acosta was Che's first wife, *mother of Hildita my half-sister, I have found a photo of her, (Wish I could hug her.) with Alberto Grundy. In this photo she looks so sweet, I wish I could have met her; it is said that she is dead, there are photos of her grave. (Who knows so many have used this way to gain another identity- just wishing.) One good thing is Hildita had two children and not just one.* **"Diario de Bolivia" books.google,de/books** informed me about the brother/sister relationship.

Aurora Camacho Schmidt. She in turn is Hilda Gadea Acosta niece, my half sister's aunt.
She wrote the book **'Surviving Mexico's Dirty War.' A Political Prisoner's Memoir**.

Aurora Camacho Schmidt's photo is in an article written by Mario Vargas Llosa. The article says that she asked him to ghost write a book for her. 'Black and White.' Leereluniverso-blogspot-.com.

The photo in the article I have matched with one as she looks today. They say the lady I found with

the name '**Cata Podesta** asked for a book to be
written for her, they say she was born 1909 and died
2009. Aurora Camacho Schmidt is still alive and is a
professor of Spanish in the U.S.A.

.

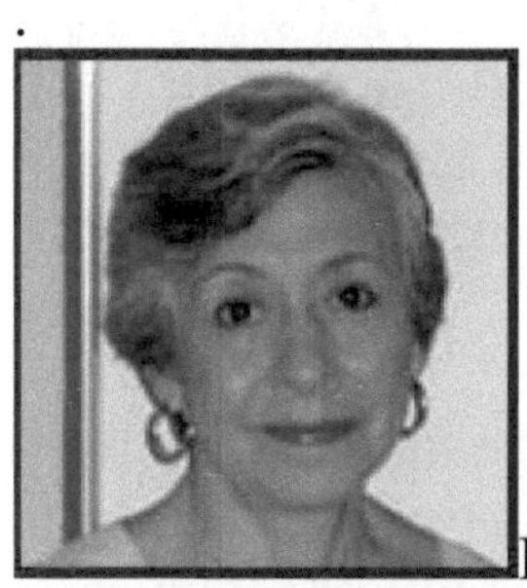Promotions Recognize Faculty
Across the Disciplines
swarthmore.edu

Cata Podesta la teorice autor del libro'Pieles negras
y blancas',…
Leereluniverso.blogspot.com

Argentina-
Jorge Luis Borges= writer/poet/journalist.
Received the Jerusalem literary prize 1971.
He was at school with Ernesto Guevara Lynch,
Che's father-who was expelled from that school for
hitting the very same Jorge Luis Borges!
   Jorge Luis Borges worked with Mario Vargas
Llosa in the National Broadcasting System of
Argentina.

Lucia Alvarez Toledo book 'The story of Che' the
editorial is by Seix Barral. (Just a remark!) This lady
is related to the de la Serna and the Llosa family, a
stronger contact than living in the same
neighborhood. (She could be the mother to Che's
half brother Fernando L. Chavez Alvarez, who I say
used other identities such as Jean Luc Godard.)
Another interesting point is she translated Alberto
Granado book, *'Travelling With Che Guevara. The
making of a Revolutionary.'* Was she part the team
making the myth?

Fernando L. Chavez Alvarez, who I say used other
identities such as Jean Luc Godard.
Just out of interest the Wikipedia tells me he spent
his childhood just outside of Buenos Aires, he was a
teacher in a high school in Buenos Aires Chivilcoy
and later in Bolivia. Interesting to read that he was a
professor of French in the National University of
Cuyo Mondoza.

Cuba-
Guillermo Cabrera Infante= writer/poet/journalist
and translator/screenplays/film critic.
Worked in Brussels/Belgium/London.
Known at one time as a Castro supporter.

Jose/Pepe Rodriguez Feo=
writer/poet/journalist/translator. Spanish to English,
liter critic.

Nicolas Guillen= writer/poet/journalist. Songwriter.
He wrote the song-Che Guevara. He was politically
active. A Cuban government minister.

Chili-
Jorge Edward Volde= writer/poet/journalist. Won
literary prizes. Chili's ambassador in
France.

Pablo Neruda= writer/poet. Diplomat. Accepted an
award from the Peruvian government.
Was a member of Salvador Allende's government.
In every Wikipedia I read I am told that Pablo
Neruda is Che Guevara's favorite poet.

Venezuela-
Republica Bolivarian de Venezula
Romules Gallegos= writer/poet/lawyer. Politian.
Was an elected president the republic. Nobel Prize
winner.

Spain-
Carlos Barral = writer/poet/journalist/actor/editor
owner of the Seix Barral orgnisation.
(Socillist party Catalonia Spain.)
To be seen in films directed by Pier Paolo Pasolini.

(The people can be connected with each other as
writers/poet prize winners- politicians
Poets like Vidadyo Telleboim. He was the Chilean
leader of the communist Party.
Nicolas Guillen received the Stalin Peace Prize.
Emir Rodriguez Monegal form Uruguay also
received liturgy prizes.
   I do not know if they drank tea together but a
network of communication has developed on the
map I have drawn on a piece of wall paper.)

Alberto Szpunberg=Albertito. This name is
coursing me some thought. Firstly he is poet, an
Argentinean, a founder member of **'Brigada
Masetti.'**
Alberto Szpunberg- Mistica, Lirica y politica -
Revista N – Clarin
www.revistaenie.clarin.com/La_Academia de_de_Pi
 A close friend of Ciro Bustos as is stated in Ciro's
own book.
   Alberto Szpunberg as an artist whose work I have
often mistaken as Ciro's work on the internet.
   (Ciro came to my notice in a paragraph in Jon
Lee Anderson book where he said, Ciro Bustos

painted wonderful portraits of people without faces. This was the remark made him interesting to me.)

There is a question in my mind- They share the same the same political stage- that they are both supposed to be Argentinean dose not bother me, but their closeness in their art work dose.

Portrait painting is an art you can learn. The fact that they have so much in common, opens the possibility that the said drawings could have been made by another hand.

Ciro Algaranaz- he is interesting as it was not clear what he was up to! I put in Ciro Bustos and Ciro Algaranaz into the network. The answers I got were, he was-

The Mayor of Camiri –
Che's neighbor in Bolivian prison!

On page three hundred and sixty-one of Ciro Bustos' book 'Che Wants To See You' ISBN 978-1-78168-096-4 tells me Ciro Algaranaz occupied the same cell as he. Ciro Algaranaz was being held for his connection to the suspected cocaine business.

Elisabeth Burgos-Debray-

Most of the folk I am looking into can be found in Elisabeth Burgos-Debray's papers in the Inventory of Elizabeth Burgos-Debray Papers. At the Hoover Institution.

Time and time again I have come across names listed there. (Just to confuse me some of the names have other spellings or different forenames or are under different names but by cross referencing

Elisabeth Burgos-Debray's lists, they tell me who was involved.)

David Stoll was not in agreement with Elizabeth Burgos-Debray over her creation of Rigoberta Menchu. David Stoll go's as far as to say it was a fabricated lie. This made heroin tortured Guatemala, coursing political unrest. The whole thing was a constructed Lie.

Elizabeth Burgos-Debray holds a box/folder:21:33 on an Acosta. This lady also constructed Daniel Alarcon Ramirez= 'Benigno' book. 'Memorias de un Soldado Cubano, 1997.

Elizabeth Burgos-Debray has for Jorge Masetti, notes, 1999 and first draft, 1999. The second draft has the same date. Box/folder:8:9-11

Thought she dose list the lawyers at the Riges Debray, Ciro Bustos trial she does not have a file for Ciro Bustos.

Chapter four
Ricardo Gadea Acosta
and my Mother's photo Album.

 RICARDO GADEA
agenciadenoticiaslima.com.pe

He is proving to be of great interest! I have
flippantly said he was Fidel Castro's contact to
Pablo Escobar, at that time I had not looked into
exactly what the connection was.
I had to chew through the history of Peru. To find
out that Hilda Gadea had been thrown out of Peru
in1949. She was living in exile in Mexico; Hilda
supported other exiles.

Luis de la Puente met Hilda in the Colombian embassy late 1954. Note he is a political activist and a Peruvian guerrilla.

Peru was a country that needed to reform: Peru had 6.000.000 farmers and 2,000,000 workers. A land rising to 3800 feet above the sea and deeply divided by ravens cut by rivers. Folk flocked to the cities at sea level looking for work and food only to have to live in slums. Only large consortiums could provide roads and bridges, trains etc. holding the folk to ransom. If I have understood rightly; a land where guerrilla attacks on the transport system would cores disruption.

Luis Felipe De la Puente Uceda (1 April of 1926 Santiago de Chuco , Peru - October 23 of 1965) was an activist , political and guerrilla Peruvian who protested against coexistence and political coalition between his party, APRA , and the forces conservative underpinning the second government of Manuel Prado Ugarteche (1956 - 1962).

IMAGENES Y TEXTOS SELECTOS: LUIS DE LA PUENTE UCEDA EJEMPLO DE AMOR AL PAIS
imagenesytextosselectos.blogspot.com
The references' come from-

LUIS DE LA PUENTE UCEDA EXAMPLE OF LOVE
OF COUNTRY

**Jose Carlos Mariategui, Luis de la Puente Uceda,
the MIR and the Peruvian Revolution**
Work compilation of texts and pictures made by
Dr. Fernando Mejía Durand in the ninth anniversary
of SAN LUIS RENACE (17 February 2002-2011)

My Mother's Photo Album.

From my mother's photos from her album.

A

B

It took me many years to find out some of the names of the folk in the photos. The photos were taken in the camp where they were preparing for the expedition with the boat 'Granma' under the guidance of Alberto Bayo. (This name appears in 'Why have their Identities been mixed with others?)

In Photo (A) Hilda Gadea is in the middle. It is not easy to see, Hilda is holding the Cuban flag.

In photo (B) the lady in the middle is my mother. Around them both are Hector Perez Marcano and Raul Menendez Tomassevich with Ricardo Gadea Acosta in the foreground. Frank Pais far right. In Photo (A) he is looking over the top of Hilda Gadea.

Chapter five.
Why have their identities been mixed with others?

Why are there so many mixed identities to be found around the 'Che Guevara' conspiracy?
In the chapter 'Interconnecting people and places' two names share the same likeness, Aurora Camacho Schmidt and Cata Podesta.

The two , Intis?

Guido Álvaro Peredo Leigue
cerrocalvo.blogspot.com

Pier Paolo Pasolini-
paginecorsare.my blog.it.

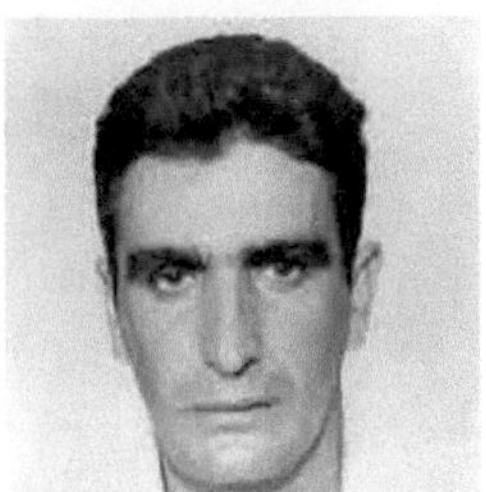

Guido Alvaro "IntI" Peredo   .
genealogiadelcheguevara.blogspot.com

   Guido Alvaro Peredo Leigue 'Inty'. 'cerrocolvo. Blogspot.com' as this program comes from Santa Clara where the Che Guevara museum is, you would think they would know! In the same program you can see Lucio Ediberto Galvan Hidalgo. He looks like Guido Alvaro Peredo Leigue 'Inti' even though his chin is missing!

I have put Pier Paolo Pasolini between the two Intis, to show the likeness between him and Guido Alvaro Peredo Leigue. As Inti or Inty was supposed to have taken over from Che Guevara after the death party, he should have the same face.

The next men are interesting-
General Enrique Jurado-   General Bayo-

ATRÁS

generalisimofranco.com ....

General Enrique Jurado.

 **Alberto Bayo, 1959 (Charlie Seiglie/Bohemia) cuba1952-1959.blogspot.com**

Alberto Bayo – Wikipedia

*de.wikipedia.org/wiki/Alberto_**Bayo***
Bayo war Sohn des spanischen Offiziers Pedro *Bayo* Guia und der aus Puerto .... Mis versos de rebeldía (Mexiko 1958); Sangre en *Cuba* (Mexiko 1958); Mi aporte a la ... El *general* que adiestró a la guerrilla de Castro y el Che, Debate 2007.

Alberto Bayo - Wikipedia, the free encyclopedia

*en.wikipedia.org/wiki/Alberto_**Bayo***
He was born in *Cuba* and studied in the United States and Spain. *Bayo's* most ... the same period. Alberto *Bayo* died a *General* of the *Cuban* Armed Forces.

This man's profile is interesting! He was noted for his acts in the Spanish Civil War. He was the general that to trained the men for the Granma trip to Cuba. 1956. This man's image does not match that of General Bayo shown in Che Guevara's own account (OTRA VEZ).

Alberto Bayo as seen in Back on the road. (otra vez) che Guevara

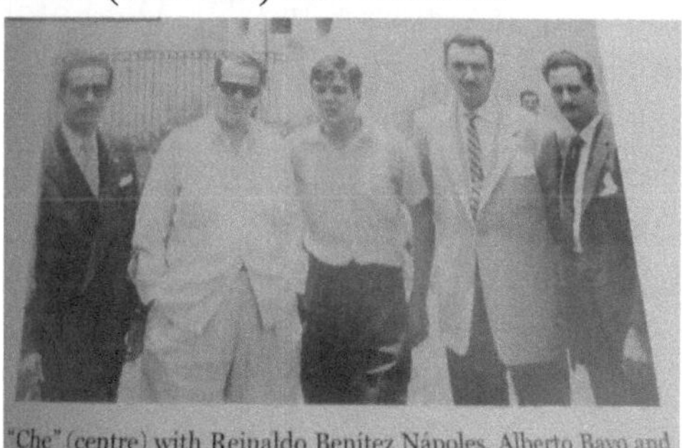

"Che" (centre) with Reinaldo Benítez Nápoles, Alberto Bayo and Universo Sánchez at the Miguel E. Schulz 136 prison.

Thesis photos are from 'Ernesto Che Guevara , Back on the road'. (Otra Vez) A journey through Latin America. ISBN 0-8021-3942-6. The book has been printed in so many versions that an ISBN number night not be necessary. Nor would an ISBN number for, 'Che Guevara- a Revolutionary Life by Jon Lee Anderson.' His book has not used the same photos but if you look in CHE Die Fotobiografie by Christophe Loving –ISBN 978-3-88897-488-5 this book dose. Next to a photo of Che up a mountain there is a group where General Jurado or General Bayo can be seen and as this photo must have been taken at the same time as the others.

I could be excused for thinking they are the same man!?
This General Bayo!?

General Bayo-

Which one was ivolved in the Spanish Sivel War? As so many have been involved in the Spanish Sival War, from reputly Che's mother as a journarlist in the war (as said by her husband), her sister's husband Cayetano Cordova Itubura was said to have been a journalist covering the war's events. General

Jurado was aclamed for his deeds in the same war as was General Bayo.

Genaral Jurado fasanated the young Che with stories of action when he took refuege with the Gervara family after having to leave Spain. We are told!

<u>VILLA GRANADILLO: EXTRANJEROS ...</u>
villagranadillo.blogspot.com/.../*extranjeros-internaci...*
05.03.2015 - *EXTRANJEROS* INTERNACIONALISTAS QUE MAS DAÑO LES HAN HECHO AL PUEBLO DE CUBA EN SU HISTORIA ...

General Bayo- went on to be a member of the new government after the revolution in Cuba. Which face did he have? His name connected to meetings held in Tarara, a mansion next to the beach about twenty kilometers from Havana, where it was reported that plans were made to create Mercenaries.
Names like Alfredo Guevara as filmmaker can be found on lists of those attending such meetings.

Just out of interest Manuel Prieres who wrote the article in the Villa Grandillo, tell us that tree Chilean communist were in this group. The Spanish Albert Bayo (Colonel of the Spanish Republic, communist, whose militarily training Fidel Castro and his men under took in Mexico).

18) Alberto Bayo (Coronel de la República Española, comunista, quien estuvo entrenando militarmente a Fidel Castro y sus hombres en México).

Bayo: Segundo de izquierda a derecha

Bayo (Segundo de izquierda a derecha) independent.typepad.com
Another pair of different men with the same names closes to Che Guevara?

Claire Sterling- this man is said to be Claire Sterling's husband.

 About Thomas Sterling · 39104. Thomas L. Sterling (* 1921; secretary, ...goodreads.com

This man looks like Claire Sterling's editor looks like Thomas Sterling! Even with bad photos the likeness to her editor Max Ascoli was an editor can be seen.
Max Ascoli-

Max Ascoli

Thomas Sterling

Max Ascoli as editor of the magazine 'The Reporter' could be seen hugging Magnani.

MEDEA 1966 REGIA GIANCARLO MENOTTI ANNA MAGNANI 1973 REGIA F ENRIQUEZ ...
archiviofoto.unita.it

Medea 1966 regia giancarlo menotti anna...

Medea 1966 regia giancarlo menotti anna magnani 1973 regia f enriquez valeria moriconi 1996 regia mario missiroli valeria moriconi altri

I saw Anna Magnani with a 'Che' and a man that looks like her husband. No not her husband but Claire Sterling's! Tomas Sterling!?

Why does this man look life Claire Sterling's husband?

This photo is from MEDEA 1966 REGIA GIANCARLO MENOTTI ANNA MAGNANI 1973 REGIA F ENRIQUEZ ... archiviofoto.unita.it

Look what happened when I looked into Claire Sterling's book, 'The Terror Network.'

Franklin Jurado- Jose Santacruz London

Look at the next person of interest, his name I found in an article written by Clair Sterling about Franklin Jurado. Who just happen to be a powerful member of the Mafia! So powerful that he also had the name Jose Santacruz London, with this name he leaded the Colomben Mafi. In Law Citations can be found some of the accusations he had to answer to.

7. Franklin Jurado businesspundit.com

<u>The washing cycle - Australian Federal Police</u>
www.afp.gov.au/media-centre/.../1998/.../washing

Franklin Jurado.

Jose Franklin Jurado Rodriguez he looks harmless; he had a Master Degree in Economics, studded at the Columbia University. He worked as a researcher at Harvard Kennedy School. And! He ran the Columbian Mafia.

Or is his name Jose Santacruz London? If they are not the same person why do they wear the same cloths? Were the photos taken on the same day?

This man is not known for being a good guy.

Cali-Kartell – Wikipedia

*de.wikipedia.org/wiki/**Cali**-Kartell*
Das *Cali*-Kartell (span. *Cartel* de *Cali*) war ein Zusammenschluss verschiedener kolumbianischer Kokainproduzenten und -schmuggler in der Stadt *Cali*.
Gründung - Organisation - Aktivitäten - Beziehung zum Medellin-Kartell

José Santacruz Londono: No. 3 of Cali Drug Cartel in Colombia rjgeib.com

Katy Jurado or Anna Magnani?

Anna Magnani-

WordPress.org

In this film Anna Magnani reveals a remarkable performer with the painful ... famouspeopleinfo.com

Katy Jurado-

Katy Jurado

Katy en *San Antone* (1953).

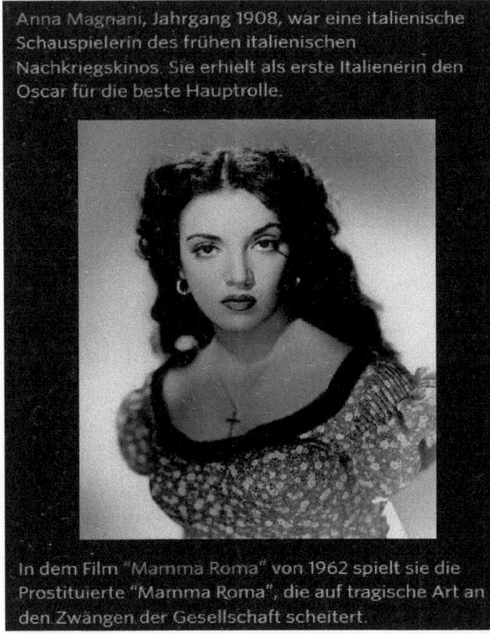

The same photo for Anna Magnani and Katy Jurado?

Why have the two ladies the same identities? I wonder why anyone would make such a mistake. And why is this kind of mistake made so often?

Chapter six.
Anna Magnani's role.
The importance of looking into this lady is because whichever name she used she also took on the role of Celia de la Serna. I have started with Anna Magnani as she and Silvana Corsini worked together with Pier Paolo Pasolini. I ended my first book having discovered her as the connection between Katy Jurado and Claire Sterling.

Anna Magnani

MEDEA 1966 REGIA GIANCARLO MENOTTI
ANNA MAGNANI 1973 REGIA F ENRIQUEZ ...
archiviofoto.unita.it

There is a muddle as to which editor or husband he is!?

This photo is from MEDEA 1966 REGIA GIANCARLO
MENOTTI ANNA MAGNANI 1973 REGIA F ENRIQUEZ ...
archiviofoto.unita.it
Chapter 'Why have their identities been mixed with others.'
Offers answers.

Anna Magnani contact with Pier Pablo Pasolini and
his to the Two Intis, that and the film 'Mama Roma'
where you can see Silvana Corsini. To suggest that
Silvana Corsini played part of one of Che's sister in
many of the Guevara Family group photos.

Che Guevara with Family by Unknown Artist
museumsyndicate.com.
If you look at this picture you will see Silvana sitting
third from the left.

I found an interesting program about Lucy Ball's husband being a Cuban film producer and a musician Desi Arnaz. To give him his full name Desiderio Alberto Arnaz Y de Ache 111. He was born in Santiago de Cuba. Inherently Lucy Ball had a fling with Fidel Castro.

Wellaware1 has a program where it states that Desi Arnaz was in Dallas at the time J F Kennedy's death. There was a moment when I thought Che was involved, I came to the conclusion that Che was wanted by Kennedy to take control of a coup code name AmWorld, Kennedy was planning to change the leadership in Cuba.

It was not the facts that Wellaware1 were showing me, I found interesting but the fact they used the same methods as I used, all be it more professionally! They looked at ears! Marched partners! I got so excited I sent them an email but I did not get a reply. One thing they do is explain the whys and wherefores for ending and starting other identities or have two or more identities at the same time.

This why I decided to look at Silvana Corsini; She had played in Mama Roma with Anna Magnani, directed by Pier Pablo Pasolini-Who I have pointed out has a strong resemblance to one of the two 'Inti's- I have put in the photos as a reminder.

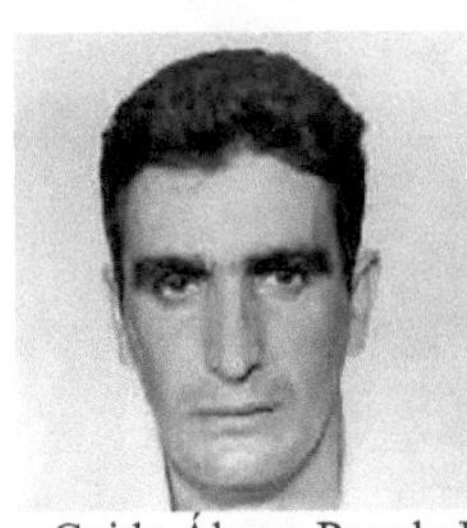

Guido Álvaro Peredo Leigue   Guido Alvaro "IntI"
Peredo   Pier Paolo Pasolini- paginecorsare.my blog.it.
cerrocalvo.blogspot.com
genealogiadelcheguevara.blogspot.com

I took Silvana's photo to match it with Beverly Aadlan, the girl friend of Errol Flynn, he made the film 'Cuban Rebel Girls' (You can find it on You Tube.) Jorge Masetti with Silvana/Beverly.

**A- anna karina jean luc godard
dancingflickr.com**

B- Mireille Darc cineartistes.com

C– Silvana Corsini-photo mamma_roma_009.jpg kebekmac.blogspot.com

D- Beverly Aadlan-pixshark.com

E- Anna Magnania-Festa della donna, a Roma nel nome di Anna Magnani tag24.it

F- Ana Maria- Che with his family and friends49 views cheguevara.sosugary.com

G- katy Jurado- Fe Esperanza y Caridad ▶KATY JURADO (3 de 3)musicamoviles.com

 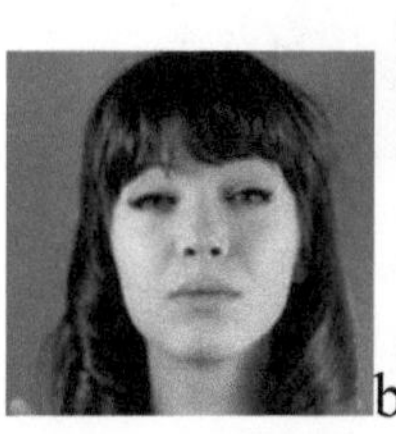 

a-anna karina   b- Mireille Darc c-Silvana Corsini

d- Beverly Aadlan   e-Anna magnai

There is a family likeness.

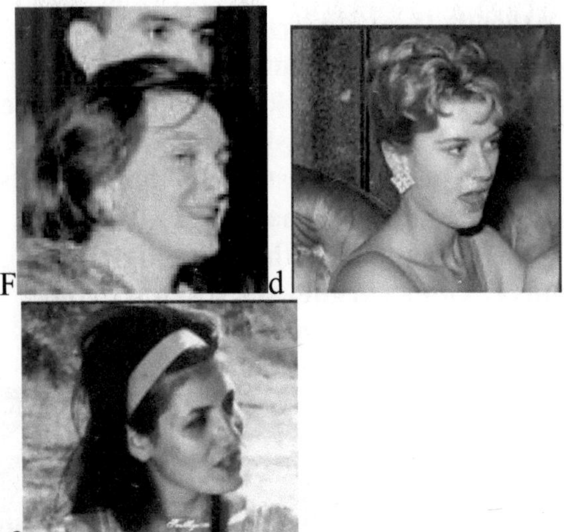

F   d

c

f- Ana Maria- Guevara   d- Beverly Aadlan
c- Silvana Corsini

g **Katy Jurado.**

Look at the lady looking into the camera I had at
first thought it was lady F- Ana Maria- Guevara
but the lady G Katy Jurado could also have played
the part. In this photo, Regis Debray and his wife
with their lawyer looking down, under the hat
without a face. But to say she played his sister
might not be a lie.

r

... su actividad "militante",se limita en los hechos, a
no dejar de publicar ...

martinezestevez.wordpress.com

The matter of the Fur coat- by the way in photo e
in the background is Jean Luc Godard

Che with his sister, Ana María

e Che with his and friends49 views
cheguevara.sosugary.com

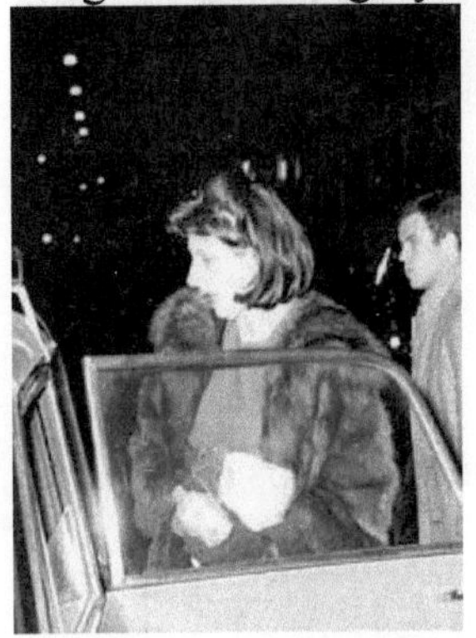

Artists in Action #221 tsutpen.blogspot.com

Small, holding, 17k smokingsides.com

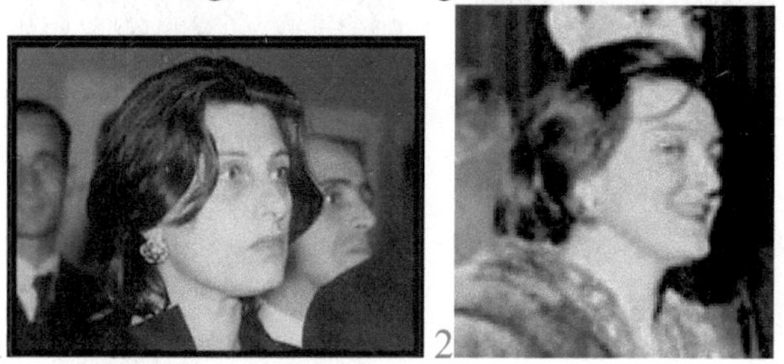

1) Picture annamagnanisito.com.
This program tells me about Anna Magnani
youth! The lady with the hat has pale eyes

were as Anna has darker eyes with the same coloring as Che. (I should know I spent months looking into his eyes and that of his mother to discover they matched mine.)

2)  Che's family and friends49 views
cheguevara.sosugary.com
Look in this program for the photo demonstrating Ana Maria- Che's sister and the coat, it is dated 1946/1950
The fur coat, would a mother and daughter share such a coat!?

.

E

F-

Note the froun.

They have one strong froun line.

Katy Jurado es.wokipedia

Anna Magnani, Jahrgang 1908, war eine italienische Schauspielerin des frühen italienischen Nachkriegskinos. Sie erhielt als erste Italienerin den Oscar für die beste Hauptrolle.

In dem Film "Mamma Roma" von 1962 spielt sie die Prostituierte "Mamma Roma", die auf tragische Art an den Zwängen der Gesellschaft scheitert.

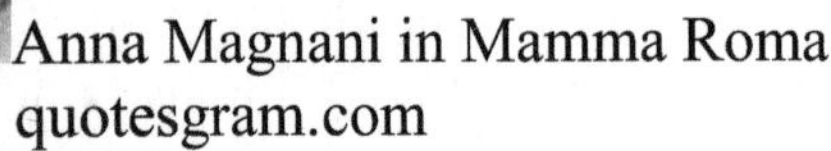
Anna Magnani in Mamma Roma
quotesgram.com

The same photo you can find it under both Anna and Katy's name in many programs. This photo with Anna or Katy has a small cross around their neck, a dress with daisies printed on it and short puffy sleeves. It was this photo that brought me to Katy Jurado.

Katy Jurado was born Maria Christina Jurado Garcia. Jurado's cousin, Emilio Portes Gil, was president of Mexico beginning in 1928. Katy Jurado, it is said studded journalism. (So has Claire Sterling.) Journalism? That was the moment I knew the ladies were one. It was not a large jump to bring the fur coat and Che's sister and Anna Magnani and Pier Pablo Pasolini together- not when Jean Luc Godard's eyes look at you over the top of Che's said sister in the aforementioned photo. Che with his family and friends49 views cheguevara.sosugary.com.

Why is it important? Because the lady under whichever name, played the part of Che's mother.
Is it just a strange coincidence with the photos of both ladies, Anna, Katy photos?
There are only a few photos showing Katy Jurado as an elderly lady, her picture profile follows her youth.

Anna Magnani picture profile show a middle aged woman. There is a program showing her as an unrecognizable child with light eyes in contrast to Anna's darker eyes.

ISOLA DEL CINEMA: Dalla letteratura con Alma Daddario al grande cinema con ...
taxidrivers.it

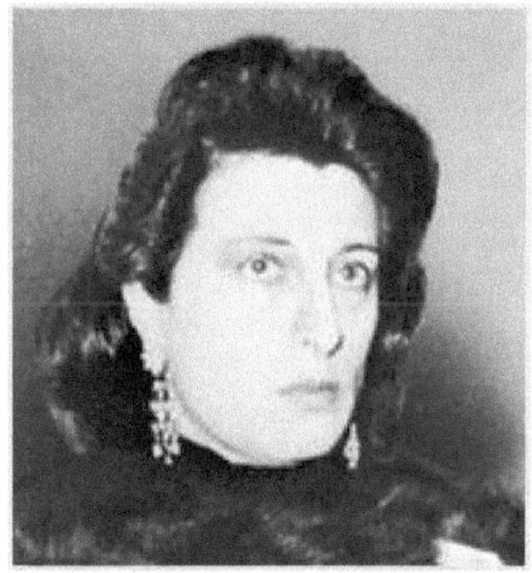

Anna Magnani
britannica.com

Celia de la Serna-

Che pictured here with his parents. His father
Ernesto Guevara said in 1969: ...

Her name they say was María Cristina Estela
Marcela Jurado García, but to Hollywood, ...
thevintagecameo.com
    Did they/she play Clare Sterling as well?

Sterling
was a journalist who lived in Italy.

She took all the "evidence" of .... bbc.co.uk

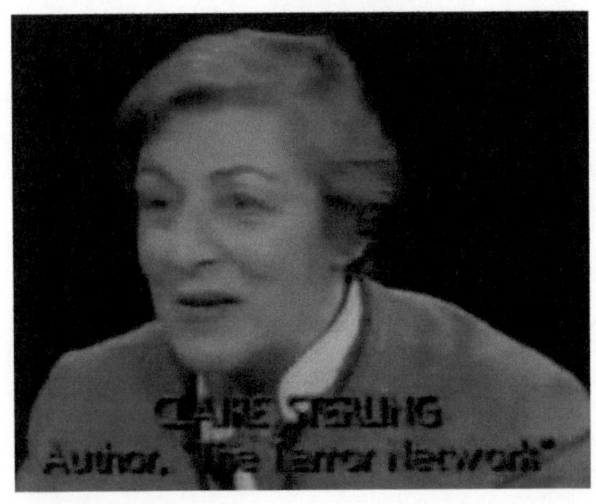

Update on "The Terror Network" - An Interview with Claire Sterling (1982)

youtube.com
They shared editors and husbands- (Why have their identities been mixed with others?)

Did she play the part of Celia de la Serna?

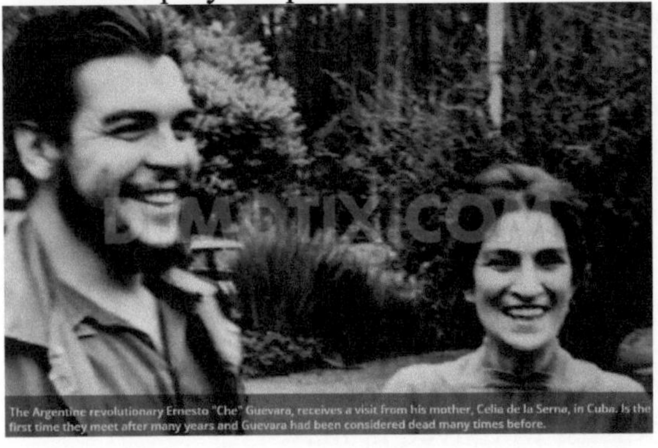

The Argentine revolutionary Ernesto "Che" Guevara, receives a visit from his mother, Celia de la Serna, in Cuba. Is the first time they meet after many years and Guevara had been considered dead many times before.

An historic look on a young Ernesto Che Guevara demotix.com

The Argentine revolutionary Ernesto "Che" Guevara, receives a visit from his mother, Celia de la Serna, in Cuba. Is the first time they meet after many years and Guevara had been considered dead many times before.

This comes from the same program as above. Note the nose!

I do not know how many times Che's mother visited Che in Cuba- but she did not seem to have many cloths as she can be seen wearing the only two out fits. Though she dose change her earrings.

 Pictured here with his parents. His father Ernesto Guevara said in 1969: ...fantompowa.net

 Llegada de padres y hermano del Che a Cuba en Enero de 1959. Foto: lanacion.com.ar

The likeness between Che and Celia can be explained in another way.

Chapter seven.
The four in one lady- Katy, Anna, Claire, Celia.

To make the case that she is a four in one lady. I would like to point out some of their connections.
Katy Jurado-
Katy Jurado studied journalism and she was the cousin of Emilo Portes Gil, who was President when there was unrest in Mexico.
Mario Vargas Llosa- is a Peruvian writer political and journalist. He directed Katy in 'Pantaleony las Vistadoras'. (He had written the novel.)
Gabriel Garcia Marquez made 'La Viuda de Montiel The Widow of Montiel is a 1979 Mexican film directed by Miguel Littin, it is based on a short story of the same name by Gabriel Garcia Marquez. It was entered into the 30th Berlin International film festival.

Director: Miguel Littin
Escritores: Gabriel Garcia Marquez, Jose Agustin

Reparto:
Geraldine Chaplin, Nelson Villagra, Katy Jurado, Eduardo Gil, Ernesto Gomez Cruz
Alejandro Parodi, Ignacio Retes, Emilia Rojas

Pais: Mexico Cooproduccion
Genero: Drama

Regis Debray was the scriptwriter of *The Recourse to the Method* (*El recurso del método*) is the Mexican-Cuban drama film directed by Miguel Littin. It is based on the novel of the same name written by Alejo Carpentier. It was entered into the 1978 Cannes film Festival. The film was also selected as the Cuban entry for the best foreign language film at the 51st Academy Awards but was not accepted as a nominee.

El recurso del método - Watch Full Movie Online FREE ...

*anontv.com/.../449754-the-recourse-to-the-**method*** - Alejo Carpentier; *Régis Debray*. Stars: *Katy Jurado* · Nelson Villagra · Ernesto Gómez Cruz ... Cast; Reviews; Comments; Images. *Katy Jurado*. La Mayorala ...

The Recourse to the Method (1978) - FilmAffinity

www.filmaffinity.com/en/film410775.html

With Nelson Villagra, *Katy Jurado*, Alain Cuny, María Adelina Vera, Salvador ... Miguel Littin, Jaime A. Shelly, *Régis Debray* (Novel: Alejo Carpentier); Music ...

Anna Magnani-

Did you know that Anna Magnani is an author? Isabella Rossellini is the one who is telling me that. Roberto Rossellini was one of the many husbands of Anna.

Roberto Rossellini's interest lay in the Italian Neorealism (Italian: *Neorealismo*), also known as

The Golden Age of Italian Cinema, is a national film movement characterized by stories set amongst the poor and the working class. He founded the Italian film company TEVERE. 1947.
Roberto Rossellini made a film with Gabriel Garcia Marquez. The Wild Bunch, with Jean Luc Godard. As it happens this is a Chillan Film.

Goffredo Alesandrini. Another husband attributed to Anna,
He was one of the most important film directors in Italian Fascism. His most remembered and important works are two anti-Communist films (combined to make up 4 hours), both based on Ayn Rand's 'We the Living'. It was turned into a pair of films, *Noi vivi* and *Addio, Kira* in 1942 by Scalara Films, Rome; despite resistance from the Italian government under Mussolini. The films were taken from theatres as the Italian Italia and German governments, who were anti -Communism, discovered that the stories also contained an anti-Fascist message. These films were re-edited into a new version which was approved by Rand and re-released as *We the Living* in 1986.

(Massimo Serato abandoned his studies to train as an actor at the Experimental Cinema Centre, he won a competition to enter Scalera Films, he became Anna Magnani partner, after the making of the film 'Meet the zoo Saponieri of Franco.' (1937), a short film funded by University groups fascists.)

Francesco Rosi-
<u>Francesco Rosi, film director - obituary - Telegraph</u>
www.telegraph.co.uk › News › Obituaries
30.01.2015 - *Francesco Rosi*, who has died aged 92, was a film director who took ... *Rosi* co-wrote Visconti's Bellissima (1951), starring *Anna Magnani,*

Francesco Rosi's films are really about the hidden ties between the Mafia and the US government following the liberation of Sicily.

Marlon Brando- was also an activist, supporting many causes, notably the African American Civil Rights Movement and various American Indian Movements.

Errol Flynn- was also a revolution supporter; he donated money to the Cuban movement, as well as producing 'Cuban Rebel Girls. In this film Beverly Aadland- Che's acting sister and Jorge Masitti or was it Jean-Louis Trintignant; can be seen acting.

Errol and Anna Magnani on set of Vulcano

Errol Magnani and Lanza theerrolflynnblog.com

Isabella Rossellini-
Isabella Rossellini's father was Roberto Rossellini,
as Anna Magnani was his wife; to see it was Isabella
telling me that Anna was an actress as well as writer.
Isabella Rossellini is the modern link to Mario
Vargas Llosa and Gabriel Garcia Marquez.

Isabella Rossellini, part two | Interviews |
guardian.co.uk Film
www.theguardian.com/film/.../0,,2074972,00.html
05.05.2007 - *Isabella Rossellini*, part two ... It's a
myth that there was no Rossellini script. .... *Anna
Magnani*, I loved her and thought she was a goddess.

Cilia de la Serna-
Cilia de la Serna Llosa: Mario Vargas Llosa first
wife Julia Urquidi Illanes informs they were friends
and that Cilia de la Serna Llosa stayed in their flat in
Paris. In the open letter- Peru 21 it states that Mario
Vargas Llosa was hospitable to *Celia de la Serna
Llosa.*

In the book written by Ernesto Guevara Lynch about his life, he says that **Che's mother at the time of the Spanish Civil war was in Spain, as a war correspondent** sent by the 'Critical' newspaper. Cilia was a correspondent during the Spanish civil war.
www.kaosenlared.net/.../80432-enestro-''che''-guevara...

Claire Sterling-
Clare Sterling informs us that she went to study Journalism. She received a master's degree in journalism from Columbia University in 1945.

Gabriel Martinez - Columbia University
*www.**columbia**.edu/cu/wallach/.../**Martinez**.html*
Gabriel Martinez. explores issues of labor relations involved in the production, maintenance, and distribution of class subjectivity. He has attended the residency ...
 Chronicle of a Death Foretold (1987), an Italian-French-Colombian co-production, directed by Francesco Rosi,

26 Apr 1990 - FILM Mafia: good for film business - Trove
trove.nla.gov.au/ndp/del/.../122103028?... -
26.04.1990 - ... recently in Sicily include To Forget Palermo by Italian director *Francesco Rosi, ... Rosi,* who won international recognition in 1963 when he

made Salva tore ... *Claire Sterling*, the American journalist author of a new book, .

New Iberoamerican Journalism Foundation

Gabriel Garcia Marqueez Foundation for New Latin Amercan Journalism.

Founder Gabriel Garcia Marquez Colombia, Carttagena De Indias. Website WWW.fnpi.org. (FNPI) is a a non-profit instution created by Gabriel Garcia Marquez in order to work for excellence in jouranalism and its contribution to progrcesses of democracy and development in Latin American countries and Caribbean, through workshops and seminars and exchanges between journalists, cooerpation between networks and incentives to professional development.

Chapter eight.
Claire Sterling one of the names in four in one Lady.

Some say she was a CIA agent, I think she was Gabriel Garcia Marquez's lady who spread his propaganda wherever it was needed, be it in her books and articles or in the American Senate.

In her book, 'Thieves World.' She writes about a man named Orlando Cediel Ospina-Vargas, of Colombia. He was the man behind Pablo Escobar's escape from the gilded Colombian prison. Orlando Cediel Ospina-Vargas had another passport which states his name was Jose Guillermo Duran of Venezuela.

After stating this, in the next sentence Claire tells me Tony Duran is the head of the Colombian delegation meeting with the Mafia in Italy.
The three names are for one man!

UN TOLIMENSE, ORLANDO CEDIEL OSPINA, ES EL PAPA ...
www.eltiempo.com/archivo/.../MAM-215062
UN TOLIMENSE, ORLANDO CEDIEL OSPINA, ES EL PAPA DE LA DROGA ... José Durán Tony es en realidad *Orlando Cediel Ospina Vargas*, de 39 años de ...

This program was nice enough to tell me about the intertwining identities. The article is dated 1992. (Did Claire know the three names belonged to one man? As they are referred to in one paragraph, I think so.)

Tony Duran was in Italy to bring together the Mafia's powerful families and Colombia's cocaine cartels.

Tony Duran-sundance.tv

Orlando Cediel Ospina-Vargas of Colombia, better known as "Tony" Duran, photographed secretly during his stay in Rome in the autumn of 1992, to negotiate a top-level partnership between the Sicilian Mafia and Colombia's main cocaine cartels. (Mario Proto)

Tony Duran-sundance.tv this internet address has another photo of him

    Tony Duran-sundance.tv this address is interesting in itself as we can wriggle back to Gabriel Garcia Marquez's film connections and the Italian Neo-Realism!
'Sundance Institute in Utah; run by the actor and director Robert Redford. Gabriel Garcia Marquez and Robert Redford were close associates.
    Those that wished to photograph men in their natural form had to leave Cuba. Tony Duran was among those that did. In Paris this kind of photograph was appreciated.

<u>Breathless (1959/Godard)/The Bicycle Thieves (aka The ...</u>
www.fulvuedrive-in.com/.../Breathless+1959+Godar...
... (2015/Lionsgate DVD)/The Encore Of *Tony Duran* (2011/Cinedigm DVD)/Hot .... with Roberto Rossellini's Rome (Open City)) launched *Italian Neo-Realism.*
<u>The Dossier | Edited by Jay V. del Rosario | Page 14</u>
https://dossiermag.wordpress.com/page/14/
Shot by Steven Klein, the adverts draw from *Italian Neorealism* cinema and that ... Photog *Tony Duran* has the honor of shooting the actor, who WWD calls "a ...

-The Terror network-
THE ROLE OF CUBA IN INTERNATIONAL TERRORISM AND SUBVERSION

Intelligence Activities of the DGI

FRIDAY, FEBRUARY 26, 1982

HEARINGS
BEFORE THE
SUBCOMMITTEE ON SECURITY AND
TERRORISM
OF THE COMMITTEE ON THE JUDICIARY
UNITED STATES SENATE
NINETY-SEVENTH CONGRESS
SECOND SESSION ON
THE ROLE OF CUBA IN INTERNATIONAL
TERRORISM AND SUBVERSION

FEBRUARY 26, MARCH 4, 11, AND 12, 1982

Serial No. J-97-97

Printed for the use of the Committee on the Judiciary

U.S. GOVERNMENT PRINTING OFFICE
WASHINGTON: 1982

HEARING

BEFORE THE

SUBCOMMITTEE ON SECURITY AND TERRORISM

OF THE

COMMITTEE ON THE JUDICIARY
UNITED STATES SENATE

NINETY-SEVENTH CONGRESS

FIRST SESSION

ON

THE ORIGINS, DIRECTION AND SUPPORT OF TERRORISM

APRIL 24, 1981

Catalog Record: Terrorism, origins, direction, and support ...

catalog.hathitrust.org/Record/006223722

Terrorism, origins, direction, and support *: hearing before the Subcommittee on ... first session, on the origins, direction, and support of terrorism, April 24, 1981.*

*Serial no. j-97-17. This is the written account of the hearing before the subcommittee on security and terrorism at which **Clair Sterling** was a witness. I use the word witness as it is the word Senator Denton used. He states that Claire Sterling has a profound background in the subjects for decision. And he informs the hearing that Claire Sterling is the author of the book, 'the Terror Network'*

The four other people who appeared as witnesses at the Hearing-

1) William E Colby-attorney at law, former Director of the Central Intelligence Agency.

2) Michael Ledeen Ph.D., modern European history, Center for Strategic and International Studies. Georgetown University.

3) Arnaud De Borchgrave- International journalist, coauthor of 'The Spike'. Associated of the Center for Strategic and International Studies. Georgetown University.

4) Robert Moss- coauthor of 'The Spike'. International journalist.

    (The Spike is a Fictionalized account of KGB disinformation.)

It is Claire Sterling who was saying on March 13th 1981 in 'The Times magazine.' that it was the USSA behind the terrorists.

At the hearing of the Senate she points the finger at Cuba. 24th April 1981.

It is Claire Sterling who informs the hearing that Ginangiacomo Feltrinelli was a hero worshipper of Fidel Castro, Che Guevara and the Cuban concept of the third world revolution. Claire Sterling also informs the comity of Ginangiacomo Feltrinelli presents at the Tricontinental Conference. And that

Ginangiacomo Feltrinelli visited Fidel Castro often. In Ginangiacomo Feltrinelli bookstores he featured the Italian edition of Tricontinental Magazine. The magazine was Fidel Castro's first official voice in the continent.

(The *Minimanual of the Urban Guerrile-* by *Carlos Marighella was also to be found in* Ginangiacomo Feltrinelli'*s bookstores. Who is telling the hearing this-Claire Sterling? And she them about Ilich Ramirez Sanchez-Carlos the Jackal; a Cuban grown hero.) (They made a film about him.)*

'The Terror Net work,' by Claire Sterling and 'Senior Service' by Carlos Feltrinelli both books state that *Ginangiacomo Feltrinelli took $50.000.000 to Bolivia.*

Despite trying very hard to get a copy of Claire Sterling's 'The Feltrinelli Case' I was not able to. But! I point out the connection.

1. Reports & Comment by Claire Sterling
Italy: The Feltrinelli Case
The Atlantic Monthly, July 1972, pp. 10-19

2. Superdams: The Perils of Progress by Claire Sterlin
The Atlantic Monthly, June 1972, pp. 35-40

It is Clair Sterling who in forms the U.S. Senate,
Subcommittee on Security and Terrorism in
February 1982. That the United States was not
immune from Cuban terrorist activity. Juan F
Benemelis in 'Las Guerras Secrets de Fidel Castro'
2002 when he published his work confirms the
subjects Claire Sterling had informed the
subcommittee hearing.

**<u>Castro and Terrorism: A Chronology -
Scholarly Repository</u>**

scholarlyrepository.miami.edu/.../viewcontent.cgi?...
von E Pons - 2001 - <u>Zitiert von: 2</u> - <u>Ähnliche Artikel</u>
10.05.2001 - *Castro and Terrorism: A Chronology.*
Eugene Pons. This Article is brought to you for free
and open access by the Institute of Cuban and
Cuban ...

    This program gives you at a glance a guide line to
Fidel Castro's activities of the times. Claire Sterling
had already stated this!

Leo Wanta, the American snake-oil salesman who stormed world money markets to crash the ruble in 1990-91.

Lee Emil Wanta

Lee Wanta supplying guns to Manuel Antonio Noriega, who was Panama's Dictator; leads us back to Gabriel García Márquez!

John Jairo Vasquez Velasquez, alias 'Popeye', was Pablo Escobar's hit-man. There is much written about him, he has not hesitated to mention who is on the list of Pablo Escobar famous friends. Manuel Antonio Noriega, Daniel Ortega he was President of Nicaragua and Gabriel García Márquez, Raul and

Fidel Castro, are in the list of political leaders who, according to John Jairo Vasquez Velasquez sponsored the misdeeds of a major terrorist in Latin America.

Pablo Escobar and his colleagues Jorge Luis Ochoa and Gonzalo Rodriguez Gacha, they took refuge in Panama, with the protection of Noriega rented a furnished house belonging to a Panamanian General for the convenience of drug traffickers.

John Jairo Vasquez Velasquez states Gabriel **García Márquez served as a courier between Escobar and Fidel Castro.**

NORIEGA, U.S. ARMS DEALER PLANNING TO BUY 5,000 ...

www.washingtonpost.com/.../**noriega**.../41e70b36-9... -

25.03.1988 - Panamanian strongman **Manuel Antonio Noriega** *is trying to arrange through ... transaction last Saturday by AmeriChina President* **Leo Wanta**.

The drug lord Pablo Escobar was hidden by Sandinistas in Nicaragua, says former buddy

El narcotraficante Pablo Escobar fue escondido en ...

www.radiolaprimerisima.com/.../el-narcotraficante-p...

05.03.2006 - **Manuel Antonio Noriega**, *Daniel Ortega,* **Gabriel García Márquez**, *Raúl y Fidel*

Castro, se encuentran en la lista de líderes políticos que, según ...

**-Thieves World' 1994-
this is another book by Claire Sterling.**

Why is Lee Wanta still interesting? He stole 2000 tons of gold. USSA gold! Lee Wanta Along with Ronald Reagan and his assistant Hillary Clinton. Claire Sterling has explained how he did it, in 'Thieves World'.

With the help of the Mafia, (Tony Duran!) every ruble was sucked out of the USSR, and the USSR's gold reserve removed from its land. What a con, USSA bankrupt! A counter reaction to Gabriel García Márquez and the Castro's plan. No longer could the USSA support their plan.

Leo Emil Wanta - Veterans Today

www.veteranstoday.com/author/**wanta**/

Leo *Emil* **Wanta** *is a syndicated columnist, former world Ambassador and Presidential Secret Agent serving under U.S. President Ronald Reagan / Totten ...*

The Story Of Leo Wanta 'The 27.5 Trillion Dollar Man' - Rense

www.rense.com/general70/**leo**.htm

In one of the most important stories of our time, **Wanta** *holds the 'finacial key' to the ... the activities of the CIA operative known as Mrs* **Hillary Rodham** *Clinton.*

Former Ambassador Says Vince Foster Was Murdered Leo ...

www.rense.com/.../formerambassadorsays.htm
Former Ambassador **Leo Wanta**, *jailed for years and framed by the Bush and Clinton ... the activities of the CIA operative known as Mrs* **Hillary Rodham** *Clinton.*

Was this why Bill Clinton band her book? 'Thieves *World' the threat of the new global network of organized crime,1994*
In Part ii selling 2000 tons of gold is the advance that the book was held back from publication.

part ii_selling 2000 tons of gold_08apr14

wantarevelations.com/.../**PART**-II_SELLING-**2000**-
...
08.04.2014 - SELLING **2000 TONS OF GOLD** *by Leo Wanta and NEW ... Link to document ~>LEO WANTA* **GOLD** *.... by* **Claire Sterling** *.... Page* **11** ...

The Role of Cuba in International Terrorism and Subversion

www.latinamericanstudies.org/terrorism.htm
THE ROLE OF CUBA IN INTERNATIONAL *TERRORISM AND SUBVERSION. HEARINGS BEFORE THE SUBCOMMITTEE ON SECURITY AND TERRORISM*

Claire Sterling's death!

New World Out of Order - Bilderberg Group - NWO3

nwo3.com/index.php/bilderberg.../podcasts-articles
2010 *Marilyn M. Barnewall* - All Rights Reserve.
Marilyn ...... At all events,
Mrs *Claire Sterling* died suddenly after her second interview with the FBI. EDITOR'S ...

William E Colby died too! Suspiciously.
(WHO MURDERED THE CIA CHIEF? - Pythia Press
www.pythiapress.com/wartales/colby.htm
William E. Colby: *A Highly Suspicious Death ... In my* **book**, *Facing the Phoenix, I described him as being a polite man who was open and approachable but ...)*

New World Out of Order - Bilderberg Group - NWO3

nwo3.com/index.php/bilderberg-group/...nwo3/pod...
This program provides another link-
Podcast *Corrections: ... I provided a link to an* **article** *about Lee Wanta by Don Nicoloff from the January 2007 Idaho Observer. ..... Lee and his* **New** *Republic* **group** *used Promis Software, which belongs to a company called Inslaw, ... At all events, Mrs* **Claire Sterling died** *suddenly after her*

*second interview with the FBI.*PERJURED
EVIDENCE AND LIES FED TO Judge Torphy's
court.
Editor's Funds to 'Resolve' previously settled
case#92CF683.

William E Colby- The CIA Chief.
Claire Sterling-   And William E Colby? The
situation gets a bit hot and pop! They have gone! At
least they did not make a film about it!

Chapter nine.
Independent men?

*The four other people who appeared as witnesses at
the Hearing* before the Subcommittee on Security
and Terrorism-

1) *William E Colby-attorney at law, former
   Director of the Central Intelligence Agency.*
2) *Michael Ledeen Ph.D., modern European
   history, Center for Strategic and
   International Studies. Georgetown
   University.*
3) *Arnaud De Borchgrave- international
   journalist, coauthor of 'The Spike'.
   Associated of the Center for Strategic and
   International Studies. Georgetown
   University.*
4) *Robert Moss- coauthor of 'The Spike'.
   international journalist.*
   *(The Spike is a Fictionalized account of
   KGB disinformation.)*

1) William E Colby-attorney at law, former Director
of the Central Intelligence Agency.
Was also a former CIA Director. On Saturday,
April 27, 1996, Colby died in what appears to be a
boating accident near his home in Rock Point,

Maryland. There was speculation that William E Colby's death was due to CIA foul play- or was it suicide? The Maryland state coroner, however, ruled that Colby had suffered either a heart attack or a stroke owing to a discernible plaque buildup in his arteries, and had fallen into the water and drowned. Most of Colby's family and his biographer viewed a suicide as completely inconsistent with his character. However, in a biographical documentary developed by Colby's son Carl Colby, he speculated that Colby had simply "... had enough of this life."
WHO MURDERED THE CIA CHIEF? - Pythia Press
www.pythiapress.com/wartales/colby.htm
William E. **Colby**: *A Highly Suspicious Death ... In my* **book**, *Facing the Phoenix, I described him as being a polite man who was open and approachable but ...*

2) *Michael Arthur Ledeen Ph.D., modern European history, Center for Strat*egic and International Studies *Georgetown University.* An American historian, philosopher and neoconservative foreign policy analyst, and writer. He is a former consultant to the United States National Security Council, the United States Department of State United and the United States Department of Defense.

When in Rome he was hired as the Rome correspondent for '*The New Republik*' and named as visiting professor at the University of Rome. In Rome Michael Ledeen worked with Italian historian Renzo De Felice in 1980, in the period leading up to the U.S. presidential elections. Michael Ledeen, along with Arnaud de Borchgrave, wrote a series of articles published in 'The New Republic' and elsewhere about Jimmy Carter's brother, Billy Carter's contacts with the Muammar al-Gaddafi.

In the early 1980s, Michael Ledeen appeared before the newly established Senate Subcommittee on Security and Terrorism, alongside former CIA director William E Colby, author Claire Sterling and former *Newsweek* editor Arnaud de Borchgrave. Both Michael Ledeen and Arnaud De Borchgrave worked for the Center for Strategic and International Studies at Georgetown University at the time. And they worked with-
<u>The Daily Beast</u>
*www.**thedailybeast**.com/*
A smart, speedy take on the news from around the world.

3) Arnaud De Borchgrave- international journalist, coauthor of 'The Spike' with Robert Moss. Are associated of the Center for Strategic and International Studies; Georgetown University.

Arnaud De Borchgrave married his wife, Alexandra Villard de Borchgrave; daughter of ambassador and author Henry Serrano Villard.

Arnaud de Borchgrave, interviewed statesmen and dictators across time zones and war zones as a swashbuckling foreign correspondent for Newsweek Magazine. He later led the Washington Times as editor during the newspaper's early years.

Arnaud De Borchgrave and Michael Ledeen worked with the 'Daily Beast.'

4) Robert Moss- coauthor of 'The Spike' with Arnaud De Borchgrave. Robert Moss is also an international journalist connected to international politicians. His subjects were Urban Guerrilla warfare. He wrote the speech for Margret Thatcher that gave her the name of 'The Iron Lady.'
Robert Moss translated- 'Short Stories' By Gabriel Garcia Marquez as well as other stories for Jorge Luis Borges.

Southern Africa: South Africa Reports Angola War Role
web.stanford.edu/.../1441-1977-02-12-FoF-a-RRW....
12.02.1977 - Another report, by **Robert Moss**, *a former editor with The Economist, was published as a series in ... Colombian author,* **Gabriel Garcia Marquez**.
Another report, by Robert Moss, a former editor with The Economist, was published as a series in the Toronto Globe and Mail beginning January 31. Moss said Cuban soldiers had been operating in Angola several months before November 5, 1975, the date on which the Cubans officially said they had decided to intervene. Moss was responding to an official account by Cuba of its role in Angola, written by the Colombian author-

Gabriel Garcia Marquez.

Amazon.com: Robert Moss - Short Stories &
Anthologies ...

www.amazon.com › ... › Short Stories &
Anthologies

by **Robert Moss** ... *Translated works from Jorge
Luis Borges,* **Gabriel Garcia Marquez**, *and other
South American magical realist authors can
transport you into ...*

<u>Here, Everything Is Dreaming: Poems and Stories
(Excelsior Editions)</u>

Apr 2, 2013 by Robert Moss.

He translated works from Jorge Luis Borges,
Gabriel Garcia Marquez, and other South American
magical realist authors can transport you into
strangely convincing fantasies for a fantastic read.
In an age of televised battles, the war for Angola
was a remarkably secret war, and the truth of what
happened is only slowly beginning to seep out. The
Cubans have just produced their authorized version,
in the form of a book-length article published by the
Colombian novelist Gabriel Garcia Marquez in the
Mexican magazine Progreso. In the midst of a
wealth of factual detail, his account is littered with
distortions and plain untruths.

Do you see names repeating themselves? It makes
my hair stand on end.

Connecting Claire Sterling and Michael Ledeen and others-

Talk:Michael Ledeen/Archive 1 - Wikipedia, the free ...

https://en.wikipedia.org/.../Talk%3AMichael_Ledee...

3.1 Dewey Clarridge On *Michael Ledeen* and "The Terror Network"; 3.2 Melvin A. .... During this Italian stint he collaborated regularly with *Claire Sterling* in ...

(In Rome Michael Ledeen worked with the Italian historian by the name of Renzo De Relice and author Claire Sterling and the former Newsweek editor Arnaud De Borchgrave. Bothe Michael Ledeen and Arnaud De Borchgrave worked for the Center for Strategic and International Studies at Georgetown University.)

Claire Sterling | The New Republic

www.newrepublic.com/tags/claire-sterling When I took over The New Republic in 1974 one of the first people I recruited--on a trip to Rome, as I recall-- was *Michael Ledeen*, a scholar of Italian fascism.

The Real History of American Relations With Iran Martin Peretz

September 30, 2009

'When Martin Peretz took over The New Republic in 1974 one of the first people he recruited--on a trip to Rome, as I recall--was Michael Ledeen, a scholar of Italian fascism. He thought it was his doctoral supervisor and his friend, the great German Jewish historian, George Mosse, who suggested that they meet. But it actually was Claire Sterling, the brave journalist of uncomfortable truths, who introduced them. Michael was then working on a book about Gabriele d'Annunzio, the futurist poet, artist, fighter pilot, political theorist and neo-fascist adventurer who led a march on Fiume to keep it in Italian hands.'

Now a connection to Gabriel Garcia Marquez- Michael Ledeen- and others!

<u>Guatemalan genocide got assist from US, Christian Right ...</u>
mondoweiss.net/2013/.../guatemalan-genocide-chris...
18.05.2013 - Neoconservative academic *Michael Ledeen*, who left the Defense .... How *Gabriel Garcia Marquez* Brought Down Samuel Zemurray, the ...

   An indication that Gabriel Garcia Marquez brought down Zemurray, overthrew the sovereign government of Honduras (in 1911), possibly had Huey Long killed, leveraged the United Nations votes needed from Central and South America to pass Resolution 181 (which acknowledged Israel's independence) and overthrew the sovereign government of Guatemala (in 1954), unintentionally

inspiring Che Guevara and Fidel Castro to
communist revolution.

I add this to show how active they were-
Michael Ledeen - Deep Politics Forum
https://deeppoliticsforum.com/.../showthread.php?...
29.05.2013 - ... Ledeen, along with *Arnaud de
Borchgrave*, wrote a series of articles ... *Claire
Sterling* and former Newsweek editor *Arnaud de
Borchgrave*.
Claire Sterling and Ledeen even appeared on Italian
television on the night of the election. They featured
as commentators from 4pm to 2am on Channel 1
which was controlled by the Christian Democrat
Party - the main recipient of CIA funds in Italy.

Michael Ledeen - Wikipedia, the free encyclopedia
https://en.wikipedia.org/wiki/Michael_Ledeen
In Rome Ledeen worked with Italian historian
Renzo De Felice, who Ledeen was ... author *Claire
Sterling* and former Newsweek editor *Arnaud de
Borchgrave*.
Both Ledeen and de Borchgrave worked for the
Center for Strategic and International Studies at
Georgetown University at the time.

Arnaud de Borchgrave - SourceWatch
www.sourcewatch.org/index.../Arnaud_de_Borchgr..
.

17.08.2009 - *Arnaud de Borchgrave* was the former editor-in-chief from 1985 to 1991 ... Robert Moss, *Arnaud de Borchgrave*, Daniel James, *Claire Sterling*, ...

Disinformation Agent

William Preston and Ellen Ray wrote a history of disinformation in the U.S.
They observed:

The greatest assistance in disinformation – especially during the current Administration – is always forthcoming from the *Reader's Digest*. In 1977 the *Times* exposed Digest editor John Barron as having worked hand in glove with the CIA on a book about the KGB. Other fraudulent journalists like Robert Moss, Arnaud de Borchgrave, Daniel James, Claire Sterling, and Michael Ledeen, among others, seem to pick up disinformation themes almost automatically. In fact, coordination between the development of propaganda and disinformation themes by the covert media assets, the overt propaganda machine, and the bevy of puppet journalists is quite calculated. A theme which is floated on one level – a feature item on VOA about Cuba for example – will appear within record time as a lead article in *Reader's Digest*, or a feature in a *Heritage Foundation report*, or a series of "exposes" by Moss and de Borchgrave or Daniel James in some reactionary tabloid like *Human Events* or the *Washington Times* or *Inquirer*. Then they will be called to testify by Senator Denton's Subcommittee on Security and Terrorism, repeating one another's allegations as "expert witnesses".

After that they are given credibility by the "respectable" Cold War publications like the *National Review*, *Commentary*, and the *New Republic*. And finally, since they have repeated the theme so many times it must be true; they are given the opportunity to write Op Ed pieces for the *New York Times* or the *Washington Post*.
— William Preston and Ellen Ray, op. cit., pp. 7-8.

Independent men-next leave!
Paul Henze-
The plot to kill the pope - Paul B. Henze - Google Books
books.google.com › Social Science › General - <u>Diese Seite übersetzen</u>
Front Cover. *Paul* B. *Henze. Simon & Schuster*, 1983 - Social Science - 216 pages ... conspiracy to murder Pope John *Paul* II and speculates on Russian motives ...

James Jesus Angleton-
books are printed by la Feltrenilli.
Ginangiacomo Feltrinelli' company!
Alexander Cockburn- CounterPunch-
connects Gabriel Garcia Marquez and Ginangiacomo Feltrinelli company.
Jeffrey ST Clair is editor of Counter Punch.

Books by Claire and printed by Simon and Schuster.

Almost President: The Men Who Lost the Race but Changed ...

https://books.google.de/books?isbn=0762784210 -
Scott Farris - 2013 - History
Alexander Cockburn and *Jeffrey St. Clair*, Al Gore: A User's Manual (Verso, ... Citizen McCain (*Simon and Schuster*, New York, 2002), and Robert Timberg,John ...

Culture Wars: An Encyclopedia of Issues, Viewpoints and Voices

https://books.google.de/books?isbn=1317473515 -
Roger Chapman, James Ciment - 2015 - Business & Economics
New York: *Simon & Schuster*, 1999. Clinton, Bill. My Life. New York: Alfred A. ... Nashville, TN: Thomas Nelson, 2012. Cockburn, Alexander, and *Jeffrey St. Clair*.

Here are more authors-

Regis Debray-
Ciro Bustos-
Felix Rodriguez-
Regis Debray : l'homme qui parlait trop -- Emrah KAYNAK

www.legrandsoir.info/regis-debray-l-homme-qui-pa...
27.04.2013 - Debray et Bustos seront arrêtés à Camiri et interrogés sans ... fautes de ses

compagnons et qui charge sans complaisance *Ciro Bustos*, ... (4) Felix Rodriguez, John Weissman, Shadow Warrior, *Simon & Schuster* Ltd, 1992.

Amazon.com: Che Guevara or Richard Nixon - Memoirs ...

www.amazon.com › ... › Memoirs
Auto-delivered wirelessly. 4.2 out of 5 stars 31. Sold by: *Simon and Schuster* Digital Sales Inc .... Jun 4, 2013 | Kindle eBook. by *Ciro Bustos* and Anne Wright.

And independent women!

Isabel Allende | Official Publisher Page | Simon & Schuster

authors.simonandschuster.com/Isabel.../1723104Ab ubakar Adam Ibrahim is the author of the short-story collection, The Whispering Trees. He is a *Gabriel Garcia Marquez* Fellow and has won the BBC African ..

Isabel Allende - Author, Journalist - Biography.com

www.biography.com/people/isabel-allende-9181801 *Isabel Allende* is a Chilean author best known for penning novels in the style of magic realism. She is the niece of former Chilean *president* Salvador Allende.

Sterling, Claire. Octopus: The Long Reach of the International Sicilian Mafia. New York: Simon & Schuster (Touchstone Edition), 1991. 384 pages.

Sterling, Claire. Thieves' World: The Threat of the New Global Network of Organized Crime. New York: Simon & Schuster, 1994. 304 pages.

Ann Wright- (Monica Ertl)
Elisableth Burgos-Debray –

Taking Charge: Every Woman's Action Guide to Personal, ...

https://books.google.de/books?isbn=1573240524 -
Diese Seite übersetzen
Joan Steinau Lester - 1996 - Business & Economics
McMillan, Terry, Waiting to Exhale, Pocket Books, *Simon and Schuster*, 1992. ... edited by *Elisabeth Burgos-Debray*, translated by Ann Wright, Verso, 1984.

Guatemalan Journey - Seite 208 - Google Books-Ergebnisseite

https://books.google.de/books?isbn=0292782993 -
Diese Seite übersetzen
Stephen Connely Benz - 2010 - Travel
Elisabeth Burgos-Debray, ed. Ann Wright, trans. New York: Verso. Montejo, Victor. ... New York: *Simon and Schuster*. Theroux, Paul. 1979. The Old Patagonian ...

Susan Sontag
<u>Remembering Susan Sontag | VQR Online</u>

www.vqronline.org/essay/remembering-susan-sontag

19.12.2006 - Remembering *Susan Sontag* .... and the Failure of the West (*Simon & Schuster*, 1995), The Exile: Cuba in the Heart of Miami (*Simon & Schuster ...*

To get even more muddled!

Counter Punch- states that Fidel Castro wrote the review for Gabriel Garcia Marques' autobiography, 'Living to Tell the Tale.' Question who is on the Counter Punch editorial?

Answer-Jeffrey St Clair and Alexander Cockburn- - -!

Chapter ten
The Workers Vanguard

The Workers Vanguard dated 25th April 1986 no. 402. Pope Plot Frame-up Flops.
"The Bulgarian Concoction- in this article Al Hage is reported to say in the first days of Ronald Ragan's turn of office; that it was their intention that 'International Terrorism would be their center of focus.

Robert Moss on 2nd November 1980 the week before Ronald Ragan's election Published in the New York Times a special entitled 'Terror: A Soviet Export'

Weeks after the president's inaugural, the 'Times Magazine of March 1981 ran the story by Claire Sterling: where she claimed to have 'Massive Proof ' that the Soviet Union and its surrogates had provided the weapons, training and sanctuary for a world terror network-
'The Terror Times' (WV No. 276, 13 March 1981)

On March the 4th 1986 Alexander Cockburn point at a nest of ideologists of terrorism including Claire Sterling, Arnaud de Borchgrave from the Washington Times. Michael Ledeen and Robert Moss, who worked with General Haig and Ambassador Jean Kirkpatrick as a team; quoting each other and becoming the authorities on the Bulgarian Connection they themselves had concocted.

In September 1982 Reader's Digest published Claire Sterling's exclusive report on the plot to murder the Pope; she used Paul Henze's research. It again it was used in NBC-TV special on the Bulgarian Connection. Claire Sterling was their consultant.
Remembering that they are the people who had given their opinions to the United States Senate on April 24th 1981!

A week after Mehmet Ali Agca shot the Pope a major scandal exploded in the Italian press!
The Italian Military and Intelligence Services were found to be riddled at the highest of leaves by members of the Masonic Loge, P-2. These members were accused of setting up a 'Super S' (super SISMI) they were accused of organizing crime and Fascist group.

Mehmet Ali Agca stated that Francisco Pazienza asked him to collaborate over shooting the Pope; Francisco Pazienza who was a top aide in the Italian Spy Agency SISMI and a member of P-2.

After the remark in 'Village Voice, 24th December 1985 that states Mehmet Ali Agca's connection to the former SISMI bigwig and had been linked to Italian fascist terrorist Stefano delle Chiaie who in turn was on the run with Turkish fascist 'Gray Wolves leader Adbullah Catli, a close associate Mehmet Ali Agca, who shot the Pope!

CovertAction (No. 23, of spring 1985): "Italian investigators have shown that SISMI. Francisco Pazienza and Michael Ledeen, perhaps working through 'Super S, together lured president Jimmy Carter's brother, Billy Carter into a compromising relationship with Co, Qaddafi during the 1980 Ronald Reagan presidential campaign." (What was reported between the sentences has not been printed in Worker Vanguard.)

- It continues-

"After Ronald Reagan's election Michael Ledeen's was more powerful than previously. He is at present working under contract to the Pentagon and the State Department.

The Workers Vanguard then continues by saying 'the Pope plotters' feed from the same trough as the witnesses at Alabama's Senator Jeremiah Denton's terrorism committee, and they all buzzed around the Georgetown University Center for Strategic and International Studies. They are named as Claire Sterling, Michael Ledeen and Robert Moss.

Arnaud de Borchgrave had also been a witness. This group attended the 1979 conference in Israeli at the Jonathan Institute (Some of the fore mentioned seemed to have been founding members. As Ronald Reagan's administration believed that the Soviet Union was the Center of International Terror Network.)"

Claire Sterling, Michael Ledeen and Arnaud de Borchgrave are not the only interesting names included in the conference. The then future vice president Bush's former CIA deputy director for intelligence Ray Cline and British M16/CIA 'asset' Robert Moss and Brian Crozier.

Brian Crozier! The Spy!

The Workers Vanguard ask the question was it all a CIA disinformation plot? They then report that Claire Sterling's group attacks the CIA for not buying their story.
In her book- 'The Time of the Assassins' 1983, Claire Sterling is reported complaining about CIA and Western secret services and the U.S spy agency's lacking of a deeper investigation.
The Workers Vanguard suggests they know why! James Jesus Angleton, they say knows the CIA is riddled with Soviet moles.
Robert Moss and Arnaud de Borchgrave were big fans of the cold war, in their joint book 'The Spike' 1980 a spy novel; Angleton is the for print of 'Nike Flowers' the head of a CIA counterintelligence who proves to gullible members of the press that the 'Western Media' is riddled with Soviet disinformation agents.

The consequence of this book was James Jesus Angleton and aid top aides were- they use the word- 'Dumped' from the CIA.

The report Fred Landis wrote in 'Covert Action (No.18, winter 1983):

"The story of International Israeli-CIA Terror Network begins with James Jesus Angleton, a former head of counterintelligence at the CIA and Catholic Zealot. While stationed in Rome he set up a network of 60 media agents and controlled CIA-Israeli MOSSAD collaboration.

Over a period of 20 years, many of James Jesus Angleton's media agents were recruited from the staff of the 'Newsweek.' (where Arnaud de Borchgrave worked for 17 years) or 'The Washington Post' in Rome, Claire Sterling was one of these; Michael Ledeen is her protégé; Robert moss is a fellow traveler."

So what was Claire Sterling role; a CIA agent or a USSR Mole or one of Gabriel Garcia Marquez's men?

A foot note.

Forrest Hylton: Political Murder in Puerto Rico - Joun

joun.leb.net/hylton09272005.html

27.09.2005 - HOT HOT HOT New *CounterPunch* Print Edition! ... Get the Email Edition of *CounterPunch* for Only $35 a Year ... *Jeffrey St. Clair* ..... Michael Ledeen and *Claire Sterling* became the sort of overnight experts on terrorism that ...

FORREST HYLTON is author of An Evil Hour: Colombia in Historical Context (forthcoming from Verso), as well as co-editor of Ya es otro tiempo el presente: Cuatro momentos de insurgencia indígena, the second edition of which is forthcoming from Muela del Diablo.

Forrest Hilton says: We often forget the anti-terrorist hysteria whipped up during the Reagan years, especially after Mehmet Ali Agca, a Turkish neo-fascist, tried to assassinate Pope John Paul II in 1981; Michael Ledeen and Claire Sterling became the sort of overnight experts on terrorism that have proliferated since 2001, insisting that a "Bulgarian connection" with Soviet communism was behind the attack. Back then, in what Noam Chomsky called the "Second Cold War," "anti-terrorism" was used mainly as a weapon in the crusade against radical nationalism in the Middle East, Central America, and Cuba. Filiberto Ojeda Ríos and those he led into the $7.2 million Wells Fargo depot robbery in West Hartford, CT, in 1983, fit snugly under Washington's "communist terrorist" rubric.

Paul B. Henze, former CIA and national security specialist ...

www.washingtonpost.com/.../paul...henze.../AG4mS.
..

02.06.2011 - *Paul* B. *Henze,* a former CIA and National Security Council specialist in psychological operations who wrote a compelling and provocative book .

Chapter eleven
Chain of events.

Claire Sterling wrote about Carlos Marighella- in 'The Terror Network.'
Anna Magnani worked with a Film producer Luchino Visonto, he in turn edited Carlos Marighella's terrorist instruction book along with the publisher Feltrinelli!
Jean-Luc Godard funded guerrilla Carlos Marighella.
Jean-Luc Godard (French director), Glauber Rocha (film director), Jean-Paul Sartre (French philosopher) Luchino Visconti (Italian director) and Augusto Boal (playwright): Direct support for guerrilla Carlos Marighella.
The Guerrilla that burned down the world- Carlos Marighella.

The Publisher Companhia das Letras launches biography 'Marighella - The Guerrilla What burned down the World' by journalist Mário Magalhães, former reporter and former ombudsman of the 'Folha de S. Paulo'. The book a documented on the guerrilla who was also a poet and composer of samba.

Carlos Marighella became famous for having created the National Liberation Action (ALN), revolutionary organization that is proposed but was unable to overturn the civil-military dictatorship installed in Brazil in April 1964. He had international support, especially Cuba's Fidel Castro, who trained and protected guerrillas, but also Italian, Giangiacomo Feltrinelli like Luchino Visconti and editor. Giangiacomo Feltrinelli, who became a terrorist and died while trying to commit a violation, maintained liaison with the Brazilian guerrilla. He was the first editor to publish "Doctor Zhivago" by Boris Pasternak, and "The Leopard", Sicilian Tomasi di Lampedusa's novel. Count Visconti, director of committed cinema, author of the film "The Leopard," gave money to ALN.

Jean-Luc Godard financiou guerrilha de Marighella - Jornal ...

*www.jornalopcao.com.br/.../jean-luc-godard-financi...*11.11.2012 - O baiano *Carlos Marighella* financiou a guerrilha contra a ditadura ... *Luchino Visconti* (cineasta italiano) e Augusto Boal (dramaturgo): apoio ...

The Brazilian Carlos Marighella funded the guerrilla war against the civil-military dictatorship in the late 1960s, with money robberies from banks and businesses. The leader of the National Liberation Action (ALN), who called himself "terrorist", also received money from Cuba. (Who plaid the military training of the guerrillas), North Korea ($ 200,000 to date) and to artists and intellectuals in Brazil and other countries.

In Brazil Carlos Marighella had the film director Glauber Rocha a permanent source of support. In

1967, he reveals to the journalist Mário Magalhães, in the book "Marighella - The Guerrilla What burned down the World", the Brazilian filmmaker sent a letter to Alfredo Guevara, head of the Cuban film institute. Intending to drive forward a violent and radical devotion; openly disseminating and justifying the creation of different Vietnams. The story was adapted into the work, "Earth Entranced".

In Rome, Glauber Rocha made the 'Collaborator' of the ALN. When he was making this film with Anne Wiazemsky, (another name used the by Che Guevara's said sister) Jean-Luc Godard was filming 'The East Wind," Glauber Rocha spoke to him, Jean-Luc Godard earmarked funds from the production to ALN.
'Restless'- Brazilian filmmaker envisioned a feature film with actress Norma Benguell holding pictures of Marighella and naked in the Andes. The project was aborted. The New Cinema Muse supported the ALN, which was considered sympathetic and hid their militants. Because of statements against the dictatorship, they kidnapped Norma and took her to the PE.
In 1970, another filmmaker, the Italian Luchino Visconti, who was filming "Death in Venice" (based on the novel by Thomas Mann, a German writer and son of a Brazilian) donated money to Marighella. Luchino Visconti had already had joined the 'ALN' with compatriot Gianni Amico, co-writer of 'Before the Revolution' and Bernardo Bertolucci, with

'Lion's Seven Heads' also linked Glauber Rocha to the ALN.

Jean-Paul Sartre began publishing Marighella texts in Europe in 1969, in the journal Les Temps Modernes. The texts were translated into French by the Brazilian guerrilla Ana Corbisier.- she can be found in Wikipedia.

Mário Magalhães, the journalist, says that the Catalan painter Joan Miró donated to the ALN sketches that yielded more than $ 3,000. In Brazil the Italian Lina Bo Bardi, author of the architectural design of the São Paulo Art Museum, hosted Carlos Marighella in its São Paulo Glass House. Where Carlos Marighella spoke with Captain Carlos Lamarca and playwright and theater director Augusto Boal; a friend of Carlos Marighella the second in command in the ALN. Joaquim Camara Ferreira collaborated with the guerrillas.

Joaquim Camara Ferreira a Brazilian politick more information in his Wikipedia.

Carlos marighalla. Carlos Marighella | baader-meinhof.com

*www.baader-meinhof.com/tag/**carlos-marighella**/* by *Carlos Marighella* Notes: Marighella's booklet was considered a sort of bible of the Baader-Meinhof Gang, among many other left-wing terror groups.

Chapter twelve.

The John Wayne and Graham Greene, Dame Margot Fonteyn, connection.

(*meaning one of the names use by the four in one lady.)

When I first looked at the cast list for 'High Noon' it was to remark on the fact that John Wayne wanted to act with Katy Jurado, I had no idea what was behind this film or another film, 'Die Hard 2'. There are threads of rumors that John Wayne and his cast in both films were involved in the unrest in Panama.

When you look up General Ramon Esperanza you are hit by the wall of 'Die Hard 2' propaganda. The film has become more predominant then the facts.

(Did they write history using the film script as a guide line?)

Eric Lichenfeld in his book- 'The Performing Arts' draws your attention to General Ramon Esperanza was a drug running dictator in the mold of Manuel Noriega. There is a lack of information about General Ramon Esperanza on the internet, I am beginning to think he might be a character of their imagination.

Manuel Noriega was arrested in December 1989, while 'Die Hard 2' was in production. He in turn had bought guns from Lee E Wanta, as stated by Claire Sterling* and others.

Manuel Noriega was dictator of Panama. The president that preceded him was Omar Torrijos Herrera among his friends were the British author

Graham Green, Fidel Castro not forgetting John Wayne.

The Island Taborcillo was given to John Wayne as a gift from Omar Torrijos Herrera; states a Wikipedia. John Wayne first wife was Josephine Alicia Saenz the daughter of the Consul General of Panama in the United States, Jose Saenz.

Graham Green was among Omar Torrijos Herrera's friends. Graham Green was a self confessed Spy. When in Mexico, publishers the Economic Culture Fund decided to publish the book about Omar Torrijos Herrera, they asked Gabriel García Márquez "what the title should be." The Colombian told them "That put simply, 'Discovering the General' and not to give him more laps." reissued the book in Spain the publisher Economic Culture Fund used the same name as in Mexico, but with two additions: a foreword by Jon Lee Anderson and an afterword by Gabriel García Márquez.

Graham Greene, Panamá y Torrijos | Cultura | EL PAÍS
cultura.elpais.com/.../1362510332_687622.html
05.03.2013 - Cuenta con epílogo de García Márquez y prólogo de Jon Lee Anderson ... escritor (y espía) inglés se enteró de que el general *Omar Torrijos Herrera,* ... prólogo de Jon Lee Anderson y un epílogo de *Gabriel García Márquez*

"Details of the friendship between the writer Gabriel García Márquez and General Omar Torrijos

Herrera were counted this afternoon during the series of talks in New Iberoamerican Journalism Foundation (FNPI) held in the city of Medellin, Colombia."
 - See more at:
https://translate.googleusercontent.com/translate_c?depth=1&hl=de&rurl=translate.google.de&sl=es&tl=en&u=http://www.prensa.com/angel_lopez_guia/Gabriel-Garcia-Marquez-Panama-Torrijos_0_4039846002.html&usg=ALkJrhjKFRX2P5SdQXsxDrarkV-bbBl2MQ#sthash.2l6TD8Cb.dpuf

Gabriel García Márquez acting as an ambassador? **(There is that man again standing on every corner.** Gabriel García Márquez.

And so is Jon Lee Anderson the writer of 'Che Guevara a revolutionary Life.'- it said he was three years in Cuba with Che's first wife to write it. He was also lived for one year in a flat above Ciro Bustos to complete the book. Coro Bustos told to me 2010.)

Omar Torrijos – Wikipedia
*https://de.wikipedia.org/wiki/**Omar_Torrijos***
Omar Torrijos beim Unterschreiben des Vertrages über den Panama-Kanal 1977 ... schenkte *Omar Torrijos* seinem Freund *John Wayne* die Insel Taborcillo. ... dass *Omar Torrijos* von *Manuel Noriega* im Auftrag der CIA ermordet worden sei.

This internet site points out Manuel Noriega was the intermediary between the then vice-president Bush and Fidel Castro in the 1980s.

The jury in Manuel Noriega trial of 10 narrowly defined drug-related counts heard nothing about his contacts with Bush or Fidel Castro. Nor did it hear about Manuel Noriega contacts with Oliver North, John Poindexter, CIA chief William Casey and other key figures in the Ronald Reagan and Bush administrations who, allegedly, connived in the supply of arms to Nicaragua's Contra rebels paid for with Medellín cartel drug cash.

Don't let Ronald Reagan's name slip by he was in close contact with John Wayne, John Wayne even writes notes to Ronald Reagan. Hand written notes with advice as to how thing should be done!

and Daniel Ortega; allowing the United States to set up listening ...

1981 Manuel Noriega becomes part of a ruling military junta after 13-year dictator and SOA graduate General Omar Torrijos Herrera dies in a plane crash, later blamed on Noriega and the CIA by other junta members.
1983-86 The US hates Manuel Noriega for: suspected spying for Fidel Castro and Daniel Ortega; helping Cuba circumvent the US economic embargo; helping to get weapons for the Sandinistas and for the guerrillas in El Salvador and Colombia; transferring high technology to Eastern Europe.

Reagan/Bush officials put him back on the US payroll, again reportedly at more than $100,000 per year. *San Francisco Chronicle*, 6/11/87

The US loves him for: spying on Fidel Castro and Daniel Ortega; allowing the United States to set up listening posts in Panama, with which they monitor sensitive communications in all of Central America and beyond; aiding the American warfare against the rebels in El Salvador and the government of Nicaragua (facilitating the flow of money and arms to the Contras, allowing the US to base spy planes in Panama, in clear violation of the canal treaties, giving the US permission to train contras in Panama, and spying in support of American sabotage inside of Nicaragua) *Newsweek*, 1/15/90

I am thinking! If Che Guevara's Life/Death was a film script, other film scripts would have been useful in making another World Order.

At a time when Panama was under the world's eye I did not expect to see- Margot Fonteyn name appear!

Margot Fonteyn was involved in plot with Castro to overthrow Panama, documents reveal
By Daily Mail Reporter
Updated: 11:08 GMT, 28 May 2010

Margot Fonteyn was involved in plot with Castro to ...

www.dailymail.co.uk/.../Margot-Fonteyn-involved-...
28.05.2010 - Plotters: Roberto Arias (left) and *Fidel Castro* sought to recruit an army to ... the coup was linked to actors including *John Wayne* and Errol Flynn ...

I found that the British born ballerina Dame Margot Fonteyn had been heavily involved in a plot with Fidel Castro to overthrow Panama's government, previously secret files have revealed.

The renowned dancer was arrested by the Panamanian authorities in April 1959 after her husband launched a failed coup attempt, using 125 Cuban revolutionaries.

Margot Fonteyn confessed to Foreign Office minister John Profumo – (who was involved in a notorious sex scandal of his own.) - That she met Fidel Castro and took part in a mission to assemble rebels and weapons at sea, for an attempted invasion of Panama.

A Panamanian conspiracy:
Dame Margot Fonteyn was involved in a coup with her husband Dr Roberto Arias and Cuban dictator Fidel Castro to overthrow Panama. Show files, released by the National Archives in Kew, west London.

Fonteyn was 39 and an internationally celebrated prima ballerina when she was arrested and held for questioning in Panama City prison on April 20, 1959, provoking huge publicity worldwide.

On April 19 the couple failed to turn up for a reception in Panama for the visiting Duke of Edinburgh hosted by the British ambassador, Sir Ian Henderson. As she and her husband, Dr Roberto Arias, the son of a former Panamanian president, had set out to sea in their yacht Nola, ostensibly on a fishing trip but in reality to gather men and arms for the coup.

Sir Ian Henderson wrote: "My conversation with Dame Margot convinced me, if I needed convincing, that the Arias family ware conspiring against the Government and that she, herself had at least on arrival here complied in their rebellious designs. She knew that her husband was gun-running, she knew that he was accompanied by rebels and at one point she used her yacht to decoy government boats and aircraft away from the direction which her husband was taking." Sir Ian Henderson did not regard her conduct as fitting for a British subject, let alone one who has been highly honored by Her Majesty the Queen.

Among the Plotters were Roberto Arias and Fidel Castro, they sought to recruit an army to help them carry out the coup. Margot Fonteyn was advised not to return to Panama for a considerable time, as her husband was on the run!

After returning to Britain, Margot Fonteyn met Office minister John Profumo and his actress wife Valerie at their home and gave them an extraordinary account of her part in the failed coup.

There is a memo about the meeting where John Profumo admitted that he had to pinch himself several times to make sure he was not dreaming the 'comic opera story' which she unfolded. The ballerina told the Conservative minister she and her husband met Fidel Castro after travelling to Cuba at the start of 1959.

Dame Margot Fonteyn said that during their visit to Cuba in January, Fidel Castro had promised help to her husband in his aims to overthrow the existing regime in Panama.

Fidel Castro was behind this coup, even though he disclaimed all knowledge.

Margot Fonteyn stated that the Cuban invaders were just soldiers of fortune who were prepared to go to war anywhere they were asked. She stated that quite a large-scale operation had been planned but that it had gone wrong at the last minute.

Margot Fonteyn explained that the coup was linked to actors including **John Wayne** and **Errol Flynn** came about after Panamanian officials found her husband's address book, which contained details both of rebels supporting his plot and of Hollywood stars with whom he had worked in the past.

The ballerina told Foreign Office minister John Profumo, her husband, Roberto Arias was prepared to go to any extremes to help the ordinary common people of Panama' who were 'having a very raw deal'. Dr Arias did not intend to nationalize the Panama Canal and did not want to be president.

Margot Fonteyn stated that it was 'immensely expensive' for her husband to have to pay for all the arms and ammunition for the operation, which were 'frequently mislaid and lost' by the rebels and had to be replaced out of his own pocket.

A note on the file shows that the Foreign Office debated whether to tell the US about the confirmation that Castro was involved in the Panama coup plot; given that Margot Fonteyn had spoken to the minister in confidence.

An official wrote: 'I dare say it would not matter much if wc do not pass on this piece of information to the Americans.'

Margot Fonteyn, who was born Peggy Evelyn Hookham in Reigate, Surrey, in May 1919, went on to reach even greater creative heights through her acclaimed partnership with Russian dancer Rudolf Nureyev, beginning in 1962. She returned to Panama with her husband for the final years of her life and died there in February 1991.

(Errol Flynn- This is not the first time his name has come up.)

John Wayne şi Margot Fonteyn, mercenarii lui Fidel Castro
*www.cotidianul.ro/**john-wayne**-si-margot-fonteyn-...*
- Cea mai mare balerină britanică a secolului XX a fost implicată într-o tentativă de lovitură de stat în Panama, pusă la cale de *Fidel Castro*. Suspectaţi în acest ...

-
- The Autobiography of Fidel Castro
- *https://books.google.de/books?isbn=039306 8994 -*
- Norberto Fuentes - 2010 - Fiction
- They bombarded you all day with Errol Flynn and Tar- zan and *John Wayne* and then they were scared silly when you picked up your weapons. Wherever you ...
Read more:
http://www.dailymail.co.uk/news/article-1282113/Margot-Fonteyn-involved-plot-Castro-overthrow-Panama-documents-reveal.html#ixzz3kI2ebHZR

This autobiography author is Norberto Fuentes, I have come across him many time in my research!

Dame Margot Fonteyn involved in 'highly reprehensible' plot to overthrow Panama government.
<u>Telegraph.co.uk</u> **vom 28. Mai 2010**
From 1942 to 1946 ***Roberto Arias*** edited La Hora, a family-owned newspaper. He then entered Panama's diplomatic service as counselor in the Panamanian Embassy in Chile. He returned to journalism a year later, and served as a delegate to the United Nations General Assembly in 1953.

 Now start looking for the man standing on the corner-

<u>Los Medios de Comunicación Social en Panamá | EL ...</u>

www.ellibrepensador.com/.../los-medios-de-comuni...
30.06.2009 - Su accionista más importante fue Tomas Gabriel Altamirano Duque, ... Dr. *Harmodio Arias* Madrid (ambos fueron Presidentes de la República), y por .... que dirige el Periodista y Escritor colombiano *Gabriel García Márquez*.

Newspapers, weeklies and magazines that are distributed Foreign Panama are:

The most important are the American newspapers

like The Miami Herald, El Nuevo Herald, The New York Times, the Washington Post, The Washington Times, the Wall Street Journal, the magazine Neewsweek etc. They are also marketed in Europe, such as ABC, El Pais (Spain), Le Monde, Le Monde Diplomatique (France), the Economist, the Time (UK) and Le Republica, Le Osservatore Romano (Italy) and the magazine Change directed by journalist and Colombian writer *Gabriel García Márquez*. There are also several newspapers in the Chinese language, the large Chinese-Panamanian community. And there are several international magazines on fashion, culture, entertainment, etc. concentrates
International news agencies and news channels exhibition:

(The magazine Change directed by journalist and Colombian writer *Gabriel García Márquez!*)

They belong to the Reuters UPI, Associated Press, Agence France Press, the Central News Agency (EFE), Prensa Latina (Cuba), Xinhua (China), Russian news agency (TASS), German Press Agency important (DPA) Italian News Agency (ANSA), Spanish News Agency (EFE) etc. Panama also have correspondents in the news channels ABC, NBC, CNN, CBS and Univision (US), BBC (British), TVE (Spanish), Televisa (Mexico) and RAI (Italian)

Newspaper El Panama America: Journal of the standard type, excellent quality and various sections. Target market is the middle and upper class. Its owners are the arias of the family, Dr. Arnulfo Arias Madrid and his brother Dr. Harmodius Arias Madrid (both President of the Republic) are connected, and therefore has good relations with the Panamanian Party (Arnulf Ista, right), which was the main opposition against the military regime and ruled Panama after the US invasion with President Endara (1989-1994), and who with President Mireya Moscoso (1999-2004), which in turn is the widow of Dr. Arnulfo Arias Madrid excluded. Its main owner is Rosario Arias de Galindo, the daughter of former President Dr. Harmodius Arias.
Need I say more?
Just a little cream on the cake-
In Critica Libre Journal: Journal of Boulevard- State the Arias family and the Panamanian Party connected and ruled the country with President Mireya Moscso the widow of Arias Madrid. This Journal was owned by Rosario Arias de Galindo, the daughter of former president Dr Harmodius Arias.

Graham Greene, wrote a book, 'Discovering General Omar Torrijos exmandatario.'
The introduction recounts how and why Graham Green spying involvement.

The interesting thing that I noted is the epilogue and prologue ware by Jon Lee Anderson and Gabriel Garcia Marquez.

Efrain Omar Torrijos Herrera (1929-1981) was the "Maximum Leader of the Panamanian Revolution" and, according to Graham Greene, wanted the whole Central America to be free from any interference by the United States.

Chapter thirteen.
The connection to Carlos Cardoen.

Chilean gun-runner Carlos Cardoen.
The Financial Times reported.
 Carlos Cardoen was a CIA front man used by Presidents Ronald Reagan and Bush 1st, to funnel cluster bombs and other weapons secretly to Saddam Hussein during the Iran-Iraq War. The connection to and from Max Marambio is made clear when you

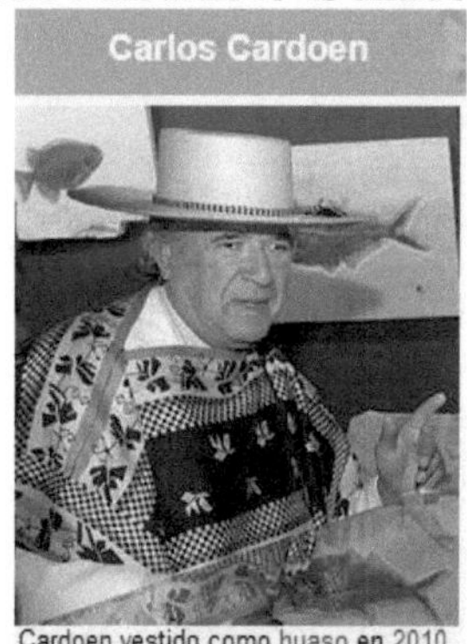

Cardoen vestido como huaso en 2010.

look into in-

Sería Chile refugio de familiares de Fidel Castro tras su muerte noticiasmiami.blogia.com

Fidel-Death Rumors!

Rumors of the physical disappearance of Fidel Castro were increased as a massive exodus of senior leaders of the Cuban Revolution and their families; mainly Chile and the United States was observed.

Local TV revealed details on current purchases of property, car and house on the border of Chile and Argentina, which have been largely facilitated by Chilean businessmen Max Marambio, founder and owner of Corporacion Cimex Havanatur and Carlos Cardoen, a sinister character wanted by the FBI after his participation in the sale of cluster munitions during the Iran-Iraq conflict in 1989.

According to the TV report, Chilean sources claim that these properties are being equipped for the family of Fidel and Raul Castro in the event of a convulsive state of Cuban society from the formalization of the death of the Cuban leader.

The Cuban Intelligence has reinforced the presence of senior officials of the Cuban Intelligence in Santiago de Chile, such as Rafael Suarez Tabares, current consul of Cuba in Chile, who would be carrying out an operation of transferring $ 80 million disbursed to perform these operations in the Andean country; with the personal jet flown by Max Marambio.

Fernando Garcia, former Prime Secretary of the Office of Interests of Cuba in USA, was expelled when the crisis of American spy Ana Belen Montes erupted, he was the Minister of Foreign Affairs of the Embassy of Cuba in Chile which suggests that

that country would be the final destination for families Castro after his physical disappearance, which, according to the newspaper El Pais.

Claire Sterling was well aware of Carlos Cardoen's conections
[PDF]<u>September 11 Commission Report Revised December 008</u>
911americanuked.com/download/1_September_11_ Report.pdf
28.08.2011 - It is the profile an international hit-man, not unlike Carlos the ...... Authors quote from a book by an American journalist, *Claire Sterling*, which ...... He then became involved with *Carlos Cardoen* and Swissco Management, and ...

The September 11 commission report make interesting reading!
THE SEPTEMBER 11 COMMISSION REPORT
Page 257
"Porter Goss was a young CIA officer assigned to JM/WAVE.
Goss had, by his own accounts, been recruited to the CIA while in his third year at Yale University. His two years of military service were, in all likelihood, actually CIA assignments. In 1961, Goss was officially brought into the CIA and sent to JM/WAVE. He later would continue to participate in the anti-Castro operations, based out of CIA stations in Haiti, the Dominican Republic, and Mexico. Later, Goss was sent to London and then Paris,

where he was involved in the infiltration of labor organizations, until he developed a near-fatal infection and was forced, officially, to retire from the spy world. In his role in JM/WAVE, Goss served with some of the CIA's most hardened Cold Warriors, including Miami Station Chief Theodore G. Shackley, later a central figure in the Iran/Contra debacle; (and) *Felix Rodriguez,* another leading Iran-Contra player;...." (The Coming Senate Battle: Open the Porter Goss File Part 1, Jeffrey Steinberg, Michele Steinberg and Scott Thompson, Executive Intelligence Review September 3, 2004.

"According to Al Martin, in 1983 Goss was involved in Iran-Contra profiteering with Jeb and Neil Bush's Destin Country Club development fraud – a fraud out of which he made about $3 million illegally. He then became involved with *Carlos Cardoen* and Swissco Management, and the fraud that Swissco Management committed, not only in Florida, but throughout the United States, in those so-called illicit 'tax-swap deals,' which Senator Bob Graham of Florida also profited in." (Prime Suspect of the Largest Mass Murder in U.S. Nominated to Head C.I.

A., Carol Brouillet, Fourth of July, 2004)

"Chalmers is a longtime denizen of the Labyrinth. In the mid-1980s, he joined up with Chilean gun-runner Carlos Cardoen, the Financial Times reported. Cardoen was a CIA front man used by Presidents Ronald Reagan and Bush Ist to funnel cluster bombs and other weapons secretly to Saddam

Hussein during the Iran-Iraq War." [UN oil for food scandal, Global Eye, Gut Check, Chris Floyd, April 22, 2005.

Two more useful addresses. With names of old friends-Frank Sturgis, Carlos Cardoen, Claire Sterling, *Felix Rodriguez-*

George Bush: World Class Monster - Voxfux
www.voxfux.com/.../bush_world_class_criminal.ht...
Bush reportedly coordinated *Frank Sturgis*, as well as Watergate team ...... to Iraqi Dictator Saddam Hussein via *Carlos Cardoen*, a Chilean arms dealer with ...

- La Sociedad de La Mentira - Scribd
https://es.scribd.com/doc/20147109/La-Sociedad-de-La-Mentira
24.09.2009 - Con George W. Bush en la Casa Blanca, a Frank Carlucci, un viejo amigo ...... particularmente su investigación de *Carlos Cardoen,* un fabricante de ...... Sin embargo, convenir con el ex agente de la CÍA *Frank Sturgis* en que ...... de *Claire Sterling* sobre el crimen organizado global Thieves World (1994).

"According to a 1995 deposition by Reagan national security aide Howard Teicher, CIA Deputy Director Robert Gates was part of a secret operation in the 1980s to funnel sophisticated military equipment to Iraqi Dictator Saddam Hussein via Carlos Cardoen, a Chilean arms dealer with close ties to the murderous General Pinochet. "Under CIA director Casey and Deputy Director Gates, the CIA authorized, approved and assisted Cardoen in the manufacture and sale of cluster bombs and other munitions to Iraq," Teicher wrote in the affidavit submitted as part of an arms-smuggling case in federal court."

Chapter fourteen.
Max Marambio- Fidel Castro's 007 Agent and Gabriel Garcia Marquez's close friend.

I am not joking when I say Max Marambio was an agent for Fidel Castro look in-

Las mil caras del chileno con más llegada en La Habana   baracuteycubano.blogspot.com

To link Max 'Fats' Marambio with the Cuban revolution can be traced back to a trip he made to Havana with his father, Joel Marambio in 1966; who was the socialist deputy of Colchagua, (a wine growing region in Chili.) Max Marambio fell under the influence of the revolution and its ideals, he went to the University of Havana and joined the guerrilla training camps inspired by the example of Che Guevara.

Max Marambio took the idea of revolution with him when he returned to Chile. He entered the MIR ,

Movimiento de Izquierda Revolucionariafull and became its leader. He was also a member of GAP, 'Grupo de amigo peronales.'
Max Marambio was Salvador Allende's personal body guard.

It is said about Salvador Allende that he was murdered by the orders of Castro. The other rumor was he committed suicide (I have forgotten where I saw that remark.) As head of one of the largest snakes of journalism, it was Gabriel Garcia Marques who announced to the world that Salvador Allende was murdered.

La verdadera muerte de un presidente, según Gabriel ...

*www.naranjaplatano.com/muerte**allende**.htm*
... de la muerte trágica de *Salvador Allende, Gabriel García Márquez* escribió un ... Sin duda alguna Gabriel García es un gran escritor en cuanto al uso del lenguaje. .... Luego todos los oficiales, en un rito de casta, dispararon *sobre* el cuerpo.

In the early nineties, when keeping a low profile, Max Marambio was commissioned by the government of Cuba to sell their former embassy in Chile. It was a silent business management full of symbolism. It was in that house street Ponds, near the corner of Pedro de Valdivia with Pocuro, where the head of security group President Salvador

Allende aloud Cubans to offer armed resistance in the days after the coup.

By the early 1975 with the twin brother, Patrick and Antonio 'Tony' de la Guardia and Max Marambio became part of commercial and secret military operations. They were three years working in Angola, Palestine, Lebanon, Korea, Central America and Europe. They all were involved undercover missions "internationalist assistance" to the liberation struggles.

In Chile Max Marambio had been with the Chilean Special Forces and the elite military corps Cuba. And he had worked with two of its most important official: twins Patrick and Antonio "Tony" de la Guardia, who in 1989 would be arrested and prosecuted for drug trafficking in Havana with General Armando Ochoa. The first would receive 30 years in prison in what became known as the No1 Cause. 'Tony' and Ochoa received the death penalty.

It might not be incorrect to say Fidel Castro felt his authority was under threat by the twins. It has been proven that Max controlled Fidel Castro's accounts in Switzerland. It has also been suggested Max bought land in Chili on the behalf of the Castro family in the event they had to go into exile.

Max Marambio owns half of Cuba's business it was easy for him to move monies here and there. This was happening at a time of conflict in the Cuban government and the world was watching.

So write a script! Max falls out with Castro, Max take his and Castro's money out of Cuba. Castro makes claims of corruption and fraud against Max, even sentences him to prison in his absences. Waite a few years, Max claims compensation for being falsely acquiesced- more money flows out of Cuba. In Journal 'New Action,' brings information to back this idea up.

Baracutey Cubano: MAX MARAMBIO EL GUATON Y LA ...

baracuteycubano.blogspot.com/.../max-marambio.ht...

06.07.2007 - *Pero* un chileno radicado en Cuba que perteneció *al MIR* y que participó en operaciones de la "solidaridad internacionalista cubana"
"New Action" has shown the figure of Max "The

Guatón" Marambio had been commissioned by the Castro family to acquire land for them in Chile. In previous years they had written about his business with the Cuban tyranny and described as one of the great Cuban proxies used by Fidel Castro to hide and move their enormous fortune.

Chile's Max Marambio faces criminal charges in Cuba. - The ...

www.thefreelibrary.com › ... › *September 1, 2010*
Free Online Library: Chile's *Max Marambio* faces criminal charges in Cuba. ... government and Marambio's Chilean *International* Network Group (ING). ... *Angel Domper* is a former business associate of Marambio, who went on to ... export firm, *TJP* Internacional, supplying Cuba with Chilean-made packaged food products.

Max Marambio Wins Arbitration Against Cuba in ...

www.havanatimes.org/?p=75487
31.07.2012 - *Max Marambio* Wins Arbitration Against Cuba in International Court ... and held $23 million of his assets, according to the Chilean *newspaper*.

The General Manager of TJP a company and business associate of Max, Angel Domper Cavalla were married to Celia Guevara.

Max's company ING- 'International Network Group' its purpose of producing Latin American Films. This is interesting in its self, when you enter this company's name in the internet how's face do you see!? Gabriel Garcia Marquez.

This is a man you can write a book about! He is a real 007 man; his life appears between the shrouds of smoke a steam train would make! I can only say at this point that this man is as capable as Gabriel Garcia Marques to control the propaganda machine.

Max has used at least five diffract names-
1)-Carlos Alfonso Gonzalez or Carlos Alfonso.
2)-As Luis Rodriguez he had a Cuban Passport.
3)-Segum Pascual-
4)-Pero El Guaton- is a nickname 'the fat man.'
5)-Ariel Fontana- is an alias for Max Marambio-
(you can be excused if you think it is a name of a film.)

1)-Carlos Alfonso Gonzalez or Carlos Alfonso.

<u>J-97-97-2 - Latin American Studies</u>
www.latinamericanstudies.org/terrorism/role2.htm
The owner of Havanatur was *Carlos Alfonso Gonzalez*. He has been identified by the U.S. State Department as a Cuban intelligence agent. Havanatur.

The owner of Havanatur was Carlos Alfonso Gonzalez. He has been identified by the U.S. State Department as a Cuban intelligence agent. Havanatur's president, Charles Romeu, has along with Carlos Alfonso Gonzalez, been indicted by a Federal grand jury for violations of the Trading with the Enemy Act.

2) Luis Rodiguez with this name Luis Rodriguez he held a Cuban Passport.

Max Marambio - Wikipedia, la enciclopedia libre

*https://es.wikipedia.org/wiki/**Max_Marambio***
Joel *Max Marambio* Rodríguez (n. Santa Cruz, 1947) es un empresario, productor cinematográfico y político chileno. En Cuba desarrolló una exitosa carrera ..

'As a film producer he owes much to Gabriel Garcia Marquez, as well as Fidel Castro. It was through he met Fidel García Márquez in Havana, and through the latter he came to produce 'Difficult Amores,' a series of six films financed by Spanish Television and whose screenplay was written by Gabriel Garcia Marquez.

In 1988 Max Marambio inaugurated its film producer cartel, which meant the opening of International Network Group ING, and simultaneously producing consortium through which met its core businesses.

Max Marambio's contribution to film the television series followed 'Nazca' (1990), the Spanish Benito Rabal, about a group of adventurers researchers walking Latin America; and the production of 'Alkyl me to dream' (1992), directed by Brazilian Ray Guerra and based on a story by Garcia Marquez. Marambio appears in the credits as executive producer.

3) Ariel Fontana- is an alias for Max Marambio- (You can be excused if you think it is a name
                                    of a film.)
    In his role as film producer he comes in contact with Katy Jurado-

<u>catalogo del festival.pdf - Festival del Cinema Latino ...</u>
www.cinelatinotrieste.org/.../catalogo_cinelatinotrie s...
Miguel Littin, quien será el Presidente del Jurado. Oficial del ...... Boy Olmi, Lalo *Mir*, Victoria. Carreras, Leo .... *leader* sindacale cocalera e voce del popolo indigeno. "Quello che *mi* ha ...... Sánchez, Reynaldo Miravalles, Raúl Pomares, *Katy Jurado*,. Alain Cuny ...... Produttore: *Max Marambio*, Luis Reneses. Produzione: ...

4) Segum Pascual-
    Carlos Alfonso Gonzalez name wanders into Segum Pascual- with this name we meet up again with **Tania Bunke/Susan Sontag. Max's role is not**

as film producer or publisher but as trainer. It is from him they say she learned international telegraphy, Morse-Code; to establish contacts with Venezuela and other Latin American countries.

Guerrilla training required theory and practice of various military matters: arm and disarm light weapons, shooting, explosives, tactics, hiking and survival exercises in the mountains where water and food must obtain. One of Tania's instructors in these areas was
Carlos Alberto Gonzalez Mendez (Pascual). He was the teacher of explosives; the classes are conducted in an operational house located near Highway noon, west of the Cuban capital in June 1963.

Tania, la guerrillera - Ocean Sur
*www.oceansur.com/media/fb_uploads/pdf/**tania-guerrillera.pdf***
Tania *al* Memorial Ernesto Che Guevara, enclavado en la ciudad de Santa .... la estancia en Cuba de Haydée *Tamara Bunke* Bíder, ahora conocida en todo el mundo como ...... *Carlos* Alberto *González* Méndez (Pascual). Él fue su profesor de ...

The interesting thing about this book is that it us written by Ulies Estada. He was said to be close to Tania Bunke, so close they were planning a life together. It is also said he was to go to Bolivar with Che Guevara but did not go as it was thought his dark skin would show him up. Ulies Estrada also talks about Max Marambio and their activities in Chili.

5) Pero El Guaton

<u>Marambio y Cuba: ¿por qué ese divorcio brutal ...</u>

*https://aquevedo.wordpress.com/.../**marambio**-y-cub...*18.04.2010 - Las aristas que persiguen a *Max Marambio* en Cuba ... El "*Guatón*" libró, según Fuentes, por Fidel y el castigo fue .... *Max Marambio* (63), el ex fundador del *MIR* y de la guardia .... de *Regis Debray* y también ex luchadora de la causa latinoamericana, quien conoce a Marambio desde su adolescencia.
- The edges chasing Max Marambio in Cuba ... The "Fats" book, according to sources, was Fidel and punishment .... Max Marambio (63), former founder of the MIR and the guard .... Regis Debray and former fighter of the Latin American cause who knows Marambio since his teens.

This program is interesting as it brings together many issues I have been talking about.
Ileana's wife of Argentinan Jorge Masetti, a former Latin 'Americanist guerriler' and founder of the Cuban agency Prensa Latina, also had occasion to meet Marambio in their olive green years with Special Forces. She states Max Marambio was officer with the rank of major.

The Masetti's and the De la Guardia are not the only ones who know these episodes in the life of the Chilean businessman. Max Marambio has always had high level contacts in Cuba; he has dual citizenship, Chilean and Cuban. He was very young when he came to Cuba and was trained there. Cuba is where he had developed all his qualities, both as a politically militant and as a businessman. Both talents were developed in closes contact with Fidel Castro.

Anthropologist Elizabeth Burgos- former wife of Regis Debray states- 'They have known Max Marambio since his teens.' They must have known the man of many talents, with extraordinary business acumen and a man of action, which was the main requirement for   promotion in the Cuban regime. Elizabeth Burgos-Debray also states Max Marambio knew how to be pragmatic and knows how to move in different medias.

El veraz - San Juan, Puerto Rico: Articulo: ¿Quién es ...

*www.elveraz.com/NORBERT0.htm*Uno de ellos es el empresario *Max Marambio* -ex jefe del GAP, guardia personal de ... Según relata en el libro, Marambio o "*Guatón*" (ahora investido con el grado de mayor del .... Lo mismo está ocurriendo con Mitterrand y con *Régis Debray*.

'Truthful - San Juan, Puerto Rico: Article: Who is ...

www.elveraz.com/NORBERT0.htmUno of them is businessman Max Marambio a former head of the GAP, bodyguard ... As told in the book, Marambio or "Fats" (now invested with the rank of major of .. .. The same is happening with Mitterrand and Régis Debray.'

Carlos Wotzkow

*www.intelinet.org/sg_site/.../sg_**wotzkow**_spy.html*
Carlos Wotzkow, admirador de los artículos de
Servando González ... Burgos se casó con *Regis
Debray* cuando éste se encontraba cumpliendo su
condena en ...
If anyone doubts that it is relatively easy to get to a
website and change information within it, I provide
some links so you can see how easy it is:
<http://www.2600.com/hacked_pages/>
<http://www.g4tv.com/techtvvault/features/3418/Ha
ck_This_Site_pg2.html?detectflash=false>
<http://www.unknowncountry.com/news/?id=515>

Chapter fifteen.
What a circle to find!

Fernando Gutierrez Barrios-Mexico secret Police-Carlos Delmar Jurado-

What a circle to find! Studding Max Marambio has led me to Fernando Gutierrez Barrios who was the head of the secret police of Mexico and the go-between the CIA and Fidel Castro!

Fernando Gutierrez Barrios gets Fidel Castro out of prison to be able to take the Granma to Cuba.

Absuelto por la historia - Granma
www.granma.cu/granmad/secciones/fidel/
Ramón Chao: Palabras en el tiempo, Argos Vergara, España, 1984, p. .... *Fernando Gutiérrez Barrios*: Diálogos con el hombre, Editorial Planeta, México, 1995, p. ... Gustarle al Papa y a Fidel el *Chan Chan* es como gustarle al mundo entero.

CIA | Diario de Cuba
www.diariodecuba.com/etiquetas/cia.html
... Manuel Martín Medem *Luis Posada Carriles* Manuel Buendía México Miguel ... Olivares Bolivia Chile CIA *Ciro Bustos* Clodomiro Almeyda Ernesto Guevara ...

Jose Manuel Martin Medem spoke about his newly published book executions of drug trafficking: the cases of Arnaldo Ochoa and Antonio de la Guardia. The best kept secrets of Fidel Castro.'

"Gutierrez Barrios worked with Fidel Castro to get him out of jail when he was arrested in Mexico while preparing the landing of the Granma. And he was the mediator who simultaneously solve the drug charges against Fidel and against the governments of Ronald Reagan and Miguel de la Madrid. US and Mexico presidents also related to the murder of Camarena and Buendia. The same solution in all cases was applied: state officials were involved in the US, Mexico and Cuba without "authorization governments."

Then there is Gabriel García Márquez, next to Fidel Castro in those days.

While looking in and around this I found the name of Carlos Delmar Jurado-
Carlos Delmar Jurado, at this point I do not know if there is a direct relationship with Katy Jurado-one of the four in one Lady. Look at what the German Wikipedia says about him.

Carlos Delmar Jurado studied in Mexico City at the Escuela Nacional de Pintura, Escultura y Grabado "La Esmeralda" in María Izquierdo. From 1955 to 1960 he was a member of the Taller de Gráfica Popular (the People's graphic workshop, TGP). 1957 there was the first time a solo exhibition of his works in Chiapas instead.

During the Cuban revolution Jurado worked in Cuba. In Guatemala, he was sentenced as a result of its revolutionary commitment to death, but pardoned at the request of his wife Chichai Jurado back.

At the University of Veracruz in Xalapa, he became director of the art school. Where he founded the art magazine Zeta.Carlos Jurado (* 3 November 1927 in Mexiko-Stadt) ist ein Künstler Mexikanischer.

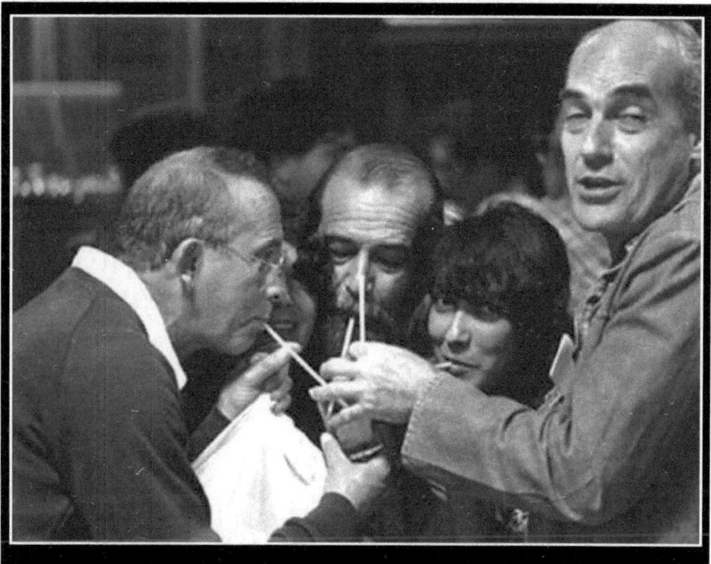

Carlos Jurado, Korda y Betty, esposa de Pirole.
Cuba La Habana 1984

 Korda nov84 cuba
fotoperiodismo.org

As you can see him with Korda the man who took the photo of Che Guevara the hero; don't tell me he did not know Gabriel Garcia Marquez.

And then I find his name involved in Watergate!

<u>CIA Cryptonyms - Mary Ferrell Foundation</u>
https://www.maryferrell.org/.../CIA_Cryptonyms.ht..
.
DRE delegate *Carlos* Bringuier had the famous altercation with Lee Oswald in New Orleans in the ..... LIRING-3, *Carlos* Delmar *Jurado. ...* LITEMPO-4, *Fernando Gutierrez Barrios*, head of the Mexican secret police (DFS) from 1964 to 1970, ...

<u>005n2pol</u>
www.jornada.unam.mx/2000/10/03/005n2pol.html
03.10.2000 - Ť Montemayor señala a Gutiérrez Barrios como uno de los responsables ... del 68, aunque el historiador Carlos Montemayor aclaró que, con base en ... de la masacre, entre los que mencionó a *Fernando Gutiérrez Barrios*, así ... García, el artista plástico *Carlos Jurado* y Luis González Souza, entre otros.

It was Carlos Delmar Jurado that integrated- not
the right word- the Mexican consulate worker Sylvia
Duran; she was responsible for Lee Harvey Oswald!
We are back in the circle of J F K's assassination.
Where, the same names appear in/at Che Guevara's
death party.
Some of whose names show up in the Bay of Pigs
adventure and are repeated in the 1973 Chilin coup
d'etat and Salvador Allende's demise. And if that
was not enough you can find them repeated in the
Watergate scandal!
*Luis Posada Carriles- Frank Sturgis -Olando
Bosh-Felix Rodriguez.*
Carlos Delmar Jurado- Active in the Mexican labor
movement representing actors and production
workers. He was a founding member of the STPC
(Union of Cinema Production Workers) and a
national director of ANDA (National Association of
Actors).

whowhatwhy.org

This program has a lot to say about Carlos Delmar
Jurado.

(Privileged authors, those who (unlike the rest of us) are able to interview CIA officers and quote from unreleased classified documents, continue to dominate the US media with their dance between "Phase-One" and "Phase-Two" accounts of Oswald. Gus Russo, for example, writes about the "tantalizing leads about a possible Cuban conspiracy with Lee Harvey Oswald." He claims, very misleadingly, that "The CIA was unsuccessful in preventing the arrest of Silvia Durán, which (although opposed by the CIA in Washington) had in fact been ordered by CIA Station Chief Scott.

Referring to the questions prepared by Scott about possible Cuban or Soviet involvement, he calls them the "most critical questions surrounding the assassination." Russo states, against the available evidence, that "Duran's Mexican interrogators chose not to ask" them. To assert this, he has to overlook the contrary testimony of Durán herself, partially corroborated **by a CIA informant (LIRING-3, since identified as Carlos Delmar Jurado**), whom Russo cites elsewhere as "a CIA contact viewed as very reliable by the agency.")

Watergate-

To go back to Max Marambio and his position as Fidel Castro's banker; it has been proven that Castro paid a sum of money to the Democratic Party. It had also been stated that the Watergate burglars where to retrieve the evidence of this transaction.

With Ann Wright involvement with the Democratic Party we are going around in circles again! I state that Monika Ertl became Ann Wright, Ann Wright was the woman who translated Ciro Bustos' book 'Che Wants To See You' she is the same Ann Wright who was an active member of the Democratic Party at the time of Watergate. Association is explained in 'Spies-CIA-Lies-Terrorist-Che Guevara.'

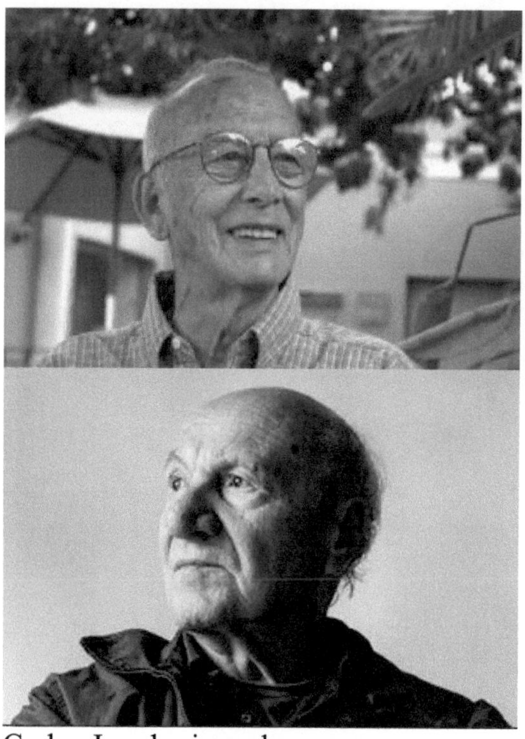

Carlos Jurado- jornada.unam.mx
Ciro Bustos   soli.nextrob.in

And then, when I looked at some of Carlos Jurado's photos I found one with that writing, I attribute to Che or Che/Bustos/Debray syndicate. Explained in Spies-CIA-Lies-Terrorist-Che Guevara.

I cannot at this point cross out the possibility that Carlos Delmar Jurado is one of the two brothers that Katy Jurado is said to have. (If one is Che!) But Emilio Portes Gil a president of Mexico and long serving minister is said to be her cousin. And as such he would have been in contact with Fernando Gutierrez Barrios, Mexico's secret police leader.

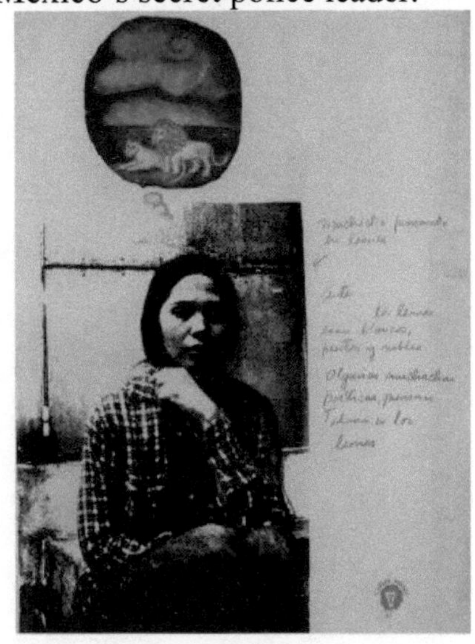

Carlos Jurado. Muchacha pensando en leones. Fotoserigrafía. 1976 Col. del artista

Look at the hand writing, it is like that of Che's.

muchacha pensando
en leones

Anita

los leones
eran blancos,
fuertes y nobles

Algunas muchachas
poéticas, piensan
Tpiensa en los
leones

Moisés: 157

Ordena los hom-
bres suficientes para ha-
cerles la casa a los zapateros
si no entorpece otros traba-
jos más importantes.

En la primera
oportunidad hay que
hablar con Benítez. Se
lo dicen.

C.

Junio 11/48

... a location in the East of Cuba, the Sierra Maestro, dated November 1958.
pfcauctions.com

Carlos Jurado, maestro de la fotografía estenopeica
oscarenfotos.com

Look again at Ciro Bustos's

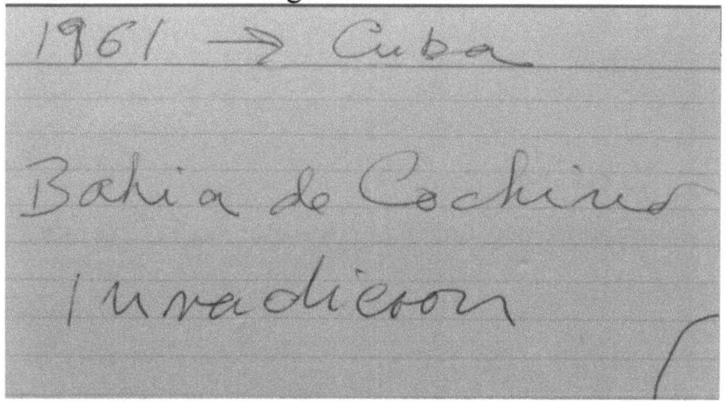

Al doctor Hugo Pesce, que provocara, sin
saberlo quizás, un gran cambio en mi
actitud ante la vida y la sociedad,
con el entusiasmo aventurero de
siempre pero encaminado a fines más
armónicos con las necesidades de
América, fraternalmente

"LA GUERRA
DE GUERRILLAS"

A Camilo

por CHE GUEVARA

Written by Ciro Bustos- a copy I have.

Chapter sixteen
The Writers-Translators

Gabriel Garcia Marques- writers-translators-

Ann Wright has written and translated many books;
here is list of who she translated for.

Ernesto Che Guevara. –
The Motorcycle Diaries.
 A Journey around South America.
          By Ernesto Guevara Lynch- (Che's farther.)
Elisabeth Burgos-Debray- Rigoberta Menchu.-
          I Rigoberta Menchu: An Indian Women in
Guatemala.

Ramon Chao. –
          The Train of Ice and Fire-
          Because Cuba is You.

Ciro Bustos.-Che Wants to see You.
               Foreword by Jon Lee Anderson,
Jon lee Anderson-
          'Che Guevara. A revolutionary Life.

(Jon Lee Anderson spent three years with Che's
second wife while writing it, and for one year he
lived in the flat above with Ciro Bustos.)

Rigoberta Menchu.-Crossing Borders.

Isabel Allende-
        Mexican Bolero.
        Mexican Bolero by Angeles Mastretta and
Ann Wright
        Isabel Allende was the daughter of Salvador
Allende.

Books by
Ann Wright-
                The Assassination of Lomumba.
                With Ludo De Witte.
Dissent: Voices of Conscience.
                With Susan Dixon and Daniel Ellsberg.
(Daniel Ellsberg connected to Watergate.)

Jon Lee Anderson- Che Guevara. A revolutionary
Life.

Ramon Cho-   Las Andaoluras Del Che.
                Che Guevara Voage a Mobocydette.
                Allende 1970,1973. With Pierre Kalfon.

Alberto Granado- Travelling With Che Guevara.

Question- How many people have written the
Motorcycle Diaries?????
Ann Wright- Ramon Chao- Ernesto Guevara Lynch-
Ernesto Che Guevara-Alberto Granado.

The Bolivian Diaries-

(The Bolivian diaries there were three originals and then more- conclusion= all are fakes.

 As there are so many versions of the trip around South America, and looking at the list of who wrote them or translated etc- Conclusion. All are fakes. (Alberto Granado's book was translated by Lucia Alvarez de Toledo-The mother of Che's half brother. Is she related to Jorge G Castaneda?)

Jorge G Casaneda-
MANUAL DE ORGANIZACIÓN DE LA EMBAJADA DE MÉXICO EN FRANCIA- this document explains Jorge G Casaneda's father was Jorge Casaneda y Alverez de la Rosa was Mexico's extern minister and ambassador in Paris, 1983-1989. (Indicating his contacts to the Mexican government.)

Jorge G Castaneda- The Life and Death of Che Guevara. Companero.

    (A)<u>Castañeda: inteligente arrogancia | Letras Libres</u>

www.letraslibres.com › Revista › Libros
"Conmigo, [*Gabriel*] *García Márquez* fue a la vez generoso al extremo, interesado, ... Hay que estar agradecidos con *Jorge G. Castañeda* porque ha ofrecido en ...

Castaneda has always seduced by his intelligence and his facility with words in Spanish, English and French. He became a favorite of Mexican themes of media as *The New York Times, Le Monde, El País Newsweek* and political commentator. He had close relations with such contrasting characters as Carlos Fuentes and Gabriel García Márquez, Regis Debray and Jose Cordova. There was a time when almost no international media could do a story about Mexico without citing Castaneda.

Algunos nudos: Jorge G. Castañeda | Cultura y vida cotidiana
cultura.nexos.com.mx/?p=8588
22.06.2015 - *Jorge G. Castañeda* es un demócrata que tira más a la izquierda, así se .... Yo me encontraba con *Gabriel García Márquez*, Carlos Monsiváis y ...

9781157440307 - People from Guadalajara: Katy Jurado ...
diebuchsuche.de › Suchen › Vergleichen
Katy Jurado, Ricardo Lancaster-Jones y Verea, El Satanico, Jose Pablo ... Luis *G.* Abbadie, Oswaldo Sánchez, Xavier Martínez, Salvador Toscano, José ... Ángel de Quevedo, Daniel Guzmán, *Jorge Castañeda*, Kristian Álvarez, Karla Carrillo, ..
In his book Jorge G Castaneda, 'Che Guevara Companero,' he writes about the encounter with Fernanado Guterrez Barros and Fidel Castro at the Santa Rosa ranch in Chalico. Fidel Castro's training camp before sailing with the Granma.

What are the connections between Jorge G Castaneda and Ramon Chao? Not really expecting a reply. Reading through-

I find they are friends, Ramon Chao knows him will enough to know why he was nicknamed blonde, "El Guero" is not a surprise. But when Jorge G Castaneda and Ramon Chao were living in Paris, Ramon Chao was in charge of Jorge G Castaneda's home when it was ransacked by the French secret police. In fact he chats on about what the secret police took with them. Was it because they saw Regis Debray, Mitterrand adviser had been there? What Ramon Chao dose say is that Jorge G Castaneda was the intermediary between Latin American guerrillas and the President of France. It would not be surprising, since his father, Jorge Castañeda y Álvarez de la Rosa, was one of the main promoters of the meetings of Esquipulas, where the peace agreements were prepared. Esguipulas is in Guwatmarlia.

Ramon Chao-
Who is Ramon Chao? I did not come across him till I started to look for links between authors and translators. I started with Ann Wright and found Ramon Chao, who brought me back to Jorge G Castaneda! This left my breathless as I met on the

way through my research other folk I have spoken about before.

Ramón Luís *Chao* Rego (born 1935) is a Spanish journalist and writer. He won the Premio de Virtuosismo for Piano in 1955. So Wikipedia tells me.

The address below states he wrote the foreword to a version by Alberto Granado

latinoamericana von granado - AbeBooks
www.abebooks.de/buch-
suchen/titel/latinoamericana/autor/granado/
Latinoamericana : Journal de voyage von Granado, A and Che Guevara *und* eine große Auswahl von ähnlichen neuen, gebrauchten *und* antiquarischen ... Préface de *Ramon Chao*. ... Latinoamericana due *diari per un viaggio* in *motocicletta,*.

    In the next address you can find versions translated by Ann Wright printed by publisher Feltrinelli.

Latinoamericana. Un diario per un viaggio in motocicletta ...
www.book-info.com/isbn/88-07-81259-2.htm - Diese Seite übersetzen
Un diario per un viaggio in *motocicletta*« (19. Auflage) aus ... *Ramón Chao* (afterword), Ernesto Che Guevara (author), Martine Thomas (translator) Mille et *une* ...

    Amazon has to offer-

Voyage à motocyclette : Latinoamericana

6 giu. 2001 di Ramón Chao e Ernesto Che Guevara.

There are so many versions of this book written by-
translated by- Question who really wrote it?
I hope you have not lost interest in Ramon Chao as
he can be seen with Gabriel Garcia Marques.
 A member of UNEAC the union of writers and
Artist of Cuba.
As Ramon Chao talks about Jorge G Castaneda in
his blog, he also tells of his friendship with Regis
Debray and President Mitterrand.

La verdad de Castañeda | Ramón Chao

*https://**ramonchao**.wordpress.com/.../la-verdad-de-
c...*
03.04.2012 - *Jorge Castañeda* (padre) fue uno de los
grandes diplomáticos que tuvo México, equiparable
a figuras como Alfonso Reyes y Amado Nervo, ...

**Just to point out who sells his
books.**

Ramon Chao - Feltrinelli

*www.**lafeltrinelli**.it/libri/**ramon-chao**/205386*
Tutti i libri di *Ramon Chao* in offerta; acquista
online a prezzi scontati su La *Feltrinelli*.

Libri Letterature di Ramon Chao in Offerta | LaFeltrinelli

*www.**lafeltrinelli**.it/libri-letterature-**ramon-
chao**/c.../1... -*

Siti del Gruppo: LaFeltrinelli · Giangiacomo
Feltrinelli Editore · LaEffe - Canale 50 · Fondazione
Giangiacomo *Feltrinelli* · Antica Focacceria San
Francesco.
Antes de ir por el premio, en un salón del Gran
Hotel posaron para la foto: ...
jetset.com.co
This photo shows the long association with Gabriel
Garcia Marquez. Ramon Chan is ducking under the
tall man with his hand in his pocket.

📷 Antes de ir por el premio, en un salón del Gran Hotel posaron para la foto: (sentados) Ramón Chao, Pablo Leyva, Magda Oliver, Manuel y Marie Claire de Andreis, Gonzalo García Barcha, Eligio García Márquez, Tachia Quintana, Charles Rosoff y Myriam de García. (De pie) Mauricio Vargas, Jaime Castro, Hernán Vieco, Gloria Valencia, Plinio A. Mendoza, Mercedes Barcha, Germán Vargas, Gabo, Alfonso Fuenmayor, Tita Manotas, Álvaro Castaño y Álvaro Mutis.

Jon Lee Anderson-

Jon Lee Anderson- Che Guevara. A revolutionary Life. Talking about Jon Lee Anderson, he has written the foreword to 'Che Want To See You' by Ciro Bustos translated by Ann Wright. Next point is, Jon Lee Anderson spent three years with Che's second wife Aleida March. In fact his children had the same nanny as Che's children. To take the association a step further, Jon Lee Anderson spent one year living above Ciro Bustos in Malmo. (If Jon Lee Anderson had not remarked that Ciro Bustos painted wonderful painting of people without faces I would never have noticed him!

Elisabeth Burgos-Debray-

Jorge Masetti- and Banigno- Elisabeth Burgos-Debray- transcribed and edited books by Daniel "Benigno" Alarcón Ramirez and Jorge Masetti, former Cuban officials who broke with Castro and went into exile. Her papers contain drafts of these books.

__Inventory of the Elisabeth Burgos-Debray Papers__

www.oac.cdlib.org/findaid/ark:/13030/.../entire_text...

Régis *Debray* and *Elisabeth Burgos-Debray* were later divorced, and ... by Daniel "Benigno" Alarcón Ramirez and *Jorge Masetti*, former Cuban officials who ... Aguilar Castro, Joaquin *Ricardo*, 1993-1995 ..... Dutch *translation*, 1983 and 1993.

Pierre Kalfon-
Pierre Kalfon- <u>Allende Chile: 1970-1973</u>
<u>Il Che: Una leggenda del secolo</u>
he has a long list of Che books.

<u>Il Che: Una leggenda del secolo - Google Books-</u>
<u>Ergebnisseite</u>
https://books.google.de/books?isbn=8858821130 -
<u>Pierre Kalfon</u> - 2011 - Biography & Autobiography
Una leggenda del secolo *Pierre Kalfon* ... 266 Jean-
Pierre Clerc, Fidel de Cuba, cit., pp. 312-313. 267
Max Marambio, colloquio con l'autore, Santiago
1993.

Look there is Max Marambio again------
Ann Wright again------
While looking through the Mary Ferrell
Foundation files after finding Carlos Delmar Jurado
name is there, (see- What a circle to find.) I put in
the name of Ann Wright, remembering that the
Operation 40 was a CIA formed assassin group.
Among its members are those we all ready know,
they run through the Bay of Pigs attack on Cuba,
Kennedy's death, Che's death party, trouble in Chili
and Salvador Allande's death, Watergate. And now I
find Ann Wright's name again this time it is because
she has written about the assassination of Patrice
Lumumda the first elected leader of the Cong.

Operation 40 - Wikipedia, the free encyclopedia
*https://en.wikipedia.org/wiki/**Operation_40***
Operation 40 was the code name for a Central
Intelligence Agency-sponsored counterintelligence
group composed of Cuban exiles. The group was
formed to ...

The Assassination of Lumumba by Ludo de Witte;
Ann ...*www.jstor.org/stable/3097312*
By Ludo De Witte; trans. by *Ann. Wright* and
Renee Fenby. .... Lumumba's assassination.6 It is
now available in English *translation* as The ... pen
of *Col.* FredEric ...

Short list of internet address- Gabriel Garcia
Marquez. Elizabeth Burgos-Debray. Ciro Bustos.
Che Guevara.

 Gabriel Garcia Marquez.
At Tranquilina's Knee - London Review of Books
www.lrb.co.uk/v05/n10/g.../at-tranquilinas-knee
... Mendoza in conversation with Gabriel Garcia
Marquez translated by *Ann Wright* ... Perhaps
Colonel David Morgan doesn't know that what
Garcia Marquez told .... by telling us of the wooden
translation of what is easy conversational prose, ...

Garcia Marquez, Gabriel 1928 - Encyclopedia.com
*www.encyclopedia.com/.../garcia-marquez-gabriel-
...*
No One Writes to the *Colonel* and Other Stories
(includes "No One Writes to the .... Mendoza
(interviews), Oveja Negra, 1982, English *translation*
by *Ann Wright* ..

Gabriel (Jose) Garcia Marquez - Student Resources
in Context
ic.galegroup.com/.../ReferenceDetailsWindow?...
Leaf Storm recounts the story of a *colonel* and the
inhabitants of a small town, ... Mendoza
(interviews), Oveja Negra, 1982, English *translation*
by *Ann Wright* ..

In-madbookcollection.blogspot.com
García Márquez, Gabriel, & Plinio Apuleyo
Mendoza. *The Fragrance of Guava: Plinio Apuleyo
Mendoza in Conversation with Gabriel García
Márquez*. 1982. Trans. Ann Wright. London: Verso
Editions, 1983.

Che Guevara-The Motorcycle Diaries: A Journey
Around South America
by Ernesto Che Guevara, Ann Wright (Translator),
Ernesto Guevara Lynch

Ernesto Guevara Lynch- Young Che.
(see Ernesto Guevara Lynch- Che Guevara's Father
was an actor too!)

Ciro Bustos-
<u>Che Wants to See You - VersoBooks.com</u>
www.versobooks.com/.../1432-che-wants-to-see-yo...
by *Ciro Bustos* Translated by *Anne Wright*
Introduction by Jon Lee Anderson ... *Ciro Bustos*
was Che Guevara's Argentinian lieutenant, fighting
beside El ...

Elisabeth Burgos-Debray-
<u>I, Rigoberta Menchu: An Indian Woman in</u>
<u>Guatemala ...</u>
www.amazon.de › ... › Spezifische Gruppen › Frauen
... *Elisabeth Burgos-Debray*, Rigoberta Menchu,
Ann Wright: Fremdsprachige ... An Indian Woman
in Guatemala von *Elisabeth Burgos-Debray*
Taschenbuch EUR ..... story was lost in *translation*,
as is always the case with books in *translation*,.

<u>I, Rigoberta Menchú - Goodreads</u>
www.goodreads.com/.../233292.I_Rigoberta_Menc...
Bewertung: 3,7 - 3.016 Abstimmungsergebnisse
In 1983 Elisabeth Burgos met the 23-year-old
Rigoberta Menchu and spent a week ... [Book transl.
into English by *Ann Wright*. ..... someone and then
translated by another person, I wonder how much is
lost in *translation*. .... I, Rigoberta Menchú: An
Indian Woman in Guatemala - Rigoberta Menchú,
Elisabeth Burgos-Debray ...

I, Rigoberta Menchú - Goodreads
www.goodreads.com/.../233292.I_Rigoberta_Menc...

Bewertung: 3,7 - 3.016 Abstimmungsergebnisse
In 1983 Elisabeth Burgos met the 23-year-old
Rigoberta Menchu and spent a week ... [Book transl.
into English by *Ann Wright*. ..... someone and then
translated by another person, I wonder how much is
lost in *translation*. .... I, Rigoberta Menchú: An
Indian Woman in Guatemala - Rigoberta Menchú,
Elisabeth Burgos-Debray ...

David Stoll-
David Stoll has been very public in his opinion that
Rigoberta Menchu's story is a fake.
The whole story has been proved to be a lie.

David Stoll - InfoRapid Knowledge Portal
en.inforapid.org/index.php?search=David%20Stoll
... Nobel Peace Prize laureate Rigoberta Menchú
wrote with *Elizabeth Burgos*. ... author and
anthropologist *Elizabeth Burgos*, "Me llamo
Rigoberta Menchú y así .

If you are not happy about those connections then
there is Ann Wright's connection to Daniel Ellsburg!
It was his psychiatrist office that was broken into in
the Watergate complex.
In the **Mary Ferrell Foundation** description on
Watergate they also suggest the brake in was to
locate materials showing that the Democratic Party
was receiving funds from Fidel Castro.
(I have made the same assumption when writing-
Spies-CIA-Lies-Terrorist-Che Guevara.)

Not forgetting I think Ann Wright took that name
after she no longer was able to use the name of
Monika Ertl. Full explanation in the above book.

Roberto Moss- translated Gabriel Garcia Marquez's
stories and articles- (See 'Independent Men.')

Just to add Feltrinelli' name-
Latinoamericana. Due diari per un viaggio in motocicletta ...

www.book-info.com/isbn/88-07-42069-4.htm
Un diario per un viaggio in motocicletta [Universale
Economica *Feltrinelli*] P. Cacucci ... Ernesto
Guevara, Alexandra Keeble (*translator*), *Ann Wright*
(*translator*)
The motorcycle diaries [Verso]

www.book-info.com/isbn/1-85984-942-3.htm -
Un diario per un viaggio in motocicletta [Universale
Economica *Feltrinelli*] P. Cacucci ... Ernesto
Guevara, Alexandra Keeble (*translator*), *Ann Wright*
(*translator*)

Lucia Alvarez de Toledo-
Lucia Alvarez de Toledo- La History Del Che
Guevara.
Author of 'The story of Che.' Forward by Gabriel
Garcia Marquez.
(A Worked for-the National Broadcasting System of
Argentina. Editor and translator of- Young Che by
Ernesto Guevara Lynch, Che's father.

Mother of-   Che Guevara's half brother ,
Fernando L Chavaz Alvarez.
(B) translator of- Travelling with Che Guevara. By
Alberto Granado.
(C) Friend of -   Liaison officer *Ciro Bustos.*

(A)   <u>bol.com | the story of che guevara | Boeken</u>
      www.bol.com/nl/s/engelse.../index.html
(B)   The Story of Che Guevara | *Lucìa Àlvarez De
      Toledo* ... Featuring a foreword by *Gabriel
      Garcia Marquez*

      (B)
          Cuñado de Ernesto "Che" Guevara. Integrante
de una familia tradicionalmente **...**
          e.sb-10.com

(c) <u>The Story of Che Guevara: An Interview with Lucía Alvarez ...</u>

*alborada.net/**lucia-alvarez-de-toledo**-the-story-of-ch...*

24.11.2010 - [*Lucía Alvarez de Toledo* is the author
of 'The Story of Che Guevara', ... As I have said in
my book, then Argentine liaison officer *Ciro
Bustos,*

Se presentó Gabo periodista en la Feria de
Guadalajara.cinereverso.org

I find that the association between Jon Lee
Anderson go's back as far as 1955. Jon Lee
Anderson was one of the jury that selected Gabriel
Garcia Marques' book for the Guadalajara
International Book Fair (FIL). Organized by
Iberoamerican Journalism Foundation (FNPI) it is a
foundation which Gabriel Garcia Marquez is very
closely associated with.
It all seems to be a bit of a joke to me.
 : During the presentation to Gabo the journalist,
an anthology of the best journalistic texts from the
greatest Colombian writer of the twentieth century.
Were selected and annotated by Jon Lee Anderson,
Martin Caparros, Alma Guillermo Prieto, Antonio
Munoz Molina, Juan Cruz, Juan Villoro, Alex and
Hector Abad Grijelmo Faciolince, among other
writers and chroniclers of the singular group of
friends or "buddies polygraphs" the Nobel Prize for
Literature:

'The power of Gabriel Garcia Marquez.'
I add this as a point of interest as this is the book Jon Lee Anderson has written about Gabo! Not only did he write a book about him, he, Jon Lee Anderson spent several months living in Gabriel Garcia Marquez's home while he, Jon Lee Anderson wrote Gabriel Garcia Marquez's Biography.
It does seem he did not have a home of his own.

"Gabriel Garcia Marquez was actively opposed to the extradition of Pablo Escobar the drug baron, to the United States. The book 'Chronicle of a Kidnapping' published in 1996, by Gabriel Garcia Marquez.
Reconstructs the kidnapping of 10 people ordered in 1990 by Pablo Escobar, the then head of Medellin cartel. The book is based on extensive interviews with victims of kidnappings and
those who participated in the endless negotiations that led to their release. The
main characters are very well-connected journalists and politicians, people from the

social and professional areas where García Márquez
and Mercedes moved.

Politics and journalism have occupied most of the
time since Gabriel García Márquez became the
majority shareholder of the weekly news 'Change.'
Change bought with money from the Nobel Prize,
which remained deposited in a Swiss bank for 16
years. "I swear it's true; He forgot that money."

Is how Jon Lee Anderson expresses the strange
situation of forgetting you have so much money in
the bank! But there again this man does not have to
worry about money, only manipulating nations.
(Just to add a little remark of my own- Kidnapping,
the book is to be found in Guantanamo Bay top
security prison! Strange place to find this book.)

In Jon Lee Anderson's –
**0802135587 - Anderson, Jon Lee - Che
Guevara: A ...**
www.euro-boek.nl/boek/isbn/0802135587.html
Afterword by *Mario Vargas Llosa*. 248 pages.
paperback. 0292715331. keywords: Literature
Translated Peru Latin America. inventory # 38059.
FROM THE ...

Jon Lee Anderson gives you the very strong
impression that he has known Gabriel Garcia
Marquez for some considerable time. Just to
complete another circle Mario Vargas Llosa has
written the afterword to 'Che Guevara. A
revolutionary Life.'

(Not forgetting Mario Vargas Llosa was the one that informs us that the mother of Che stayed in his flat in Paris!)

El PODER DE GABO. In this article Jon Lee Anderson explains how, the guerrilla organizations and the Army National, ELN combined with the Cubans and with inspired by Che Guevara, mixed in the fray of drugs and trafficking. By the early 80s, when the Cali and Medellin cartels had become powerful; Colombia was producing 80 percent of the cocaine consumed in the United States as well as heroin. Colombia's military says it needs help to fight the guerrillas to defeat them would end the drug trafficking. The border between the activities of drug traffickers and guerrillas became even more tenuous after Pablos Escobar's death. By the mid nineties the drug business was divided among a large number of mini-mafias, paramilitary the guerrillas themselves. The FARC, the wealthiest guerrilla organization in Latin America, controlled an area where much of the cocaine consumed in the world is produced. It was believed that it had 15,000 armed combatants, while the ELN had 5,000. Both groups would the pay wages to their members and are financed by numerous criminal activities including collection of taxes on the production of heroin and cocaine. Kidnapping for the collection of ransom and extortion of money from US and European oil companies, to change protection of its mining operations and its pipelines.

US Congress assigned $ 289 million to the Police and the Colombian army, making Colombia the third largest recipient of US military aid US after Israel and Egypt. This aid package was to rid Colombia of its problems.

'Gabriel García Márquez has been closely involved in the peace negotiations. He presented to the then Colombian president Andres Pastrana, Fidel Castro, who could facilitate talks with the guerrillas. He also helped to restore good relations between Washington and Bogota. Bill Richardson, Us energy secretary, stated that Gabriel Garcia Marques was a catalyst in the peace talks.

Gabriel García Márquez was invited several times by President Clinton to the White House with his friends. It was stated, that not only had the US President in mind the objective of obtaining a negotiated agreement between the guerrillas and the Colombian government, but also to achieve an improvement in relations between the United States and Cuba. "America needs the participation of Cuba in the Colombian peace talks because the Cuban

government has the best contacts with the guerrilla;
Gabriel Garcia Marques is said to have explained.
Cuba is perfectly located just two hours by plane,
where Colombian president Andres Pastrana could
at any time, carry out all meetings required and
returned without anyone knowing.

If Jon Lee Anderson is so will informed of
Gabriel Garcia Marquez's busyness then you can
defiantly call him one of Gabriel Garcia Marquez's
men.

Chapter eighteen.
`My Friend Che´ by Ricardo Rojo

`My Friend Che´ by Ricardo Rojo is a book I
looked at with interest, is a very clever book it
leaves room for others to write their versions. It dose
however tell you clearly what is going on in the
political circles of the time in question.

This book is dated May 1968, it must have been
written to try to explain some of the issues that did
not match at the time. Though others have made
statements that do not match with Ricardo Rojo,
they have however built on what he has said.
The Bolivians had had a revolution in 1953 and had
reformed its land ownership.

One issue that Ricardo Rojo makes clear is Fidel
Castro did not abandon Che in Bolivia.
Fidel Castro was negotiating with the Bolivian
Communists. Mario Monje as Secretary General was
at the beginning of December 1966 in Havana to
discuss the problem the Communists of Bolivia
faced. Should they support the guerrilla movement
they would risk working against the instructions
from Moscow.

Fidel Castro could not ignore the pacts between
the Latin American Communist Parties and
Moscow; he needed the support of the Bolivian
Communist to help the Che' guerrillas movement.

*Ricardo Rojo states that, Fide Castro was asking
Mario Monje to let Political Leadership of the Latin*

*continent to be transferred from Moscow to Havana.
This is a hefty statement!*

The next statement Ricardo Rojo makes is: Mario Monje was prepared to resign his post of Secretary General of the Bolivian Communists enabling him to follow the guerrillas, in this position he could negotiate with other groups. Ricardo Rojo states Mario Monje wanted the leadership for both the Military and Political operation carried out on Bolivian territory.

I have to quote the exact words Ricardo Rojo says Che Guevara used in his book-
"My failure would not mean that the fight can't be won. Many failed trying to climb Everest, but Everest was finally conquered."

Ricardo Rojo continues by saying the following dawn Che Guevara managed to hear a broadcast of a speech by Fide Castro from Havana. (26th of July 1966) he was speaking to those gathered to celebrate the eight anniversary of the triumph of the revolution. In this speech he says-
"In whatever part of the world Major Ernesto Guevara and his companions are, our message is especially warm. The Imperials have killed Che many times in many places, but we hope someday, when imperialism least expects it. Major Ernesto Guevara will be born of his ashes, like the phoenix, a fighting, healthy guerrilla.

Ricardo Rojo states that this speech brought volunteers, he names Moises Guevara who on January 19.1967, introduced himself to Che

Guevara. Ricardo Rojo also states that negotiations continued in Havana. The one of the two leaders of the Bolivian Communists party that traveled to Cuba was Jorge Kolle. Simon Reyes was the Secretary of Relations for the Union of Mine Workers. (From the Mine Union it was hoped volunteers would come.)

We have been told Castro abandoned Che without add, but it was the problems between the Bolivian Communists that left the guerrillas without the Communist Party organization for supplies or communication lines.

This situation is ideal to set the death scene for an up and coming hero! He is cut off so we think. Camiri is a proximally one hundred kilometers from La Higuera. Camiri where Regis Debray and Ciro Bustos were on trial!

Ricardo Rojo says Che could fly a plane he had learned a fly a twin motored Cessna, and could take control of a Britannic. Che/Ciro could pop over anytime to play his role in the death scene using a car or a plane.

Dated in book 1944/1957. From Cochabamba to the Argentinean border.

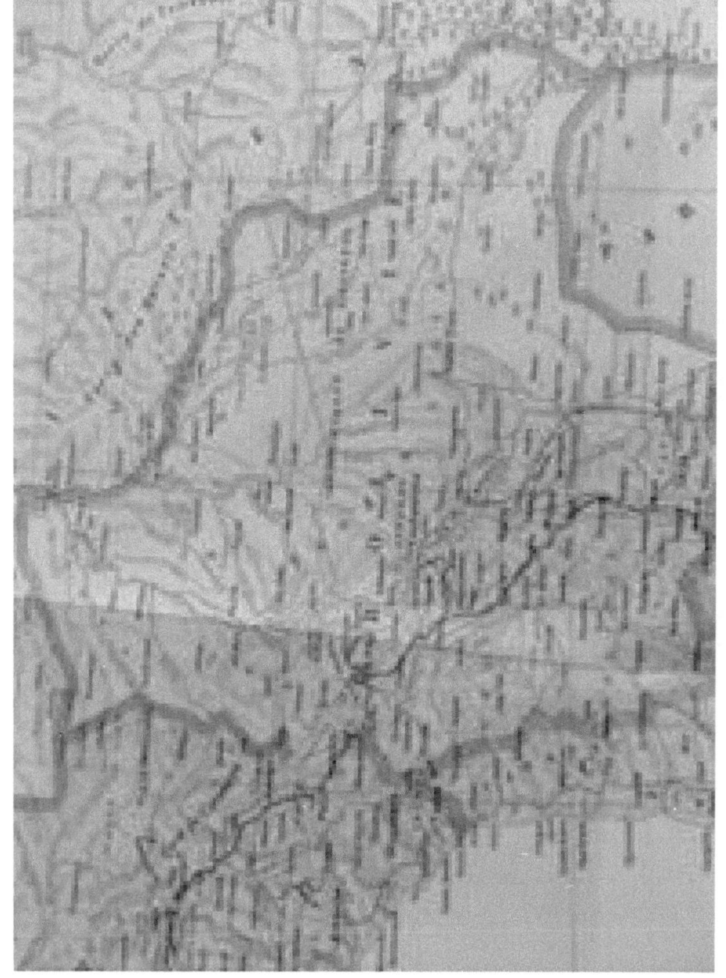

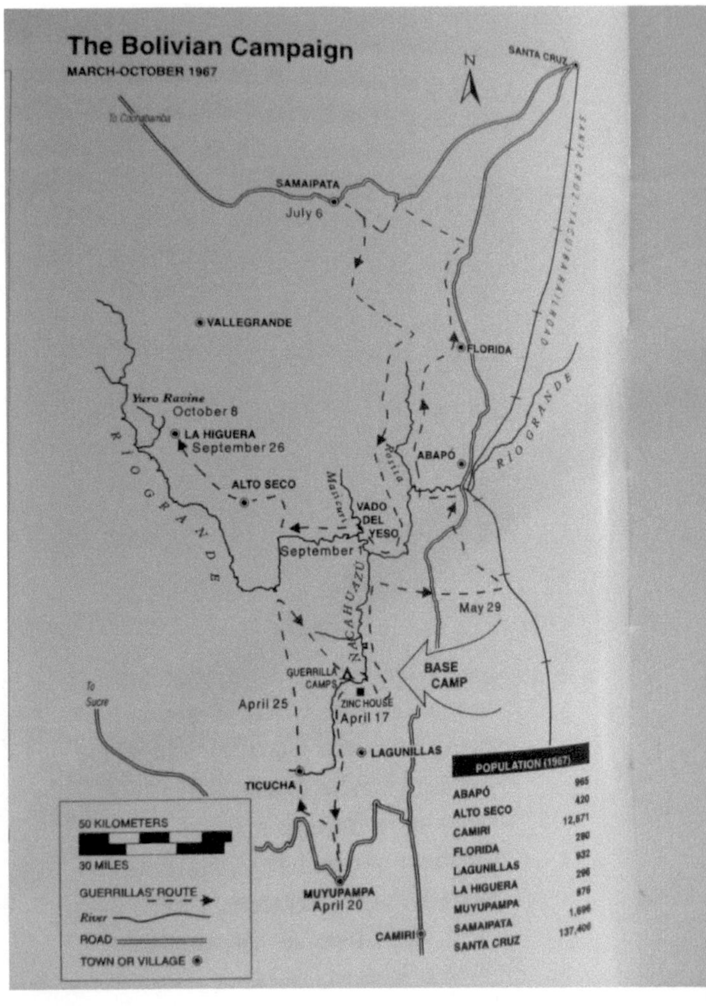

Ricardo Rojo tells us this as he says he is Ciro Bustos' lawyer! Why dose Regis Debray's wife Elisabeth Burgos Debray not state that in her

papers? She dose however have a file for him
Box/Folder: 13: 60 Rojo, Ricardo, 1967-1968

Ciro Bustos names Jaime Mendizbal as his defense lawyer! As dose Elisabeth Burgos Debray in her papers, she uses news papers from the trial. (From those photos of the trial, I state he is acting as a brother of Che Guevara!)

In 'Che Wants To See You' which is Ciro Bustos' book of events it does not mention Ricardo Rojo as a lawyer but as his friend. The decryption Ciro gives is of Ricardo Rojo can be seen in 'My friend Che.'

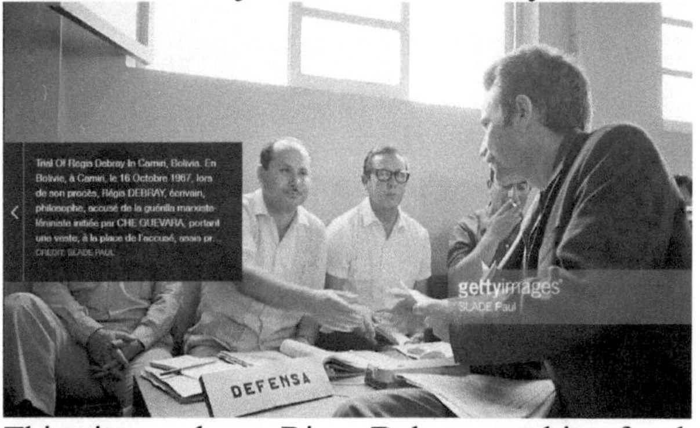

This picture shows Riges Debray reaching for the hand of Ricardo Rojo.

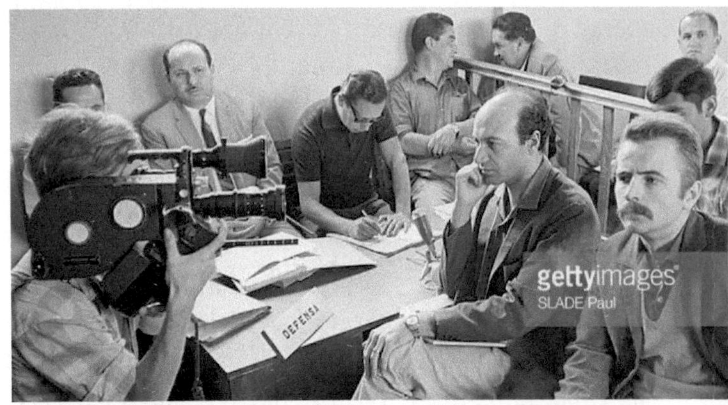

This photo shows Ricardo Rojo with his back to the wall, Ciro/Che looking at the camera man next to Riges Debray.

<u>Website mit diesem Bild</u>

Trial Of Regis Debray In Camiri, Bolivia. En

Bolivie, à Camiri, le

gettyimages.co.uk

<u>Website mit diesem Bild</u>

Pero sobretodo, el profundo amor con que se refería
no solamente por su ...

manigna.blogspot.com

This photo can also be found in 'My Friend Che'.

It is safe to say he was present at the trial.

    Ricardo Rojo states in his foreword that Salvador
Allende read the first draft of his book!
Ricardo Rojo states many times he was a friend of
Salvador Allende.
Salvador Allende was to supply Ricardo Rojo with a
letter addressed to a socialist lawyer in Guayaquil
asking him to help Ricardo Rojo in any way he
could. As Ricardo Rojo suggests that 'Che' is with
him at the time, this implies that the assertion
between Che Guevara and Salvador Allende was a
long standing one.

   In **<u>VILLA GRANADILLO: EXTRANJEROS</u>**

...

*villagranadillo.blogspot.com/.../extranjeros-
internaci...*

05.03.2015 - El fotógrafo *Alberto* Korda del
periódico Revolución, quien con su cámara .... a un
tío materno, periodista y comunista: *Cayetano*

Córdoba Iturbe, quien ..... Conociendo ahí al republicano Coronel *Bayo*, quien a la sazón funge ... "The above translated- Photographer Alberto Korda of Revolution, who with his camera .... to a maternal uncle, a journalist and Communist: Cayetano Córdoba Iturbe, who ..... Knowing there the Republican Colonel Bayo, who was then serves .."

They state that Salvador Allende Gossen gave money to Ernesto Guevara and letters of recommendation for subversive journeys in Latin America. They suggest the year is 1952.

As a political refugee in 1953 as a lawyer Ricardo Rojo says he met Che Guevara in La Paz, Bolivia. Ricardo Rojo was a lawyer active in a commission formed by the largest opposition party in Argentina- the Ragical Civic Union- its purpose was to defend political and union prisoners.

Caribbean Military Legion-
Caribbean Military Legion was formed in Cuba by when Carlos Prio Soccarras was Presadent and while Romulo Betancourt and Juan Bosh were living in Havana. One of its members was the President of Costa Rica, Jose (Pepe) Figuers.

In 1952 when Batista took power in Cuba the leaders of the Legion abandoned Cuba to take refuge in San Jose de Costa Rica, where Ricardo Rojo says he and Che met the Venezuelans Romulo Betancourt and Raul Leoni as well as the Dominican Juan Bosh. All three would become presidents of their countries in the following years Ricardo Rojo informs us. As there was a Caribbean Military Legion and the Dominican director had an embryonic military organization in the Caribbean teaching hundreds of young men to use modern weapons.

I am not surprised the CIA was present in Guatemala, Ricardo Rojo is telling of his meetings with ambassador this, and president that, while he and Che take refuge in Guatemala.

The Argentinean Chancellor Osequeda seems to have paid Ricardo Rojo boarding house bills.

The Argentinean Ambassador Nicasio Sanchez Torance has brought the Argentineans Yerba Mate (tea). The ex-Pressident, Juan Jose Arevaldo told Ricardo Rojo and Che he had returned from Chile where he was Guatemala's ambassador; as one his relatives had died. On finding out Ricardo Rojo was in Guatemala he diced to look Ricardo Rojo up, he even go's so far as to ask them to lunch!

Two young men of apparent no consequence are hobnobbing with the political elate. This was said to be before Che Guevara has even met Fidel Castro!

Hilda Gadea.

Ricardo Rojo mentions the Peruvian members of the APRA. The American Popular Revolutionary Alliance and that Hilda Gadea was an unselfish companion of the Peruvian exiles in Guatemala. She was working for INFOP an institute created to stimulate agrarian and industrial production. Remember who her brother is! Ricardo Gadea Acosta.

Looking at what Ricardo Rojo tells us about himself; he says he was at the Colombia University, where he attended a Professor Frank Tannenbaum's classes on Latin American Politics. This in the university grounded by Gabriel Garcia Marques?! A lot of the people I am talking about went there! Ricardo Rojo suggests he was there in 1955.

Arturo Frondizi happens to be a close friend of Ricardo Rojo! Arturo Frondizi is only the man who becomes Argentinan President in 1958... Such good friend Arturo Frondizi arranges to bring Ricardo Rojo from of exile in New York.

Arturo Frondizi - Wikipedia, the free encyclopedia

*https://en.**wikipedia**.org/**wiki**/**Arturo_Frondizi***
Arturo Frondizi Ercoli, GCMG (October 28, 1908 – April 18, 1995) was the President of Argentina between May 1, 1958, and March 29, 1962, for the Intransigent ...

Ricardo Rojo informs me that Jorge Masetti was an Argentinan journalist and he was Che's correspondent in West Germany. Ricardo Rojo was Argentin's ambassador to West Germany in Bonn. He tells of two reformist presidents, Arturo Frondizi- Argentina and Janio Quadros of Brazil tried to mediate between the United States and Cuba. And that the coexistence of a pact between the United States and Russia made it unlikely a war would be made over Cuba. This was happening at the time Che was Minister of Industries. Ricardo Rojo was to elaborate on an extensive memorandum for Che on Cuban relation with West Germany. (In this time Fidel Castro was disusing Brazil with the Chinese.)

It is more what this book does not say that is interesting for someone that was intimate with someone else it lacks the personal feel, it does however tell what is happening in the world at the time. He only mentions Ciro Bustos three times one of which is in the foreword, stating he was Ciro Bustos's lawyer. Regis Debray is named as a very close friend of Castro's. As for Tania Bunka (Who's other identity was Susana Sontag) he says her body was carried away by the rivers' water.

Ricardo Rojo has a lot to say about Che's death scene, I was wondering how he could know so much!? Has he written the script? Was he paving the way? He is sitting not a hundred kilometers away with the main actor! No wonder there was a smile on their faces they had just pulled off the best bit of theater.

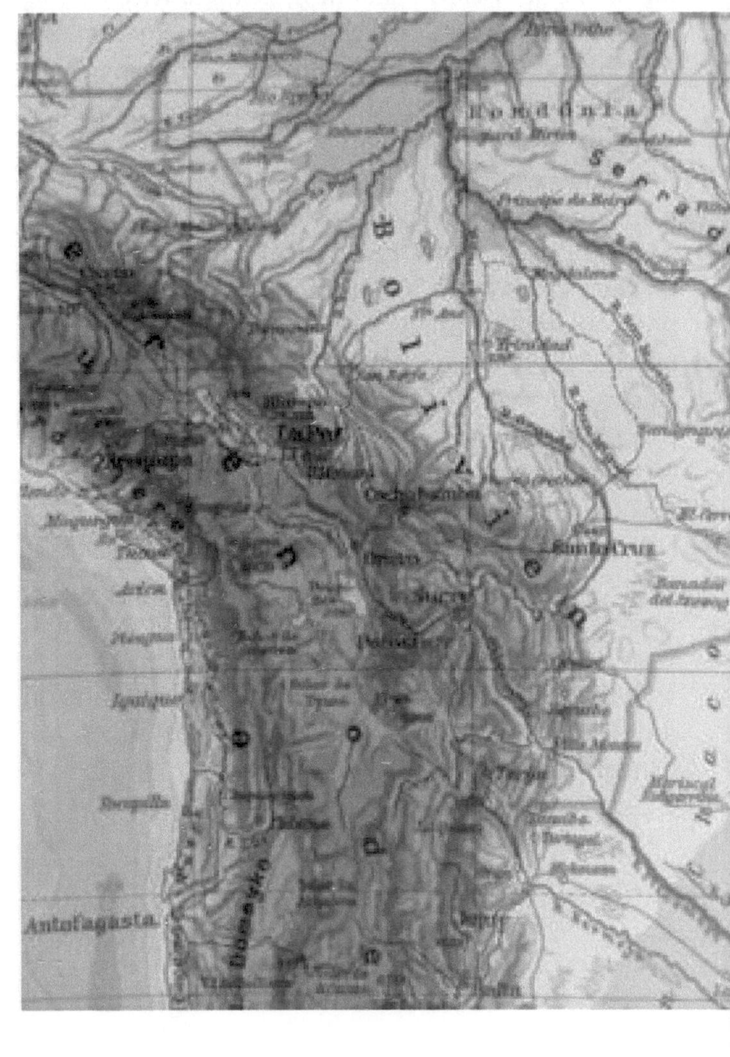

Chapter nineteen.
Paco Ignicio Taibo 11 is a Gabo man.

The friendship between Gabriel Garcia Marquez is to be seen as the two families take a meal together with their common interest in the film industry. Bill Clinton is one of their mutual friends.

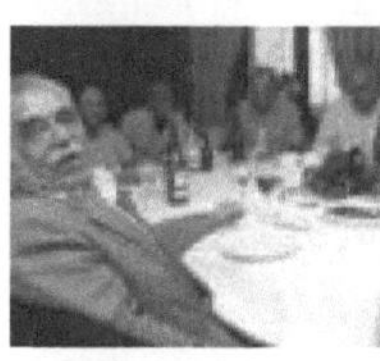 Más fotos ...lne.es

Paco Ignicio Taibo 11 is a Mexican author, a journalist, a screenwriter. He was a foreman on the jury for the film festival in Havana 2007. His father Paco Ignicio Taibo 1 is a film maker who ran many of the film festivals in and around Mexico.

Paco Ignicio Taibo 11 is of Spanish, Mexican, Italian descent, it is not surprising to see his name connected to films involving Anna Magnani. To connect him to Katy Jurado was not as complicated as it first appears; he wrote a book about Maria Felix, her husband was Agustin Lara. Who just happened to have been the conductor of the orchestra that Katy Jurado's mother was supposed to have sung with!

elpais.com/diario/1983/.../431474412_850215.html 04.09.1983 - ... Gianneti *Anna Magnani* L'acttrice, la donna, *il* mito; L'automovile; La sciantosa; Un ... por los autores mexicanos Luis Orozco y *Paco Ignacio Taibo*. ... Samuel Fuller, *Ignacio Taibo*, Monte Hellman, Graciela Borges, Diego .

Paco Ignicio Taibo 11's name can be connected to Portes Gil, Katy Jurado's cousin. His book about Mexican unrest, it is centered Pancho Villa. Pancho Villa was one of the leaders of the Mexican resolution 1879-1923. Portes Gil holds the president's post for two years 1928.
Por Ignacio Paco Taibo II Con ciertas fotos tengo una relación de amor muy ...
diasdehistoria.com.ar

This address shows an article he wrote about Korda' famous photo of Che that Feltrinelli sent around the world. The world is small!

Guevara, Also Known as Che (9780312206529): Paco ...

Amazon.com: Guevara, Also Known as Che (9780312206529): Paco Ignacio ... Mexican novelist and historian *Paco Ignacio Taibo* II here captures the life and character of *Che Guevara*, the .... *11* of *11* people found the following review helpful. Paco Ignicio Taibo 11, as it happens to have written a book or two on Che Guevara. 'Ernesto Guevara, Tanbien concido como el Che.' To see he has written an article on Korda's famous photo of Che Guevara printed by Feltrinelli does not lead me to be surprised that his books have also been published by Feltrinelli.

... dinero para la guerrilla ...
martinezestevez.wordpress.com

Martin Zestevez In the article to be found in the above address the writer tell us that he has some interesting ideas. He tells us that Che had the use of a radio station to publicize his men's action in the Sierra Maestra. He used his channel to overturn operating government's propaganda.

Martin Zestevez remarks about over four hundred books that had been transported to the guerrilla zone- their guerrilla camp. He names two Cubans, Pombo and Tuma as the men who were responsible for their part in organizing the urban guerrilla network in Bolivia, July 1966 in La Paz. Among their duties was the purchase of second hand books form kiosks around the city. The books were to serve as a teaching aide for ideological and political education of the guerrillas.

Riges Debray and Ciro Bustos were captured on April 19th 1967. Their capture was to prove more interesting as they told their captives about the books. It is said that Ciro Bustos proceeded to draw maps to show where the books were located. The books were evacuated to the Command of the Fourth Division based in Camiri. In CAMIRI!

Martin Zestevez goes on to on to say he was assigned to find the books in 1996, he knew of their existence in 1984. He checked the inventory left by the guerrillas in caves but the books without exception were not to be found. They had been neglected by the Armed Force; they did not provide librarians or archivists for their administration. (There is only a list to say they existed!)

Che Guevara was supposed to have in the time he spent in his camp Nancahuazu written his diary, read 19 books a month, transcribe works of Leon Trotsky, and run a revolutionary struggle! When he was said to have been captured he had in his backpack no less that 108 documentary pieces. (Running around a jungle I would have left the notebook of poems out! Talking of the note book of poems- 69 poems written by Che at this time have been translated by Paco Ignicio Taibo 11. Paco Ignicio Taibo 11 publishes them. (I have to ask how did he get hold of them? Unless he was part of the propaganda teem!?)

Paco Ignicio Taibo 1, Paco Ignicio Taibo 11 and family are on Gabriel Garcia Marquez's team

Martin Zestevez informs us that all that has been rescued; be it books or documents or the documents prepared by the Armed Forces and the Bolivian guerrillas fitted into a metal draw. That they have gone missing, stolen misplaced or have been destroyed. Even the war trophy, a set of surgical instruments that were in a showcase in Camiri, Command Headquarters of the Fourth Division have disappeared.

There have been attempts to locate and reconstruct, what now is called, 'The Historical Archive of the Armed Forces.' Martin Zestevez also mentions that letters written by the guerrillas did not reach their destination because the postmen Regis Debray and Ciro Bustos failed to deliver them! Others were also found in Che's backpack. (No wonder he could not run away he was held down by letters, poems and books!)

It is Paco Ignacio Taibo 11's book that Pierre Kalfon uses in his book, 'Ernesto Che Guevara. ` For Che's troubles in the Congo; and Frank R Villafarn's book 'Cold war in the Congo'. The confrontation of Cuban Military Forces, 1960-1967.

Frank R Villafarn was born in Cuba 1944, a writer of Cuban history.

Max Marambio and Paco Ignacio Taibo names also can be found in these books.
How did I find Ignacio Paco Taibo 11? I found this connection when I read revue written by Ion Mihai Pacepa entitled 'Who was the real Che?'

Chapter twenty.
Who was-is the real Ion Mihai Pacepa?

Just read Ion Mihai Pacepa's Wikipedia profile-he was a top KGB man till he defected to the United States in 1978. There after he worked with the CIA. The CIA described his cooperation as "an important and unique contribution to the Unites states.

Ion Mihai Pacepa - Wikipedia, the free encyclopedia

*https://en.**wikipedia**.org/wiki/**Ion_Mihai_Pacepa***
Ion Mihai Pacepa (Romanian pronunciation: [iˈon miˈhaj paˈtʃepa]; born 28 October 1928 in Bucharest, Romania) is a former three-star general in the ...
Activity in the Romanian ... - Defection - Writings and political views

Former Soviet spy: We created Liberation Theology ...

www.catholicnewsagency.com › News › US
01.05.2015 - *Espionage* deep in the heart of Europe. Secrets in the *KGB*. Defection from a communist nation. Ion Mihai Pacepa has seen his share of.

I fell of my seat when I read his Wikipedia profile as it covers most of the issues I have stumbled over.
In the article the 'Sward and the Shield'. I noticed the remark, 'All this is no more than what Claire Sterling said in 'The Terror Network.'

<u>The Sword and the Shield</u>

members.iglou.com/jtmajor/Mitrokhn.htm
THE SWORD AND THE SHIELD: The Mitrokhin
Archive and the Secret History of the KGB ... In
1998, in woods near the city of Berne, Swiss
security forces exploded a ..... (All this is no more
than what *Claire Sterling* said in The Terror
Network.)

Just going through Ion Mihai Pacepa's Wikipedia
you are told the Carlos the Jackal was asked to
assassinate him. Wasn't Carlos- the Jackal said to be
one of Fidel Castro's toys? I do not know if Lee
Harvey Oswald was one of Castro's toys! Could
Nikita Khrushchev ordered the assassination of
Kennedy, but was unable to stop Lee Harvey
Oswald? Ion Mihai Pacepa says in his book,
'Programmed to Kill: Lee Harvey Oswald, the
Soviet KGB, and the Kennedy Assassination.' That
the KGB's fingerprints were all over Lee Harvey
Oswald and his killer Jack Ruby.

Michael Ledeen former adviser for terrorism to
President Reagan has written review on Ion Mihai
Pacepa's book. (Claire Sterling and Michael Ledeen
gave evidence to the Warren Commission.)

Ion Mihai Pacepa alleged that the Soviet Union
tried to discredit the Papacy. He says he was caught
up in an effort to smear the Vatican, by portraying
Pope Pius X11 as a coldhearted Nazi sympathizer.
(Claire Sterling has written on this subject.)

Ion Mihai Pacepa also wrote another article that is of interes,t in this all too brief description of him-
Who is Raul Castro?

Who is Raul Castro- A tyrant only a brother could love. (http://article . nationalreview.com) I want to point out at this stage that Romania- Bucharest has a large Cuban Embassy.

FrontPage Magazine - Who Was the Real Che?

archive.frontpagemag.com/readArticle.aspx?ARTID

...

23.01.2009 - By: *Ion Mihai Pacepa* ... working undercover as a writer—I. Lavretsky, in a book entitled Ernesto *Che Guevara*, which was edited by the KGB.

Ion Mihai Pacepa's article has so many interesting remarks. One of which is that the Castro brothers who feared any liberalization, decided to plaster a romantic revolutionary façade over their communism. "Operation Che." was launched to the world by 'Terrorist' Regis Debray. His release from a 30 year prison sentence after serving three years was due to the intervention of French philosopher Jean Paul Sartre- a communist romantically involved with the KGB.

Ion Mihai Pacepa also states that Jean Paul Sartre ideologue of the Baader Meinhof terrorist band. (But Ion Mihai Pacepa does not mention Ciro R Bustos.)

Ion Mihai Pacepa tells of an intelligence officer Alberto Korda, a Cuban. He worked as a photographer for the Cuban newspaper 'Revolucion'. He produced the romanticized picture of Che.

Ion Mihai Pacepa states that the photo was introduced to the world by a KGB operative, an undercover as a writer- I. Lavretsky- he wrote the book, **'Ernesto Che Guevara, which was edited by the KGB.**

(I have read this work; it is of interest as it too questions the reality of Che Guevara's Death Party.)

Ion Mihai Pacepa dose give Feltrinelli credit for flooding the world with Alberto Korda's Che Guevara photo.

Ion Mihai Pacepa states that General Aleksandr Sakharovsky believed that Fidel Castro was just an adventurer! But he was impressed by Che Guevara and Raul Castro's devotion to communism. The two were brought to Moscow to be indoctrinated and trained. They were given a KGB adviser before they were returned to the Sierra Maestra. Their KGB adviser in the 1950s and 1960s was Nic′kolay Leonov.

Former Soviet spy: We created Liberation Theology | Veritas ...

*veritas-vincit-international.org/.../**former-soviet-spy-**...*

09.08.2015 - A *former KGB Spy* has recently claimed that Liberation Theology - condemned by ... *Ion Mihai Pacepa* on *Raul Castro's* yacht in Cuba, 1974.

Who is Raul Castro? A tyrant only a brother could love.

Who Is Raúl Castro? | National Review Online

www.nationalreview.com/.../who-ra-l-castro-ion-mi...

by *Ion Mihai Pacepa* August 10, 2006 3:17 AM. A tyrant only a brother could love. ... I met *Raúl* many times, both in Cuba and in Romania.

What a title for an article- A tyrant only a brother can love! Ion Mihai Pacepa goes on to state Raul Castro transforms a paradise into a shambles. He worried that Raul Castro turn Cuba into a tyranny. Ion Mihai Pacepa says he met Raul Castro many times in Cuba, Romania and Moscow, as Raul was responsible for the Cuban intelligence service- 'The Direccion General de Inteleigencia.' In the early 1970s Raul Castro entered into a drug venture with Ion Mihai Pacepa former service-
'The Departamentul de Informatii.'
Ion Mihai Pacepa and Raul Castro were close enough to work, talk, and fish; challenge each other on the firing range. Have fun with their Alfa Romeo cars. Ion Mihai Pacepa states Raul was always under the influence of alcohol and self-importance. But Raul Castro is generally perceived as a colorless

minister! But was also the brutal head of one of
Communism's most criminal institutions-
'The Cuban Political Police.'
(At first I was confused reading Ion Mihai Pacepa
articles, but now I understand why Gabriel Garcia
Marquez needed to take Fidel Castro under his wing.
There were not just two giants playing for power;
South America had a giant as well, Gabriel Garcia
Marquez.)
Did Nikita Khrushchev really dream of going
down in history as the Soviet leader who installed
Communism on the American continent, as Ion
Mihai Pacepa says? He remarks at the closeness
between Nikita Khrushchev and Raul Castro. Where
they obsessed with espionage and counterespionage?
It was Nikita Khrushchev that brought Raul Castro
to Moscow in the 1950s secretly. At Nikita
Khrushchev's order Raul Castro was given an
intelligence adviser: Nikoaly Leonov. He was the
best expert on Latin America the-
''Pervoye Glavnoye Upravleniye.' could provide.
Their influence in the course of Cuban revolution,
political kidnappings were introduced.
In 1962 Nikita Khrushchev appointed Aieksandr
Shitov as his ambassador to Cuba and KGB adviser,
soon after they started secretly building rocket bases
in Cuba.
Ion Mihai Pacepa states it was Nikita Khrushchev
and Raul Castro with Aieksandr Shitov that pushed
the pushed the world to the brink of nuclear war, not
Fidel Castro.

Aieksandr Shitov became Salvador Allende KGB adviser. This made Ion Mihai Pacepa believe that Raul Castro was holding the reins of the Cuban revolutionary wagon.

Ion Mihai Pacepa says he was administering the money Romania was making from its own drug trafficking in 1970s. In 1972 the Castro brothers and Romania's Ceausescu laid the foundation for a bilateral drug venture. They wanted to flood the world with drugs. The Castro brothers said-"Drugs could do a lot more damage to imperialism than nuclear weapons could. Drugs will erode capitalism from the inside."

1972 saw Raul Castro according to Ion Mihai Pacepa, work around the clock to expand Cuba's political influence in South America and the Third World. Countries like Nicaragua, El Salvador and Angola were influenced by their movements of Liberation. Raul Castro had his military and advisers and instructors in Palestine. The Palestine Liberation Organization bases had established close cooperation with Libya, South Yemen, and the Polisario Front for the Liberation of Western Sahara.

By the Mid 1970 Ion Mihai Pacepa and the Departamentul de Informatii Externe were working with Raul Castro to support the Revolutionary Armed Forces of Colombia, a Marxist, anti-American insurgency organization whose task it was to spread Communism to South America.

Ion Mihai Pacepa was to defect in 1978, he moved from the Romanian KGB and its Soviet connections to jump into bed with the CIA! He was no longer able to access inside information about Raul Castro's export of terrorism and Revolution.

Ion Mihai Pacepa states that in 1994 Raul Castro was in Bucharest to get intelligence and political support for the 'National Liberation Directorate'. An intelligence group tasked to coordinate Cuba's guerrilla and terrorist training camps.

Raul Castro, so Ion Mihai Pacepa says took credit for unrest in Nicaragua and Grenada. He also took credit for killing 197 people in Colombia in 2001, the same group kidnapped 13 Colombian lawmakers from a government building, they held Colombian presidential candidate Ingrid Betancourt.

(Lillian Betancourt was one of the wealthiest people in the world at this time, she headed the French cosmetic company, and she was Ingrid Betancourt's mother. I had though her money was supporting some of the events in and around this time, as her name can be connected to Jean Luc Godard and his film productions: Ciro Bustos-Sacrificio.

Ion Mihai Pacepa also remarks that Hugo Chavez the president of Venezuela, who idolized the Castro brothers, had threatened to stop exporting oil to the U.S. Hugo Chavez had intended to start a conventional war against his neighbor Colombia! As Colombia was the U.S. main ally in the region!

05.05.2015 - *Ion Mihai Pacepa* fue general de la policía secreta de la Rumania ... *Ex espía* de la *Unión Soviética*: Nosotros creamos la Teología de la Liberación ... creado por la KGB con ayuda del *"Che" Guevara*; y la Organización para ...
LIBERATION THEOLOGY-

The concept of the movement of the LIBERATION THEOLOGY has made me think. The movement was born in the KGB, it name was invented by KGB. During the years the KGB had a penchant for movements of 'Liberation.' They were involved in Colombia, Bolivia.

Yasser Arafat was helped to create the Palestine Liberation Organization. They were a few Liberation movements born in Lubyanka- the headquarters of the KGB.

Ion Mihai Pacepa clams that the KGB took control of World Council of Churches, in Geneva, Switzerland; to use it as a cover to turn the LIBERATION THEOLOGY as a revolutionary tool in South America. World Council of Churches was the largest international organization after the Vatican ecumenical, with 550 million Christian of various denominations in 120 countries.

Ion Mihai Pacepa tells us that KGB created a religious organization called 'Christian Peace

Conference' its employees were soviet intelligence officers undercover!

'Christian Peace Conference' official task was to reduce poverty. Recognize new religious movements, encourage the poor to revolt against- 'institutionalized violence of poverty.'

Now I can understand the need to drain the Soviet Union assets. The fact that Leo Emil Wanta worked out a scam to crush the ruble in 1990-1991 is explained by Claire Sterling in her book 'Thieves World.'

Ion Mihai Pacepa is a Gabriel Garcia Marquez man, is hard to say, but he was a man of that time.

If the world was an orange; despite its segments it is still an orange. Even if it's bad bits need cutting out it is still an orange. This world is bazaar!

Chapter twenty-one.
A Fake!

It was Ion Mihai Pacapa that reported about a trip Raul Castro was supposed to have made in 1953. The name Nikolay Leonov or (Nicolai Leonov) reminded me of a photo that had puzzled me before.

Alfredo Guevara, political commissar of the Cuban cinema ...

www.thecubanhistory.com/.../alfredo-guevara-politi...
20.04.2013 - *NikolaiLeonovRaulCastroJoel*[1] Fidel Domenech. Nikolai Leonov and Raul Castro on their way back from the Praga "Congress" in 1953 when ...

Exgeneral de la KGB cuenta sus vínculos con Raúl Castro

*www.martinoticias.com/...**raul-castro**.../96677.html*
15.06.2015 - *Su* amigo Nikolai Leonov, *exgeneral* de la *KGB* y exdiputado a la Duma, es el autor del libro, que presentó en Moscú el canciller Serguei ...

It is said to be of Fidel Domenech, Nikolay Leonov and Raul Castro. Fidel Domenech, a Captain in the Cuban military.

Ion Mihai Pacapa said that Nikolay Leonov- was the KGB's adviser to Che Guevara and Raul Castro in the 1950 and 1960s.

The next person in the photo is said to be Raul Castro. But I did not think it was Raul Castro! I would have said it was Che! If it is Che then it would mean that the Guevara part began in another way.

Depending in which program you are reading, they are going to or coming back from participating in the establishment of the Preparatory Committee for the IV International Youth Festival that was held in Bucharest. Either in May or April or even August.

It is stated that Raul Castro was on that ship, 'Andrea Gritti' coming or going to or from Havana and Bucharest.

Yet another program says that Raul Castro could not go to this youth festival as he was prevented from attending due to the assault on the Moncada Garrison.

<u>Historia de los Festivales Mundiales de la Juventud y los ...</u>
*www.**granma.cu/granmad**/.../16**festival/historia**.htm l*
Praga 1947: 1 *Festival Mundial* de la *Juventud* y los Estudiantes ... *historia* dos meses después le impediría a Raúl asistir al IV *Festival Mundial* de la *Juventud* y ...

Fun when historians cannot agree with each other!
The Photo-
The first thing is it is not Raul Castro-
Secondly the Photo is a fake-   -A FAKE-
Why is it a Fake?

    Three men standing in a next to each other,
apparently not touching each other.
I enlarged the photo to have a better look at the face
of the man on the right. I was surprised to see a
thumb and two fingers around the man's right arm!
Fidel Domenech hands are on the ship's rail,
Nikolay Leonov hand you can see on his hips,
whereas the third man has his hands behind his back.
All men are enjoying the sun in their swimming
trunks. So where is the man that the fingers belong
to?

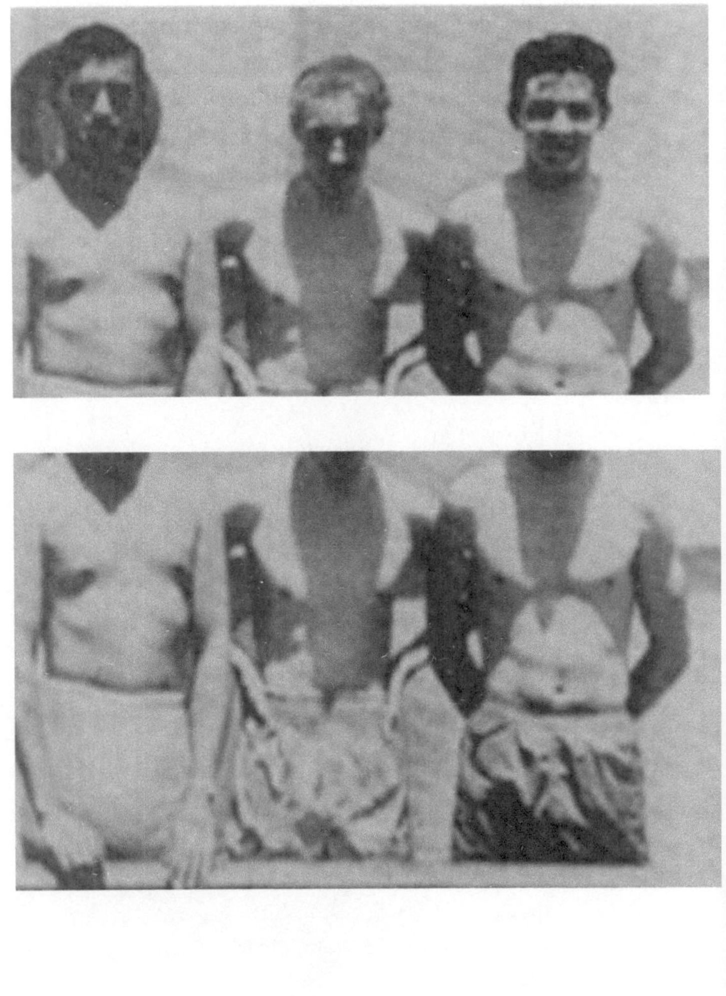

On the arm are two fingers and a thum.

"I know the files of Mrs. Maria Theresa Proenza, I saw her lying down smoking marijuana with the Mexican painter, even with clothes on Frida's bed, unsuccessful attempts to recruit her, as well as those of Eusebio Lopez Azcue, who really was Victor Pina Cardoso, Consul of Cuba in Mexico quine next to Colonel Nicolai Leonov directed the operation to assassinate to John F. Kennedy."

This remark came from a replay in <u>Joaquín Ordoqui and the "greatness of the revolution"</u> Dose seam everyone knows everyone.

El blog de Tania Quintero: Joaquín Ordoqui y la "grandeza de la ...
taniaquintero.**blogspot**.com/.../**joaquin-ordoqui-y-la-grandeza**-de... ▾ Diese Seite übersetzen
01.02.2016 - Joaquín Ordoqui y la "grandeza de la revolución" ... Mesa, que Roberto Fandiño tecleó para dar copias a Chomón, Alfredo Guevara y el G-2.

El blog de Tania Quintero: febrero 2016
taniaquintero.**blogspot**.com/2016_02_01_archive.html ▾ Diese Seite übersetzen
29.02.2016 - Web, taniaquintero.blogspot.com ...... Joaquín Ordoqui y la "grandeza de la revolución". El miércoles 24 de septiembre de 2014, el periódico ...

Chapter twenty-two.
Fake Photos

Looking at the photo with the three fingers that do not have a body to belong to, I decided to take another look at other photos.

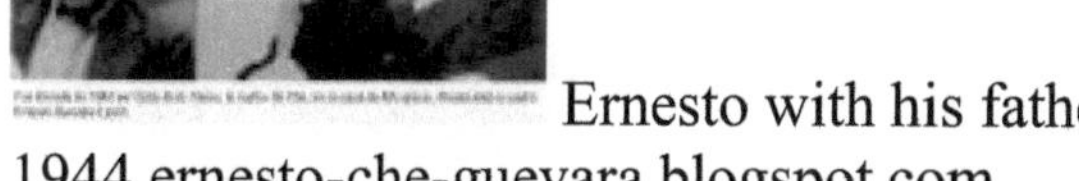 Ernesto with his father in 1944 ernesto-che-guevara.blogspot.com

Fue tomada en 1944 por Celia de la Serna, la madre del Che, en su casa de Alta gracia. Al lado está su padre Ernesto Guevara Lynch

Just look at the opportunity this photo offers! Two photos can be joined.

 1936 yılında ailesiyle birlikte. Guevara öğrencilği boyunca Latin

...devrimcilik.blogcu.com

In this photo the shadows do not match- the rail across the small boy in the foreground and the shadow of the rail by a young Che!? And the small boy in the foreground left leg is in the water as Che's should be!

The Congo Diary!
Congo Diary: The Story of Che Guevara's "Lost" Year in Africa (Centro de Estudios Che Guevara) Paperback – December 27, 2011
by <u>Ernesto Che Guevara</u> (Author), <u>Aleida Guevara</u> (Foreword)

Featuring a foreword by Gabriel Garcia Marquez ("Che Guevara in Africa"), this book fills in the missing chapter in Che Guevara's life as head of the secret Cuban force that went to aid the liberation movement in the Congo against the Belgian Colonialists in 1965. The idea was to prepare a group of Cubans for the mission to Bolivia, as well as to assist African national liberation movements.

This diary remained unpublished for decades because of its controversial content, but, like his other diaries, reveals Che's great literary gift, his razor-sharp intellect, his dry wit, and his brutal honesty. Because this diary deals with what Che admits was a "failure," he examines every painful detail about what went wrong in order to draw constructive lessons for future expeditions.

This publication of the complete *Congo Diary* has been thoroughly revised by Che's widow, Aleida March, and published in association with the Che Guevara Studies Center in Havana.

Features:

Forewords by Gabriel Garcia Marquez ("Che Guevara in Africa") and Che's daughter, Aleida Guevara

Twenty-eight pages of unpublished photos
Extensive notes and glossary explaining Swahili terms
Back cover by Nelson Mandela and Gabriel Garcia Marquez

You can see Che sitting to one side reading, without straining you can also where two photos have been joined together. In the foreground you can see a twig confirming the join.

This file photo taken in 1965 photo shows Cuban-Argentinian guerrilla leader   ...newvision.co.u

As I do not have access to the originals I cannot answer arising questions nor can I answer all the questions I need answers for. But I can through doubt on what we are expected to believe. I could add many other examples. If you are not looking for fake photos you don't see them.

Two examples of the death face of Che, where the line of a contact lens can be seen.

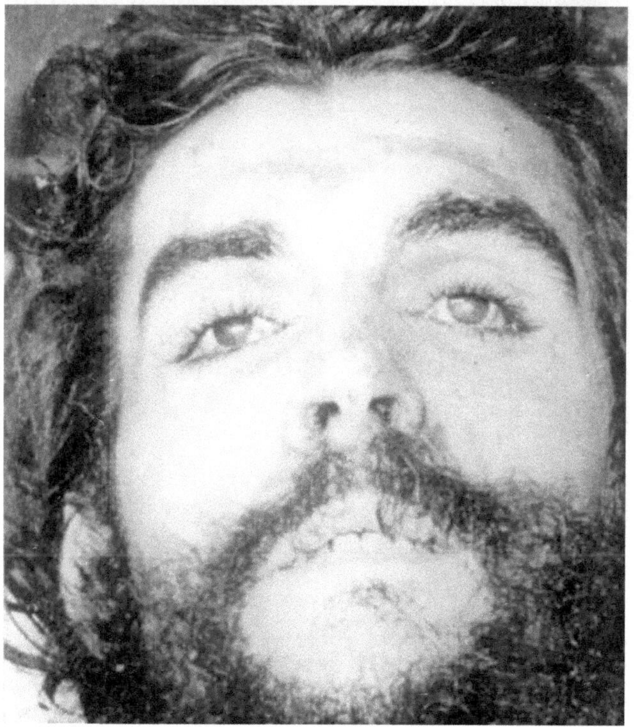

Volvieron a Camiri y le iban dando algunos dolares, 5 a veces por su ayuda,
...museochqguevaraargentina.blogspot.com

Loading zoom.
articulo.mercadolibre.com.ar

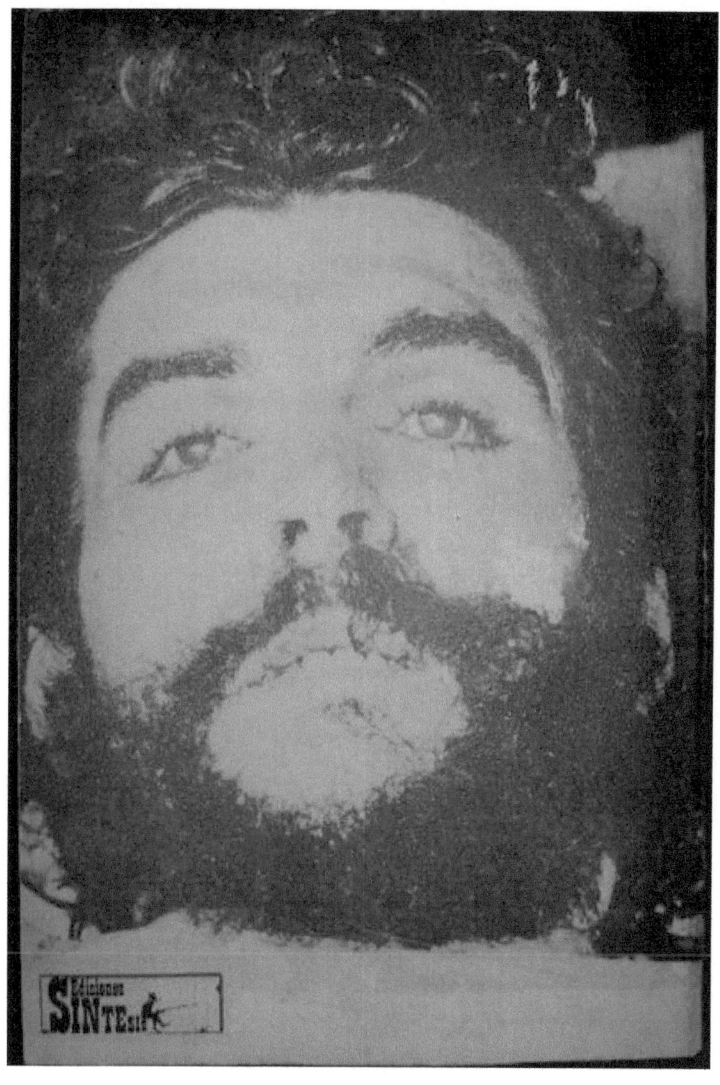

The examples are to demonstrate that there are fakes to be found. The question is WHY?

To talk about fake Photos is a subject that has to be look at from another point of view, what do the scriptwriters want us to see? I have been through a sea of photos that are supposed to mark the death of a hero. But as the death party was planed and paid for in advance! Giangiacomo Feltrinelli took $50,000,000 to La Paz.

$50,000,000 is a lot of money even now! Giangiacomo Feltrinelli's trip to Bolivia is well known; Clair Sterling and Carlo Feltrinelli as well as his wife Inge Schönthal also reported the Giangiacomo Feltrinelli withdrew the large sum of money. (Inge Schönthal continued to run the publishing house grounded by Giangiacomo Feltrinelli after his death.)

To sit and try to decide which photos are fakes and those that are not is a waste of time. They like the Bolivian Diaries they can only be fakes- as the event they were printed for was a fake in its self.

There can only be one hand written Bolivian Diary, the moment more appear then it/they are faked. When there are inconsistencies in the Death party photos- such as different backgrounds, differing from blue and gray, to having graphite and then not! Different objects, unnamed folk standing about, the only consistent figure is Che, with or without his eyes open and reflecting light. (No matter how many photographers there were at a wedding the same people and objects are to be found in all their pictures, even if taken from different points of view. With such differents in the photos it can explain the different dates that were given to the death day. The fact that the walls do not match could mean that the scene was played in different locations. With Ciro Bustos and Regis Debray acting at the much published court case only a few miles down the road, to distract any observer, they were not in prison at that time but living next door. (Stated in Ciro's own book; this statement can be confirmed in other's statements)

Cars, Tana's black Land Rover was able to use the good road next to a gas pipe line, there were even light airplanes in use by the civil and military alike. The actors were using the military accommodation across the road from the court. You can confirm in newspapers from the time that Che Guevara was unknown in Bolivia. Elisabeth Burgos-Debray's folders have copies of this.

Now I know they are actors on a film set, to see young men point their guns at a body is funny. Had I been there I would have laughed; they would have need to find away to stop me! It is fair to say there have been fake photos made for other reasons.

¿Quién mató al Che?
atilioboron.com.ar

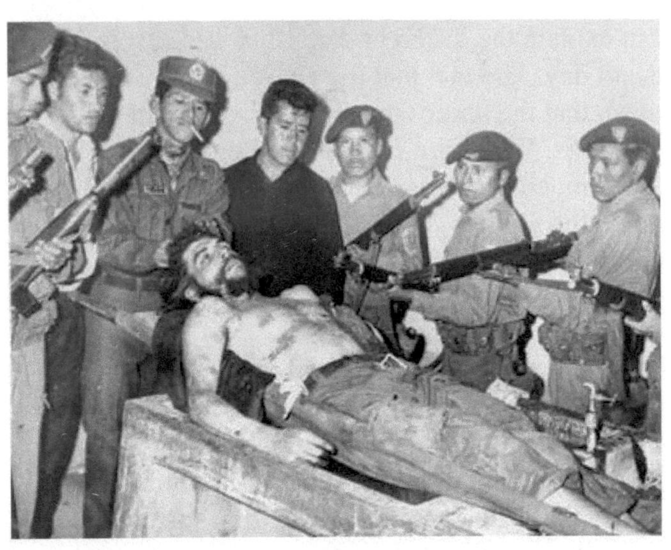

Marcelo Fernández-Zayas.
Marcelo Fernández-Zayas another Gabriel Garcia
Marquez man? He has written articles confirming
Felix I. Rodriguez's part. Marcelo Fernández-Zayas
even states he was there swapping cameras with
Nino de Guzman!

OTHER ARTICLES IN THIS SERIES ON CHE
GUEVARA: Che Guevara himself was betrayed
Che Guevara: Who was the victim?
Marcelo Fernández-Zayas
http://www.amigospais-guaracabuya.org/

For an event that was supposed to be secret there
were a lot of invited guests!

Felix I. Rodriguez, recounts his life in a book published by Simon and Schuster. (The same publisher as Claire Sterling and others in this complot) in 1989 under the title 'Shadow Warrior - Shadow Warrior'. Felix I. Rodriguez has the same code name as Ciro Bustos. As confirmed in 'Weg Der Revolution Che Guevara' www.icestorm.de. This film also shows the two men who played military advisers and integrators for the CIA. Their faces can be seen at the court case where they are acting as the accused lawyers. The taller one takes on the role of an 'INTY' and Pier Paolo Pasolini took on the role of the second 'INTY'. (see 'Why have their identities been mixed with others?)

Also in the film there is a scene where a jubilant man-Che Guevara is bouncing up and down; it is on the occasion of Benigno Dariel Alarcon Ramirez and others return from Bolivia vir Chili with Salvador Allende's help.

Che Guevara was betrayed itself
Marcelo Fernández-Zayas

'Marcelo Fernández-Zayas states on October 8, 1967, in a place not too far in Vallegrande area, the headquarters of the Eighth Division of the Bolivian army under Colonel Joaquin Zenteno Anaya . In the same place he was, installing radio equipment in the Bolivian aircraft, Captain Felix Ramos Medina, whose real name is Felix Rodriguez Mendigutía.

This is a Cuban American veteran of the Central Intelligence Agency (CIA), an expert in counterinsurgency, who was advising the Bolivian army fulfilling the request of La Paz to Washington.' He states also, the CIA intervened on behalf of Debray. Rodriguez confirmed the involvement of a CIA agent in favor of Debray, who worked under the name of Gabriel García García, whose real first name is Julius.

Ciro Bustos states in his book he had a contact-Gabriel Garcia!? Here is a Gabriel Garcia-whose real first name was Julius!? According to Marcelo Fernández-Zayas he was a CIA Agent. To decide if they are one and the same I leave it up to you.

Felix I. Rodriguez is someone that has been on the scene from Kennedy's death and Che Death party Watergate and shared the same publisher as Clare Sterling, given evidence in the Senate as she has. Plays cards with Dariel Alarcon Ramirez 'Benigno'.

Dariel Alarcon Ramirez 'Benigno' and Felix Ismael Rodriguez Mendigutía met up in Paris- so states Marcelo Fernández-Zayas on Octber 14, 1996. To play cards!?

This brings me back to where I started! I started with the Film 'Schnappschuss mit Che' by Wilfied Husismann. Where Ciro Bustos leaves prison with a full head of hair; which was strange for a man that had gone to prison as a bald man.

Félix: Es la única y la ultima foto de el vivo en cautiverio.

baracuteycubano.blogspot.com

'Schnappschuss mit Che' by Wilfied Husismann provides the evidence that the snap shot with Che Guevara is a FAKE. It has Felix Ismael Rodriguez

Mendigutía standing next to the condemned man, Che Guevara.

There only has to be one faked photo that brings down the house of cards.

There is one more photo I want to show you that is this one with Juan Antonio Rodríguez Menier, Félix Rodríguez. Juan Antonio Rodríguez Menier is the former high-ranking Cuban intelligence officer and co-founder of Cuba's secret Service.
Look what they are doing with their fingers.
Serves us right we have been hoodwinked!

Juan Antonio Rodríguez Menier, Félix Rodríguez redcarpetreports.de

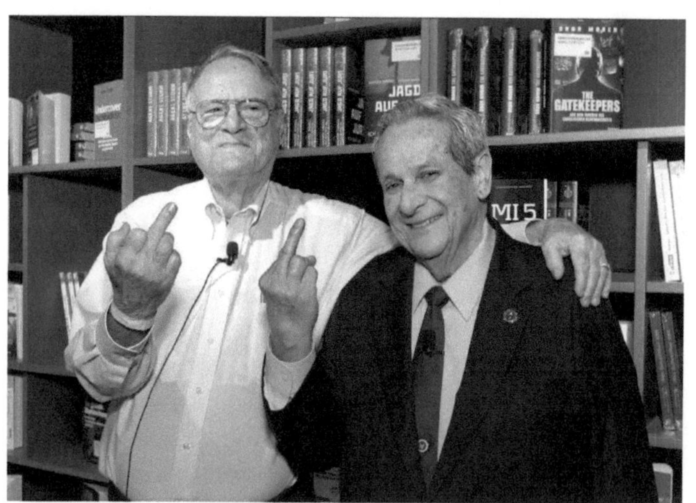

Chapter Twenty-Three.
The Guantanamo Bay question.

   Has anyone asked the question, why are the Americans in control of Guantanamo? America imposed an embargo on Cuba, but still use the province of Guantanamo for is military base in the natural lagoon for its warships, and US have placed their renowned prison in its middle. It is a prison that takes theorists from all around the world. A prison that does not have a reputation of being a holiday camp!
   President Obama's election cry was to close the prison camp; at the end of 2015 (time of writing.) this has not happened.
   As I start to look into this, the first thought that comes to mind is this is like suing someone for keeping rabbits in their house, but you are putting their rabbit muck on your vegetable garden.
   You would not think that this question would be so difficult to answer, but after a week of rummaging through net sights, Guantanamo there was only a few points of interest.
The first I found in-
'The White House Years.' By Henry Kissinger.
White House Years: The First Volume of His Classic Memoirs
https://books.google.de/books?isbn=0857207105 - Henry Kissinger - 2011 - Biography & Autobiography

In his 1971 conversations with *Régis Debray*— at a time when he was, in fact, ... or with Fidel Castro's restraint with respect to *Guantanamo*.5 The only inference ..

I can understand why Regis Debray was conducting conversations with Henry Kissinger over Salvador Allende. But I am not so sure why they are discussing Guantanamo Bay, other to say there was a lot of activity, but it does not answer the question as to why the base is tolerated by all sides.

This is the remark Henry Kissinger made-
'Salavdor Allende had pointed out that it is tactical nesscessity to to take controal of the Government. Salavdor Allende comared this tactic to Mao Tse-tung decision to permit private enterprise for a few years after the communists took power in 1949 or that of Fidel Castro's Restraint with respect to Guantanamo.`

The other refarance Henary Kissinger makes about Guantanamo is-
The next remark is-
'Vorontsov informed Heny Kissinger that his governmet desired to reafirm the Kennedy-Khushchev understanding of the 1962 respedt to Cuba: "We would like to stress that in the Cuban question we proceed as before, from the understanding on this question in the past we expect

that the Amererican side will also strictly adhere to this understanding."

Henry Kissinger states he was puzzled and says so, he was not aware of any special tension over Cuba; We are not doing nothing unusal; there was no obvious reason why the Soviet Union should raise the question. Voronsov said there had been new stories, he said, about American planes to strengthen the defense of the Guantanamo Navel Base. There were also stories of alleged Soviet military activities in Cuba.

Vornosov read him a note complaining about stepp-up subversives activities against Cuba by exiles operating from Florida. Herny Kissinger asked in what way Moscow wished to conffirm the 1962 understanding and what Vorontosv thought the understanding was. He said an oral statement from Herny Kissenger would be enough. Vornosov said he took the understanding to be that the US would not invade Cuba by milatry force.'

This was said to have happened at the time of the arrangments under which the Soviet misslels and bombes were withdrawn.

An Obviation- Under the name of Luciano Monteagudo, who I believe is Jean Luc Godard, who is a founder member of ATMO a Swedish film making company, he has written an article for Pagina 12; with the text for 'Sacrificio-Who Betrayed Che Guevara.' About Ciro Bustos. A film by Erik Gandini and Tarik Saleh.

I am not surprised to see that they make other films-
Gitmo is a film about Guantanamo.

Gitmo (2005) - IMDb
www.imdb.com/title/tt0481348/
Bewertung: 6,6/10 - 271 Abstimmungsergebnisse
Gitmo (2005) Poster .... Stars: Jon Lee Anderson,
Ciro Bustos, *Régis Debray* ... Useful and probing
documentary of interrogation practices at
Guantánamo Bay.

Erik Gandini - Wikipedia, the free encyclopedia
*https://en.wikipedia.org/wiki/**Erik_Gandini***
Erik Gandini (born 14 August 1967) is an Italian-
Swedish film director, writer, and ... 3.1 Surplus -
Terrorized into Being Consumers; 3.2 *Gitmo*; 3.3
Videocracy ... death and shed new light on the role
played by French intellectual *Regis Debray*.

   A little point of interest about what have been
going on for the last twenty years-
I found this in-
The two faces of Guantanamo Bay, Cuba | Medill | Washington
dc.medill.northwestern.edu › GITMO
Diese Seite übersetzen
13.08.2015 - NAVAL *STATION GUANTANAMO*
BAY, *CUBA* – The U.S. may have opened an ...
Since the reestablishment of diplomatic *relations*
between the U.S. and .... This year they cooperated
to fight an imaginary *fire* on the fence line.

"The captain of the base, Captain (David) Culpepper, meets with the Cuban Frontier Brigade, which is their equivalent to the military on that side," Wirfel said. "It's a very professional meeting. There is never anything political talked about. It's all administrative in matter."

The goal of the meetings is to keep the border peaceful. Neither side wants an inadvertent flare-up from a misunderstanding.

"As you can imagine, when you have guards standing on the fence line face-to-face with each other, it's important that there's some communication as to what's happening on our side and what's happening on your side," said Wirfel.

The reestablishment of diplomatic relations, Wirfel said, would not affect the monthly meetings, which have been going on for 20 years.

In addition to the monthly get-togethers, there is a surprising annual joint military effort at cooperation between two countries that have not gotten along for decades.

"Every year we also do a bilateral exercise with them," Wirfel said. This year they cooperated to fight an imaginary fire on the fence line. The participants jumped back and forth across the heavily guarded border, at one point carrying a person with a simulated injury across the border into enemy territory.

To conclude it might be better to think about the embargo.

The Cuban embargo is from an outsiders point more like a dog on a lead, by that I mean sometimes the line is real tight whereas other times the line is slack. Depending on who is playing what game as to how tort the line is. In 1974 Gorge Bush Sr. is the head of the CIA; he asked Orlando Bosch to unite all the Cuban exiles- the Miami Mafia groups.

Chapter twenty four.
Ernesto Guevara Lynch- Che Guevara's
Father was an actor too!

To write down how their relationships were
worked into the making of Che Guevara was like
trying to untie knotted bits of string. So much comes
together- from drug barons, the Spanish Civil War
and those who had to leave their countries for
whatever reason.
    Writers from different countries; men burned by
the Mexican revolution. Not forgetting the film
industry that Mexico was to be proud of, with
writers and actors that could command attention
across the world.

Here are the connections we are supposed to believe.

Cayetano Cordova Iturburu-
        Carmen de la Serna, wife or aforementioned
        and sister to-
        Celia de la Serna- said mother to Che.
        Daughter of Carmen de la Serna-
                Carmen Cordova- Chichina.
                Che's cousin and first love.
        Cousin- Dolores Moyres Martin-
                aforementioned family member.

Look at this small group of said family members-
how they relate to influences of the time-

Cayetano Cordova Iturburu-
    He was president of the SADE, Argentina Society of Writers, between 1965-1969

Gabriel Garcia Marquez- was the head of the **Mexican** society of writers that lead to the foundation of the ICAIC run by Alferdo Guevara in Cuba.

Manual Barbachono Ponce- was the Mexican film producer Alferdo Guevara learnt form with Gabriel Garcia Marquez.

Paco Ignicio Taibo 11- is also a film producer and Gabriel Garcia Marques close family friend. One of his films is 'Pancho Villa' Cantinflas acted in it.

'Cantinflas' Fortino Mario Alfonso Moreno-actor and was general secretary in 1944 to the Union of film production. It is known that he was used as a double for Che.

Ernesto Guevara Lynch- Che Guevara's father was also in Show Business he chaired the committee of Republicans, gave lectures and concerts with Cuarteto Aguilat.(The Quartet Aguilar, was group who fled the troubles of the Spanish Civil War.)

Entre rejas - El blog de martinguevara - Overblog
martinguevara.**over-blog**.*es/article-entre-rejas-1178...*

18.05.2013 - Los González *Aguilar*, llegaron a la Argentina expulsados por la ... Los tíos de Carmen tenían un *cuarteto* musical, eran astros del laúd, todo ..

(Who tells us this? Ann Maria Erra second wife and Martin Guevara, his youngest son.)

Ann Maria Erra de- Ernesto Guevara Lynch's second wife, sectary.
Lucia Alvarez de Toledo- Ernesto Guevara Lynch's translator, editor and mother to Che's half brother.
Dolores Moyano Martin. Cousin- Cayetano Córdova Iturburu family.
Martin Guevara- youngest son of Ernesto Guevara Lynch.
Jorge Camarosa- 'Historias Secetas De Cordoba.'
Jorge G Castaneda-
(At first I found it difficult to understand the connections; so many bits of string!)
Cayetano Córdova Iturburu-
Cayetano Córdova Iturburu - Wikipedia, la enciclopedia libre
https://es.wikipedia.org/.../Cayetano_Córdova_Iturb
Cayetano Policinio *Córdova Iturburu* (16 de febrero de 1899, Buenos Aires, Argentina- 25 de abril de 1977, Buenos Aires) Periodista y poeta, fue uno de los...
He was president of the SADE, Argentina Society of Writers, between 1965-1969.

In 1971, it was incorporated into the *National Academy of Fine Arts*.
He married Carmen de la Serna (sister Celia de la Serna, mother of Che Guevara), his daughter is the architect Carmen Cordova
In1934, he joined the Communist Party.

The address below shows the connection to Gabriel Garcia Marques! Raul Gonzalez Tunon was also a journalist and was with Cayetano Cordova Iturburn during the Spanish Civil War.

Raul Gonzalez Tunon worked with Manuel de Falla; he wrote and directed music for the Quartet Aguilar. Manuel de Falla court the attention of Manuel Ponce.

Opus 94 - Instituto Mexicano de la Radio

*www.imer.mx/opus/*Música de España, México y Brasil: Miguel Bernal Jiménez, Manuel M. Ponce, Heitor Villa-Lobos, Isaac Albéniz y *Manuel de Falla*. Lunes 25 de enero a las ...
Ann Erra Lynch remarks on this connection.
Ann Erra Lynch de Guevara, madrastra del Che. / Belen Vargas.
1937 - 2007 :: ii congreso internacional de escritores para la ...
ddd.uab.cat/pub/expbib/2007/exili/aznar.asp.html
... Vallejo; a los argentinos *Cayetano Córdova Iturburu* y Raúl González Tuñón; ..... con toda la razón del mundo pudo afirmar el escritor *Gabriel García Márquez* ..

Thiess address state the relationships between cousins and friends, l have all read mentioned.

<u>Carmen Córdova - Wikipedia, la enciclopedia libre</u>
https://es.wikipedia.org/wiki/Carmen_Córdova
Carmen Córdova pertenecía a una familia de ideas avanzada y progresistas, hija del escritor Cayetano Córdova *Iturburu*. Creció rodeada de un mundo ...

<u>Carmen Córdova: retrato de una moderna - Página/12 :: radar</u>
www.pagina12.com.ar/.../9-1922-2004-12-31.html
31.12.2004 - Fue hija del escritor y crítico "Policho" *Córdova Iturburu* y prima del Che. Criada en la gran tradición moderna de los años '30 y '40, *Carmen*

<u>Che Guevara: A Biography - Seite 94 - Google Books-Ergebnisseite</u>
https://books.google.de/books?isbn=1461732069 -
<u>Daniel James</u> - 2001 - History
AnovE: Ché at age 7 with his aunt *Carmen* de la Serna cle *cordova Iturburu*, whom he idolized, and his cousin Negrita, with whom he later had a puppy-love ...

<u>Arq. Carmen Córdova. Su fallecimiento : Sociedad Central ...</u>

socearq.org/.../arq-carmen-cordova-su-fallecimiento...

Hija del poeta, escritor y crítico Cayetano "Policho" *Córdova Iturburu* y de *Carmen* de la Serna, prima hermana de Ernesto Che Guevara, *Carmen* fue socia y ..

Maria del Carmen "Chichina" Ferreyra, Ernesto` s first true love.
ernesto-che-guevara.blogspot.com

Dolores Moyano Martin-

Tribute to Dolores Moyano Martin-lcweb2.loc.gov
   Dolores Moyano Martin's detailed recollections of Ernesto Che Guevara as a boy and young man were published in the New York Times Magazine in August 1968, less than a year after his death in Bolivia. The World & I (February 1988) published

"From El Cid to El Che: The Hero and the Mystique
of Liberation in Latin America," which writer-editor
Cynthia Grenier described as a "brilliant, penetrating
analysis that links Guevara with a long tradition of
Hispanic and Latin American history and
psychology."

Jorge Camarasa-

PDF]Documento completo Descargar archivo -
SeDiCI
sedici.unlp.edu.ar/.../Documento_completo.pdf?...1
von L Otrocki - 2008 - Ähnliche Artikel
... a *Gabriel García Márquez*, "La investigación no
es una especialidad del oficio, ... El Palacio y la
Calle de Miguel Bonasso y Días de furia de *Jorge
Camarasa*.

Jorge G Castaneda

Algunos nudos: Jorge G. Castañeda | Cultura y
vida cotidiana
cultura.nexos.com.mx/?p=8588
22.06.2015 - *Jorge Castañeda* es una rara avis y su
más reciente libro Amarres ..... Yo me encontraba
con *Gabriel García Márquez*, Carlos Monsiváis y ...

Jorge G Castaneda- 'the Life and death of Che Guevara, Companero'
Jorge Germán Castañeda Gutman (born May 24, 1953) is a Mexican politician and academic who served as Secretary of Foreign Affairs (2000–2003).

On March 25, 2004, Castañeda officially announced his presidential campaign by means of a prime-time campaign advertisement carried in all major Mexican television stations.

Jorge G Castaneda wife is also interesting she is from a political active family, by this I want to point out all in the above list have political resins for building Che Guevara's young history.

'Cantinflas' Fortino Mario Alfonso Moreno-

'Cantinflas' Fortino Mario Alfonso Moreno- note-lead a strike of artists with Jorge Negrete-(**One of Katy Jurado's godfathers.)**

Biografia de Cantinflas [Mario Moreno Reyes]
*www.biografiasyvidas.com/biografia/.../**cantinflas**.h t...*
Cantinflas [Mario Moreno Reyes]. (Ciudad de México, 1911-id., 1993) Actor cómico mexicano. Se hizo mundialmente célebre con el nombre de su personaje ...

In 1944 he joined the Union of Workers of the Cinematographic Industry (STIC), founded in 1919 under the name 'Allied Employees Union of Cinematograph.' His contribution was instrumental in improving the conditions of employment of staff of the studies, as he led a planned strike, seconded by Jorge Negrete and Arturo de Cordova (with whom he maintained a strong controversy over the direction of the National Association of Actors [ANDA]).

Cine, pedagogía y exilio. Un recorrido entre España y ...
ccec.revues.org/4884
von S Sel - 2013 -
... Val del Omar escribe en Madrid su Manifiesto de la Asociación Creyentes del Cinema. http:/ (. ......

URL : *http://ccec.revues.org/4884* ; DOI : 10.4000/ccec.4884.
http://ccec.revues.org/4884

'Cantinflas' Fortino Mario Alfonso Moreno-Katy Jurado.

So close was their contact that Katy Jurado found his body after he had committed suicide!
(There are other versions of his death to be found.)

La película de Cantinflas hace olvidar la maldición familiar ...
www.elmundo.es › LOC
28.06.2014 - *Mario Moreno* Cantinflas pudo haber sido un alcohólico empedernido ... Poco después de su muerte, *Katy Jurado*, la actriz de Hollywood que ...

Lucia Alvarez de Toledo-

Lucia Alvarez de Toledo in 'interview: Lucia Alvarez de Toledo' with Mark Thwaite states- "Some years ago film-maker Pepe Gonzalez-Aguilar and I had put together the material for a documentary on Che. Unfortunately Pepe developed throat cancer and died soon after. He had grown up with Che in Cordoba (he was a Spanish Republican refugee) and had followed him to Cuba to work for the ICAIC- the Cuban Film Institute. Alfredo Guevara. (Pepe Gonzalez-Aguilar's family were members of the Quartet Aguilar.

Lucia Alvarez de Toledo- this lady has been involved in translating and editing many of the books need in this complot. A close friend to Ciro Bustos.

www.other-news.info/.../che-was-the-most-complete...

21.10.2010 - Intervew with *Lucia Alvarez de Toledo*, author of the just-published THE ... My friend *Ciro Bustos*, who was the last of his surviving comrades to ...Ernestro Guevara Lynch-Alberto Grundo-Ciro Bustos-

Spanish Civil War Generals-

A foot note to Cayetano Cordova Iturburu's stable! It is his connections the generals of the Spanish Civil War' come from!?

Look into 'Ernesto Che Guevara- back on the road again.'(OTRA VEZ) ISBN 0-8021 -3942-6 and see "Che" centre, next to him Alberto Bayo.

Who, Jon Lee Anderson states he is the Spanish general that was the trainer in the camp with Fidel Castro. Yet another Alberto Bayo is to be seen next to the Che Guevara in Cuba- Chapter 5-Why have their identities been mixed?

12

<u>Ernesto "Che" Guevara y la guerra civil española. -
Kaos</u>
*2014.kaosenlared.net/.../80432-ernesto-"che"-
gueva...*
10.02.2014 - En ese año estalla una huelga *general*,
en apoyo de los trabajadores de la .... Entre los
militares llega en 1940 *Enrique Jurado Barrio.*
(The second photo is from the above address.)

If Katy Jurado was acting as Che's mother, there
is the likely hood that one of her brothers took the
part of Che Guevara; this was the idea I started with.
It is said of Katy's mother was a singer, 'Voice of
Latin America.' On the radio station XEW-AM-
Emilio Azacarrage Vidaurreta- there is so much
written about his artists, wonder why I cannot find
even her stage name.

Emilio Azacarrage Vidaurreta was the founder of
XEW-AM and went on to command the television
stations.
Emilio Azacarrage Vidaurreta- *Belisario de Jesús
García*-Katy Jurado's uncle.

Emilio Azcárraga Vidaurreta - Wikipedia, the free ...

https://en.wikipedia.org/.../Emilio_Azcárraga_Vida u...

Emilio Azcárraga Vidaurreta (2 March 1895, Tampico, Tamaulipas – 23 September 1972, Mexico City) was a Mexican businessman, the son of Basque ...

Emilio Azcárraga Vidaurreta as founder of XEW radio worked with Belisario de Jesus Garcia; said to be Katy Jurado's uncle- her mother's brother.

(Not forgetting Emilio Portes Gill- said to be Katy Jurado's cousin. He was a top Mexican politician and was president for two years.)

RECORDANDO A LA GRAN ACTRIZ KATY... - Actores Del ...

https://www.facebook.com/.../721346127979970:0
Su tío, hermano de su madre, era el compositor y músico *Belisario de Jesús García*, que era compadre de don *Emilio Azcárraga*, el fundador de la XEW radio y ..

Constitutionalist army colonel, poet and prolific composer, was born on November 14, 1892 in Montemorelos Nuevo Leon, and died on August 31, 1952 in Mexico City, from 1908- 1910 begins his musical career, he was the son of Don Juan B. Garcia Galván and Ms. Irene de la Garza Garcia.

'Katy Jurado's uncle, her mother's brother, was the composer and musician Belisario de Jesus Garcia, who was a friend of Don Emilio Azcarraga, the founder of the XEW radio and later the Mexican television network Televisa. As beautiful teenager, Katy soon interested producers and filmmakers, who came to make deals to debut as an actress, but her parents never gave consent. One of them was the famed director Emilio "El Indio" Fernández, who offered her a role in the Passion Island (1941), a film with which was debuted for a director, her godfather and actor Pedro Armendariz. As Katy was only fifteen, she was not allowed to act in it. In 1943 she was offered another role in the film Shall Not Kill (Chano Urueta)

Emilio Azacarrage Vidaurreta-
<u>Emilio Azcárraga Vidaurreta - Wikipedia, la enciclopedia libre</u>
https://es.wikipedia.org/.../Emilio_Azcárraga_Vida u...
Emilio Azcárraga Vidaurreta (Tampico, Tamaulipas, 2 de marzo de 1895 - Houston, Texas, 23 de septiémbre de 1972) fue un empresario mexicano, magnate ...

<u>Inicios</u> - <u>Telesistema Mexicano</u> - <u>Muerte y Fundación de Televisa</u>
Look into XEW's history. XEW-AM

Its history is interesting as are the names of those involved and its political point of view.

'The Mexican state had shown clear signs of political interest representing the development of television and broadcasting. In the early twentieth century, both print and radio were monitored and censored by various institutional and extra-legal mechanisms, such as the 1917 Press Law, which was purely repressive and still valid. It was to prevent, through various mechanisms, which were instruments used to fight for political power. The second, the radio ban remained for several decades, to spread content of a political nature. The enabling state counterpart profit accumulation of businessmen and auto evidently without any limitation. Virtually consolidation presidential system combined with the political control through the hegemonic ruling party, from the National Revolutionary Party (PNR) to Party of the Mexican Revolution (PRM) to the Institutional Revolutionary Party (PRI) was developed in parallel with the decision- a peculiar television and radio formula that would fit the objectives and aims of the new post-revolutionary political system. The radio, which supposedly limited supplant the newspaper as an instrument of criticism and vigilance against governments formed from the Colony, Independence and Reform, contributed to prop up the government emanating

from the Revolution supported by a business model that almost won and transplant them US. Emilio Azcarrage Vidaurreta, owner of the XEW, learned, before the consolidation of the industry the value of combining the strategy of partnership, subordination, political lobbying pressure and economic investment, was the most visible figure who led the huge radio success not only economically.'
The station had a schedule of entertainment, where paraded figures like- Emilio Tuero , Juan Arvizu , Luis Arcaraz , Nicholas Urcelay , José Mojica , Alfonso Ortiz Tirado , Tito Guízar , Los Panchos , Maria Luisa Landin , Maria Victoria , Panzón Panseco , Los Cuates Castilla , Mario Moreno Cantinflas , Germán Valdés "Tin Tan" , Agustin Lara , Tona la Negra , Angelines Fernández , Angel Garasa , Carmen Rey , Pedro Infante , Jorge Negrete , Pedro Vargas , Jose Alfredo Jimenez , Fernando Fernández "The Crooner of Mexico" , Gustavo Adolfo Palma of Guatemala , Luis Aguilar , Eulalio González "Piporro" , Antonio Aguilar , Francisco Gabilondo Soler 'Cri-Cri " , Chip and Capulina , The Three Aces , the three diamonds , Hugo Avendaño , Amparo Montes , Hector Martinez Serrano , Juan "El Gallo" Calderon , Paco Stanley and other artists. It was directed by Jaime Almeida, Ricardo Rocha and Daniel Moreno.

Not being able to find anything about my grandmother I came to the conclusion she did not exist.

Who were Katy's godparents?

Depending from which information sores you are reading two names come up.

Pedro Armendariz and Jorge Negrete names are named as godfathers.

Pedro Armendariz- brought Katy Jurado to act in her first film as he was her godfather.

Katy Jurado - Wikipedia, la enciclopedia libre

*https://es.wikipedia.org/wiki/**Katy_Jurado***

Katy Jurado (Guadalajara, Jalisco, México; 16 de enero de 1924 .... En 1953 protagonizó El bruto, de Luis Buñuel, junto a *Pedro Armendáriz*, por la que recibió ...

(Note Luis Bunuel's name it points a finger in connecting Anna Magnaini-Itily.)

EL BRUTO Program Notes - Austin Film Society

www.austinfilm.org/page.aspx?pid=2904

The woman who would become known to the world as *Katy Jurado* was born .... including the very macho *Pedro Armendáriz* **(who had been Katy's godfather ...**

Jorge Negrete- another Godfather.

Katy Jurado - Biography - IMDb

www.imdb.com/name/nm0432827/bio

Katy Jurado was born María Cristina Estela Marcela Jurado García into a wealthy ... When movie star *Emilio* Fernandez discovered Katy at the age of 16 and .... Mexican film star and singer Jorge Negrete was her *godfather* at her quinceañera.

México en el Oscar: Katy Jurado, estrella internacional

sitioexpresodemedianoche.blogspot.com/.../el-debut...
16.01.2011 - Su tío, hermano de su madre, era el compositor y músico Belisario de Jesús García, que era compadre de don *Emilio Azcárraga,* el fundador .

The name of Katy Jurado's first husband must be menchioned at this point-
Victor Velazquez- an actor and a writer, a singer, a lawyer.

Ernesto Guevara Lynch-
   Ernesto Guevara Lynch, who played Che Guevara's father. He chaired the committee of Republicans, gave lectures and concerts with Cuarteto Aguilat. Luis Aguila was a member of this group, he worked with Agustin Lara: with whom Katy Jurado's mother was supposed to have sung with on XEW-radio.

Katy Jurado - Buscabiografías

*www.buscabiografias.com/.../6185/**Katy%20Jurado***
Katy Jurado María Cristina Jurado García Actriz mexicana Nació el 16 de ... Casada con el escritor

Víctor Velázquez para sustraerse a la jurisdicción familiar.

With all the above names I stumble on to another name- **Barnabe Jurado.**
It was when I was looking for a face of my grandmother.

Chapter Twenty Five.
Katy Jurado – Family.

Katy's name in full- Marica Cristina Estela Marcella Gacia de la Garzia. Chale Nafus tell us in the program notes for EL Bruto. Chale Nafus, he was director of Programming at the Austin Film Society.

What I really want is to find out about Katy's two brothers. But I cannot at this time find out much; only what a Wikipedia or Chale Nafus offers. There are two interesting points Chale Nufus has to say. Katy Jurado was not happy with her olive skin and her dark looks, her brothers were to be envied for their fair shins, green/blue eyes. The remark I liked the best is; the men in her family had *Lawyers degrees*.

The results of my research-
Father-Luis Jurado Ochoa. *Nothing found about him.*
Brothers- *Luis Raul.* ------- *Nothing found about him.*
    Oscar Sergio.--- Nothing found about him.
Mother- Vicenta Estela Garcia de la Garza. –
    Nothing found about her.
(As this lady was said to be a singer I thought it would be easy to find her but- She sung for the radio station in Mexico XEW. (She may have had a stage name.)
This lady singer with this reputation does not have anything written about her, other than, she was Katy Jurado's alleged mother.

Godfather- Pedro Armeadariz,
        He was a Mexican actor. Not a small fish at
        that! And his wife was actress Camelita.
            (There are more godfathers to come!)

Godfather- Jorge Negrate was a Mexican actor, who
        helped found the Union of Film Production in
        Mexico, and the National Association of Actors.

First husband- Victor Velasquez- actor and lawyer.

Uncle- Belisario de Jesus Garcia de la Garza.
        In the Military and a renowned musician.
            Mother- Irene de la Garza Garcia.
            Father– Juan B. Garcia Galvin.

Cousin – Emilio Portes Gil.
            He is an interesting addition! He was
            Mexico's president between 1928 and 1930.
            He promoted Mexican artist, sending them
            on promotion trips abroad.
            He married Carman Garcia Gonzalez Teran.

There are two photos to show a family likeness
between Uncle- Belisario de Jesus Garcia de la
Garza and Cousin – Emilio Portes Gil.

Belisario de Jesús García es.wikipedia.org

Emilio Portes Gil britannica.com

In the internet program.

**<u>Joaquín Ortega Arenas Escribe y Se Pronuncia:
octubre 2012</u>**

joaquinortegaarenas.blogspot.com/2012_10_01_arc
...

28.10.2012 - Con una corta escolta de Cadetes del
Colegio *Militar* pudo llegar hasta la ... Un interinato,
Emilio Portes Gil, y un Presidente impuesto, que tal
vez ..... "Morir por tu amor" del Maestro *Belisario*
de *Jesús García*, que tocaba con ...

There is an interesting story told by an eye
witness-

*"Alvaro Obregon won the election in July of 1928
without opponents. (He was the current Mexican
president.)*
*Alvaro Obregon Salido and Cenobia Salido
daughter of billonaire Jose Maria Salido were killed*

when more than twenty bullets were fired at a restaurant 'Bulb' San Angel. While the Orchestra played.

The Orchestra leader Alfonso Esparza Otet recounted how the assassination took place.
"I was playing a waltz 'Dying for your love' (this happens to have been written by Belisario de Jesús García) Belisario de Jesús García who was playing with us first violin when the general assistant approached me and said he want to hear 'Limoncito' I stop- Dying for Love'-
Which terribly upset Belisario de Jesús García, he stopped playing to look for his violin case.

We had played a few chords when gunfire broke out- the murderer had just shot three or four times- Look man I was in the revolution, this was a shooting, I through myself on the ground. By the way Belisario de Jesús García also dropped to the ground. Once the shooting stopped he left the restaurant carrying the empty box of the violin. The violin was lost and I had to replace it."

Belisario de Jesús García was a renowned musician as well as active in the Mexican army. Godfather- Pedro Armeadariz- as well as being an actor and Katy's godfather, he made many cereals for radio station XEW.

Radio, Music, and Gender in Greater Mexico, 1923-1946

etd.lib.msu.edu/islandora/object/etd%3A305/datastream/OBJ/view

This dissertation studies the early *history* of radio in *Mexico* by analyzing the complex ...... *Mexican* scholars, Julia Tuñón and *Carmen* Ramos Escandón, ... and U.S. born Mexicans in the United States, like Pedro J. *González* and Lydia Mendoza, ... During the transfer of power in *Mexico* from *Emilio Portes Gil* to Pascual.

This program explains how radio and cinema were part of everyday life in the changing times in Mexico. Women's roles were changing in the thirties. But what is really interesting is Emilio Portes Gil active role in supporting the arts!

"Mexican President Emilio Portes Gil extended economic and moral support to the Musical group Los Trovadores Tamaulitpecos. They went to New York-
The Mexican Government invested in oversea trips of performers and took an interest in seeing who complied with post-revolutionary government's cultural projects. They were sent as goodwill ambassadors!
The other remark I find interesting is-
This was the case with Miguel Lerdo de Tejada's orchestra who during a tour in the United States

were noted to have "Skillfully fulfilled their mission."

Ángel Agustín María Carlos Fausto Mariano Alfonso del Sagrado Corazón de Jesús Lara y Aguirre del Pino to give him his full name, it was said to have sung with Katy's mother.

Agustin Lara was one who benefited from Emilio Portes Gil's government support, he asked the Mexican consul in San Antonio, Eduardo Hernandez Chazaro for financial assistance. His company was on tour. (Haciendo Labor pro-Patria.) -conducting work for the motherland.

Strange words!? Not if you are trying to connect events and state from where Katy Jurado came from.

Chapter twenty six
The Mafia puzzle
Franklin Jurado- Jose Santacruz London

   From chapter five comes two names for one man.
I found the name Franklin Jurado in an article
written by Clair Sterling about him. He just happens
to be a powerful member of the Mafia! So powerful
that he also had the name Jose Santacruz Londono,
with this name he leaded the Colombian Mafia.
With the name Franklin Jurado, it is said he was
professor of economy, educated at Harvard.
Look what Joseph P Kennedy's Wikipedia has to
say about Franklin Jurado!
Joseph P. Kennedy – Wikipedia Joseph Kennedy
(etwa 1914)
   "Joseph Kennedy was known to transfer illegally
acquired gains from the alcohol business in legal
investments for money laundering so already at this
time. That were selected industries (stock market,
film industry and later real estate) from him for this
how today almost predestined for money laundering.
Kennedy's approach, which was first of all to
cooperate to a diversified mixture of different
sources of money to initiate to insert the second
minimum own funds, thirdly within the acquired
investments very quickly and extensively to modify
(for example, fusion, part sale, renovation), with
other investors fourth after very short time again
with very high profits to repel them, is in the
classical manner of the first stage of money

laundering model , which by the Colombian, Harvard trained economist and former money launderer for the Cali cartel, *Jose Franklin Jurado Rodriguez*, was developed, and certainly not without reason as "Kennedification stage" referred to by this. "

Joseph P Kennedy other Mafia associates were men like Frank Santra, Meyer lansky, Lucky Luciano, Just to name a few.

Joseph P Kennedy was the father of J F Kennedy

7. Franklin Jurado businesspundit.com

The washing cycle - Australian Federal Police
www.afp.gov.au/media-centre/.../1998/.../washing

Franklin Jurado

Or is his name Jose Santacruz Londono? If they are not the same person why do they wear the same cloths? Were the photos taken on the same day?

Cali-Kartell – Wikipedia

*de.wikipedia.org/wiki/**Cali**-Kartell* Das *Cali*-Kartell (span. *Cartel* de *Cali*) war ein Zusammenschluss verschiedener kolumbianischer Kokainproduzenten und -schmuggler in der Stadt *Cali*.

José Santacruz Londono: No. 3 of Cali Drug Cartel in Colombia rjgeib.com

This man is not known for being a good guy.

offensive contre le cartel de cali don chepe:le boss de jurado

archives.lesoir.be/offensive-contre-le-cartel-de-cali-don-chepe-le-...

09.01.1993 - ... le 22 juillet dernier du chef du cartel de Medellin, *Pablo Escobar*. ... à ce numéro qu'Edgar Garcia et *Franklin Jurado*, les deux blanchisseurs ...

Once established that the above man is one and the same the connection to Gabriel Garcia Marques becomes clearer. José Santacruz Londono was one of the three big bosses of the Colombian Mafia with Gilberto Jose Rodriguez-Orejuela and Miguel Rodríguez Orejuela. They are brothers! No wonder I was puzzled about their like mess.

Claudia Pilar Rodriguez

Gabriel Garcia Marques's center is Mexico City. The aforementioned Drug Barons used the Palacio de Bellas Artes to deuces matters; not a surprise as their lawyers had their offices there. (chapter 26, Palacio de Bellas Artes and chapter 27 Barnabe Jurado, will explain the Bugsy Sigel connection. if Franklin Jurado is related to Barnabe Jurado I have at this point not been able to find out.)

This address confirms this and more.

EL ESPECTADOR

Sábado 18 De Marzo, Última Actualización: 1:00 Am

Los capos del cartel de Cali |
ELESPECTADOR.COM   El
Espectador984 × 655Bildersuche
Pacho Herrera, Gilberto Rodríguez Orejuela, Miguel
Rodríguez Orejuela y José Santacruz Londoño
fueron los

"A few steps from the National Capitol, in the
Cultural Center Gabriel García Marquez, were called
the most talked-about political leaders who will seek
to make them counterweight to those two options:
the Senators Claudia López, Antonio Navarro and
Jorge Enrique Robledo; the Minister of labour, Clara
López; the former Governor of Antioquia Sergio
Fajardo; Sen. Piedad Cordoba and former Mayor of
Bogotá Gustavo Petro."

1 - **Bibliothèque et Archives Canada**

*www.collectionscanada.gc.ca/obj/s4/f2/dsk2/ftp02/N
Q57623.pdf*
von A Schulte-Bockholt - 2000 -
'The late *Pablo Escobar* Gavina seerns to share this
attitude as he believed he ...... exclusion The
Rodriguez Orejuela brothers and the late *Jose
Santacruz* ...... Bolivian drug dealers and
coorganized by *Klaus Barbie*. an intemationally
sought ...

"Letters were past from Pablo Escobar to Fidel Castro and Raul Castro by Gabriel Garcia Marquez states Popeye one of Pablo Escobar's men.

Plata o plomo | Kokain | Juni 1995 | NZZ Folio *folio.nzz.ch/1995/juni/plata-o-plomo* Kartellboss *Pablo Escobar* schaffte es bis ins Abgeordnetenhaus und nutzte die ... von *José Santacruz Londoño* und vier weiteren Bossen aus der «Capital de la .... Und *Gabriel García Marquez* «verlangt» von den Chemikern die Entwicklung ...

(Pablo Escobar made it up in the House of representatives and took advantage of... of José Santacruz Londoño and four other bosses from the «capital de la...» And Gabriel García Marquez «required» the development by the chemists...)

"I was in Mexico carrying a letter to the Nobel Laureate for Raul and Fidel Castro; a manuscript of Escobar's," Popeye said.

"When I got off the plane the Mexican police were waiting for me and took me to where 'Gabo' was signing autographs," he continued, according to Colombia Reports. "He called me aside and said, 'Popeye, where is the letter?' and I gave it to him." In the message, Popeye told Todo Noticias, "Pablo Escobar was asking Fidel for a Russian submarine to carry the drug from Mexico to Havana, and with this submarine, to Miami."

(Fernando Gutierrez Barrios, the head of the Mexican police, he happens to have worked with Carlos Delmar Jurado in the conspiracy with Lee Harvey Oswald.)
We do seem to flutering around the Kennedys.

Pablo Escobar's top hit man: Gabriel Garcia Marquez worked with El ...

www.businessinsider.com/pablo-escobar-gabriel-garcia-marquez
15.10.2015 - *Pablo Escobar's* top hit man claims literary icon *Gabriel Garcia Marquez* worked with El Patron ... *Gabriel Garcia Marquez*, a Colombian novelist and journalist, is a revered figure in Latin ... *Jose* Goitia/Associated Press.

El Carnicero y el Patrón: La conexión oculta entre Pablo Escobar y ...
Oxígeno Digital640 × 427Bildersuche

El Carnicero y el Patrón: La conexión oculta entre Pablo Escobar y Klaus Barbie
 (This also explains why you can find Klaus Barbie influence and Che's handwriting under the name of Luiz Renato Almeida Pires in 1968 Teoponte) (Spies-C.I.A-Lies-Terrorist-Che Guevara.)

1 - Bibliothèque et Archives Canada
www.collectionscanada.gc.ca/obj/s4/f2/dsk2/ftp02/NQ57623.pdf
von A Schulte-Bockholt - 2000 -
'The late *Pablo Escobar* Gavina seerns to share this attitude as he beiieved he ...... exclusion The Rodriguez Orejuela brothers and the late *Jose Santacruz* ...... Bolivian drug dealers and coorganized by *Klaus Barbie*. an intemationally sought ...

All of these men are fighting for control of the drugs? What a muddle.

Plata o plomo | Kokain | Juni 1995 | NZZ Folio
folio.nzz.ch/1995/juni/plata-o-plomo
Kartellboss *Pablo Escobar* schaffte es bis ins Abgeordnetenhaus und nutzte die ... von *José Santacruz Londoño* und vier weiteren Bossen aus der «Capital de la .... Und *Gabriel García Marquez* «verlangt» von den Chemikern die Entwicklung ...
   "However, an international legalization does not stand out, so that the disappearance of the power of the cartels is not expected. Prudent Colombians,

therefore, cling to the hope that demand is shifting to other drugs produced in other places and distributed by other traders. *And Gabriel García Marquez "demands" the chemists to develop cheap methods for synthetic cocaine production directly on the sales markets so that their countrymen no longer need this business.* There is, however, a precedent: By the end of the 1970s, Colombia was temporarily the main supplier of the US from marijuana - until the US more climate-friendly, far more potent cannabis seeds suitable for domestic cultivation were available. The Colombians were thrown out of the business overnight - but they quickly took it back with the cocaine."

So we have it again! The little man on the corner Gabriel Garcia Marques; only this time he is sitting in the middle, between bitter opponents in the Columbian Mafia, in Mexico City, he is the key man connection the Showbiz world. His throne is in the Palacio de Bellas Artes.

thieves' world - The Unmasking of Maine....and Beyond

https://unmasker4maine.files.wordpress.com/.../thieves-world-the-threat-of-the-new-glob...
Above all, *Claire Sterling* describes the great shift of worldwide criminal attention to ...... *Jurado* had been working the whole Continent when the DEA picked him up ...... crash of Sindona's *Franklin* National Bank in New York was the biggest on.

Chapter twenty seven
Palacio de Bellas Artes- Mafia Roots

Looking at the Wikipedia history of the Palaico de Arts it is difficult to define when it was used as a Hotel, it is so much more. It where Barnabe Jurado met William S Burroughs, the same place where *William S. Burroughs shot his girl friend Joan Vollmer.*

And at the Palacio de Bellas Artes, Mario Varga Llosa punched Gabriel Garcia Marquez in the eye; the famous black eye can be seen on the internet.

The lawyer Barnabe Jurado used was the same lawyer as Bugsy Siegel, Jose Vasconcelos. Jose Vasconcelos was lawyer to the top members of the mafia.

Bugsy Siegel's connections are of great interest as his girl friend was the film star actress Jean Harlow; he married the film star Virginia Hill. Bugsy Siegel had made the Palacio de Bellas Artes his home as had Gabriel Garcia Marquez.

Bugsy Siegel was the founder of the first casinos in Las Vegas.

The next address explains Jose Vasconcelos had his office in the Palacio de Bellas Artes! His office and Barnabe Jurado's and Mafia connections.

Prensa rosa, amarilla, de rojillos y rojetes – El Heraldo de ...

elheraldoslp.com.mx/.../prensa-rosa-amarilla-de-roji...
26.06.2015 - Salvó al astuto penalista Bernabé Jurado acusado de posesión de ... del Hotel Flamingo's?, propiedad de Bugsy Siegel, uno de los mafiosos ...

The association between Gabriel Garcia Marquez and Bugsy Siegel and the drug lord Pablo Escobar must have been close as Gabriel Garcia Marquez wrote the book 'News of a kidnapping.' Pablo Escobar had ten people kidnapped to prevent him from being taken to North America on drug charges. Pablo Escobar was a guest in Palacio de Bellas Artes when he made Mexico City his home town.

Pablo Escobar - CrimeTV

www.crimetv.com/page/people/mobsters/pablo.../89. ..

Bugsy Siegel ..... Gabriel García Márquez' book, News of a Kidnapping, details the series of abductions that Escobar masterminded to pressure the then ...

10 Good Cities With Bad Reputations : TripHobo Travel Blog
www.triphobo.com/.../best-cities-of-the-world-with-
14.09.2015 - ... at the Palacio de Bellas Artes, or Frida Kahlo's works at her former home. ... The city is the former hometown of drug kingpin Pablo Escobar.)

Bugsy Siegel - Wikipedia, the free encyclopedia
https://en.wikipedia.org/wiki/Bugsy_Siegel
Benjamin "Bugsy" Siegel (February 28, 1906 - June
20, 1947) was a Jewish American mobster. Seal
what known as one of the most "infamous and
feared ... Siegel traveled to Las Vegas, Nevada
where he handled and financed some of the original
casinos. He assisted developer William Wilkerson
Flamingo Hotel after Wilkerson ran out of funds.
Siegel took over the project and managed the final
stages of construction. The Flamingo opened on
December 26, 1946.

    Katy Jurado's Mother was supposed to have sung
at the Palacio de Bellas Artes. But I cannot find a
photo of her anywhere nor can I find any other
information about her!
Katy Jurado as Claire Sterling she would have
known of the Mafia connections.
As for Anna Magnani! The Palacio de Bellas Artes
was where her shoes were exhibited.

El Universal - Estilos - Los zapatos tienen su historia
www.eluniversal.com.mx/estilos/47971.html
25.03.2006 - El Palacio de Bellas Artes exhibe 80
piezas de colección creadas por ... estrellas del cine
estadounidense y europeo, como Anna Magnani.
(The Palace of Fine Arts showcases 80 pieces of
collection created by ... stars of American and
European cinema, as Anna Magnani.)

The next addresses show Clair Sterling's knowledge of the Mafia's activities.

<u>War and State Terrorism: The United States, Japan, and the ...</u>
https://books.google.de/books?isbn=0742523918 - <u>Mark Selden</u>, <u>Alvin Y. So</u> - 2004 - History
... in San Francisco, who in turn would meet with *Bugsy Siegel's* mistress, Virginia Hill. ... *Claire Sterling* estimated in 1994 that the "Triads were bringing in ...

<u>Lucky Luciano – Wikipedia, wolna encyklopedia</u>
https://pl.wikipedia.org/wiki/Lucky_Luciano
W 1957 roku *Claire Sterling*, dziennikarka (nieistniejącego już) magazynu „The ... Później w szpitalu miał odwiedzić go "*Bugsy*" *Siegel*, który widząc stan ...

<u>La Cosa Nostra – Wikipedia</u>
https://de.wikipedia.org/wiki/La_Cosa_Nostra
1940 ging *Bugsy Siegel* im Auftrag der New Yorker Familien nach Los Angeles, ... Juni 1947 wurde „*Bugsy*" *Siegel*, der in Las Vegas das Casino-Hotel ..... Hochspringen ↑ siehe Stille 1997, S. 134; Hochspringen ↑ *Claire Sterling*: Die Mafia.

Fernando Gutierrez Barrios- Mexico secrete Police- and Fernando Gutiérrez Barrios was a prominent and controversial Mexican politician affiliated to the Institutional Revolutionary Party (PRI). He was in charge of the Dirección Federal de Seguridad secret police at the midst of the dirty war (1964 – 1970), served as governor of Veracruz (1986 – 1988) and as Secretary of the Interior in the cabinet of President Carlos Salinas de Gortari. This gave him the right to have concert dedicated to him at the Palacio de Bellas Artes-

 Carlos Delmar Jurado- studied in Mexico City at the Escuela Nacional de Pintura, Escultura y Grabado. And he has exhibited at the. Palacio de Bellas Artes

Breve cronología de la fotografía - Criminalistica.mx
www.criminalistica.com.mx/.../280-breve-cronolog...
1963 El Palacio de Bellas Artes es escenario de la exposición de Arno ... Se publica El arte de la aprehensión de las imágenes y el unicornio, de Carlos Jurado ...

https://es.wikipedia.org/wiki/Abelardo_L._Rodríguez
Abelardo L Rodriguez ,Mexican president owned the land that would tune into Las Vagus.

You may be wondering why I start with this
Mexican president when I want to explain the
Mafia's roots in this. The next statement is he sent in
1929 Emilio Portes Gil abroad to study the
techniques of aviation and industry that were at the
forefront at the time. The reason he did this was the
need to transport the drugs that were cultivated in
the fields of Sinaloa. His government was known for
building air fields not roads.

Three men could not be toppled for their deals,
their names were Juan Felipe Rico and Alberto V
Aldiete, Abelardo L Rodriguez. Their lawyer was
Barnabe Jurado. (Barnabe Jurado. Part three.)

The drugs were exported to the Americans; as the
Americans faced the Nazis and the Japanese.

Abelardo L. Rodríguez, 'Embajador de la mafia', dice History ...

*www.lacronica.com/.../843234-**Abelardo-L-Rodrigu**...*

20.05.2014 - *Abelardo L. Rodríguez*, fue gobernador
de Baja California y presidente ... BC se retratan
también los personajes de *Bugsy Siegel*, Virginia
Hill y Meyer ... del territorio Norte de Baja
California y presidente interino de *México*.

Narcotráfico y sus orígenes criminales en Latinoamérica

www.perfil.com/.../Narcotrafico-y-sus-origenes-cri...
17.05.2014 - La historia de *Abelardo L. Rodríguez*,
Bugsy Siegel, Virginia Hill y Meyer ... gobernador

de Baja California y, finalmente, presidente de *México*.

ABELARDO L. RODRIGUEZ, EX PDTE. DE MÉXICO Y EX ...

enlaceinformativo.net/nota.php?id_not=22338
18.05.2014 - DE *MÉXICO* Y EX GOBERNADOR DE B.C. SEÑALADO COMO JEFE ... *Bugsy Siegel, Abelardo Rodriguez*, Virginia Hill, y Meyer Lansky son ...

From the above address' you can see members of the Mafia names appear.
Intently Shenk Agua Caliente became president of Twentieth Century Fox; he was subjected to trial like other gangsters of the period and was imprisoned until US President Harry Truman pardoned him, as well as other mobsters. He immortalized the gangster movies: Lucky Luciano, Meyer Lansky and Frank Costello. Bugsy Siegel film star wife Virginia Hill was part of this. Both Bugsy Siegel and Lucky Luciano were clients of Jose Vasconcelos and Barnabe Jurado.
(chapter five for another mafia member, Frank Jurado.)
Reading Meyer Lansky's Wikipedia you can sense the changing climate in Cuba.
Meyer Lansky was the mobs' accountant and Santo Trafficante hedged his bets when Fulgencio Batista looked as if he would be over thrown by Fidel Castro. **Santo Trafficante provided money and weapons for the Cuban revolution!**

It has been said the Fidel Castro pushed Santo Trafficante out of Cuba.
In my opinion if this was true Fidel Castro would have resaved a Mafia execution, he has not.

CIA and Kennedy.

<u>Meyer Lansky - Wikipedia, the free encyclopedia</u>
https://en.wikipedia.org/wiki/Meyer_Lansky
Lansky met *Bugsy Siegel* when they were teenagers. .... The 1959 Cuban revolution and the rise of *Fidel Castro* changed the climate for mob investment in Cuba ...
<u>Early life</u> - <u>Gambling operations</u> - <u>War work</u> - <u>The Flamingo</u>

<u>Mob Rules: What the Mafia Can Teach the Legitimate Businessman</u>
https://books.google.de/books?isbn=1101515341 - <u>Louis Ferrante</u> - 2011 - Business & Economics
Meyer Lansky and *Bugsy Siegel*, two Jews credited with the vision of Las Vegas, ... Cuban revolutionary, *Fidel Castro*, with money and guns just in case Castro ...

I mention again Jose Vasconcelos because he has a very good reason to have his offices in the Palacio de Bellas Artes; he was often to be seen with the then president Abelardo L. Rodriguez. To use his other name christen name, Eduardo Vasconcelos he was the Secretary of Public Education.

To quote his Wikipedia, Eduardo Vasconcelos was a prominent politician and Mexican lawyer born in Oaxaca, a member of the Institutional Revolution Party he occupying several positions of importance. He studied at the Institute of Sciences and Arts of Oaxaca, he had a law degree from the National School of Jurisprudence in 1907, presided in 1909 the Ateneo de la Juventud, which he founded. He was a supporter of the Mexican Revolution since its inception and later became a lawyer at the National Automomous University of Mexico. He was appointed co-director of the newspaper El Antirreeleccionista.

His Wikipedia also tells us, he was a writer. No wander he has his offices in the Palacio de Bellas Artes.

El Palacio de Bellas Artes is where Gabriel Garcia Marquez faunal was held.

I have to add something important about Fernando Barrios Gutierrez.
Not forgetting that Fernando Gutierrez Barrios- Mexico secret Police- and Carlos Delmar Jurado worked with him. Fernando Gutierrez Barrios as the head of the secret police of Mexico was said to be the go-between the CIA and Fidel Castro!

Fernando Gutierrez Barrios got Fidel Castro out of prison so he would to be able to take the Granma to Cuba...

<u>Absuelto por la historia - Granma</u>

www.granma.cu/granmad/secciones/fidel/
Ramón Chao: Palabras en el tiempo, Argos Vergara, España, 1984, p. .... *Fernando Gutiérrez Barrios*: Diálogos con el hombre, Editorial Planeta, México, 1995, p. ... Gustarle al Papa y a Fidel el *Chan Chan* es como gustarle al mundo entero.

Fernando Barrios Gutierrez was the man said to have integrated Lee Harvey Oswald's contact in the Cuban consulate.
(My opinion is someone wanted to establish a man like Lee Harvey Oswald was in Mexico City.
Strange we are back to J F Kennedy's assassination plot.)

Chapter twenty eight..
Pablo Escobar and Klaus Barbie.

There was a really strong link between Pablo Escobar and Klaus Barbie. This can be confirmed in and many other programs-

Pablo Escobar y Klaus Barbie fueron piezas claves para montar la «General ...
By Boris Miranda.

Pablo Escobar and Klaus Barbie were the key figures of the cocaine movement. Their covenants led coups, anticommunist paramilitary organization; they did business with the Vatican and other drug runners worldwide.

Santa Cruz, Panama City, Medellin and Miami were a few of the places where the scenes of this almost secret connection took place; they joined the old Nazi paten, it was one of the most sinister alliances of the last decades of the twentieth century.

Klaus Barbie and the then young Pablo Escobar controlled almost 90% of the production and distribution of the world's drugs.

Remember it was the CIA that saw Klaus Barbie was nestled in Bolivia. The Vatican clergy Krunoslav Draganovic saw to his travel papers.

Klaus Barbie was said to have helped in the capture of Che Guevara.
He sold weapons to finance the war in Nicaragua, worked with Oliver North; who had the same codenames as Che Guevara and Felix Rodriguez. As stated in 'Ultimate Sacrifice' – by Lamar Waldron and Thom Hartmann.

Noriega and the Drug Trade Database, Part II - Historical ...

historicaltextarchive.com/sections.php?action... Rondon is an OCHOA VASQUEZ frontman who appears as owner of La Guarani, ... minister following Wednesday's resignation of *Orlando Vasquez Velazquez*, who ...... of the military government with the help of fugitive Nazi *Klaus Barbie*.

Klaus Barbie arranged the meeting between Panamanian General Manuel Antonio Noriega and Pablo Escobar. Manuel Antonio Noriega was also a drug lord.
Gabriel Garcia Marquez were friends with Manuel Antonio Noriega

Klaus Barbie involved the events surrounding Teoponte; where you can find Ciro Bustos/Che

Guevara working under another name, after the death party. (See Spies-CIA-Lies-Terrorist-Che Guevara)

Klaus Barbie was the Godfather to Monika Ertl. Who in turn translates works for Ciro Bustos/Che Guevara. (See Spies-CIA-Lies-Terrorist-Che Guevara)

You can find Pablo Escobar name connected to Jorge Negrete one of Katy Jurado's godfathers and Victor Velazquez, Katy's first husband. All be it for their folk music. Bothe the aforementioned names are also renowned as top lawyers. (see The Palacio de Bellas Artes.)

When the Medellin-Pablo Escobar cartel had to move out of Bolivia the Bolivian/Colombian connection were reestablished in Mexico and Brazil.

José Santacruz Londono: No. 3 of Cali Drug Cartel in ...

*www.rjgeib.com/heroes/unanue/**londono**.html*
The Violent End of *José Santacruz Londono*: ...
Medellin was the headquarters for drug lord *Pablo Escobar,* whose rival cartel fought a terrorist war against the ...

In chapter 'Why have their identities been mixed with others?' It is clear that José Santacruz Londono other identity is Franklin Jurado. As José Santacruz

Londono he is said to have been shot on a road in the northwest city of Medellin. This city was Pablo Escobar center.

'10 Good Cities With Bad Reputations : TripHobo Travel Blog
www.triphobo.com/.../best-cities-of-the-world-with-
...
14.09.2015 - ... at the Palacio de Bellas Artes, or Frida Kahlo's works at her former home. ... The city is the former hometown of drug kingpin Pablo Escobar.)

Pablo Escobar - CrimeTV
www.crimetv.com/page/people/mobsters/pablo.../89.
..
Bugsy Siegel ..... Gabriel García Márquez' book, News of a Kidnapping, details the series of abductions that Escobar masterminded to pressure the then ...

The above address is to point out Gabriel Garcia Marques involvement. He knew so much he could write a book! 'The news of a Kidnapping.' They must have talked when they were guest at Palacio de Bellas Artes.

Gabriel Garcia Marquez delivered drug letters from Pablo ...
*colombiareports.com/**gabriel-garcia-marquez-**
delive...*

02.10.2015 - *Gabriel Garcia Marquez* delivered drug letters from *Pablo Escobar* to ... key contacts who would deliver drug trafficking *information* by letter.

In this address it is stated that Gabriel Garcia Marquez was the connection between them all!

In the book "The real Paul" Colombian journalist Astrid Legard, the hit man and right hand drug dealer, John Jairo 'Popeye' Velázquez narrates in detail the relationship between Escobar and the president of Cuba, Fidel Castro and his brother Raul.
John Jairo 'Popeye' Velázquez says, Escobar had desires of being a guerrilla, so his approach with the Cubans should not be surprising, but he was surprised by the role of Nobel Prize Gabriel Garcia Marquez, who worked as a "messenger" between the two sides.

I don't think now it is wrong to say there is a true story of partnership between governments, drug traffickers, Nazi war criminals and CIA agents intertwining with the Mafia.
I would never have found any of this out if I had not been looking for a farther. Nor met the man who told me Hans Ertl had said Che Guevara was a good husband to Monika Ertl. Klaus Barbie was her godfather. The man who told me was Klaus Barbie's son. (See Spies-CIA-Lies-Terrorist-Che Guevara)

Michael Levine connection.

Pablo Escobar y Klaus Barbie fueron piezas claves para montar la «General ...
By Boris Miranda. Had something else of interest to say, this time about Michael Levine.
Michael Levine was an undercover Drug Enforcement Administration officer for the US, DEA. He was in Argentina, 1978-1982 from there he managed to deceive the Bolivian drug lords. He used the name of Roberto Suarez. Not to be confused with Roberto Suarez Gomez. Who in his turn financed the military coup that installed a dictatorship in 1980, in which Luis Garcia Meza would be President and Suarez's cousin Luis Arce Gomez was Minister of the Interior, and so he received political protection for his enterprise.

Michael Levine was one of the most important undercover agents of his decade. He managed to incriminate bigwigs of the drug cartel. But! His government sat on the cases, releasing the detainees.

Michael Levine states the CIA was instrumental in making the General Motor of the Cocaine world. This is stated in the first paragraph of his Wikipedia. 'The Big White Lie: The Deep Cover Operation That Exposed the CIA Sabotage of the Drug War and Deep Cover: The Inside Story of How DEA Infighting, Incompetence and Subterfuge Lost Us the Biggest Battle of the Drug War. Are both books written by Michael Levine as well as 'Undercover' 1988. He explains the real partnership between his government, drug traffickers, Nazi war criminals and CIA agents.

Claire Sterling says in her notes in her book 'Thieves World.' That Richard Levine was the DEA analyst in Washington.

Chapter twenty nine
Who was Barnabe Jurado?

In- **LESSONS FROM JURY BERNABÉ (Parts One to five.)**
esquivel-zubiri.blogspot.com

The first words are- Every law student or persons engaged the practice of law in Mexico knew who the hell Barnabe Jurado was, he was known for his illustrious and immemorial actions. The press knew him as the 'Devil's Advocate' the other name he had was 'Abo-Ganster'

He had two law firms in Mexico City; his connections lead him to sponsor public figures in the world of politics and show business and they included the Mafia.

With his arguments in controversial cases, he kept people accused of theft, fraud, murder, out of prison. He had friends among politicians, union leaders, business tycoons, journalist, he had judges as friends; Barnabe Jurado's contacts were prosecutors and the police. He contacts stretched through the Judicial Police to the dreaded police of the Federal Security Service, they were in service to the courant presidents. (see 'What a circle to find! For Fernando Gutierrez Barrios- Mexico secret police.)

Barnabe Jurado was known to be an excellent speaker; he enjoyed smoking and drinking, consumed drugs. His desire for women brought him in contact with prostitutes and actresses known in Hollywood.

He practiced law in Argentina, Spain and Cuba and in the United States as well as Mexico. With a nickname of 'Abo-Ganster' he was among the drug traffickers and their hired killers. Mexican President Lazaro Cardenas del Rio and 'Caudillo' Generalissimo Francisco Franco, dictator of Spain paid him for his consulting services.

Barnabe Jurado was born in 1909. The son of Miguel Jurado Aizpuru and Dona Guadalupe Angel Jurado, they were among the 300 aristocratic families who co-governed with Don Porfirio Diaz, before the outbreak of the Mexican Revolution. 1910.

Miguel Jurado Aizpuru estate 'La Hacied de Canutillo' was under siege in 1916. 'Francisco' Pancho Villa arrested Miguel Jurado Aizpuru, he was detained by order of the revolution as he been the head of the Northern Division. Miguel Jurado Aizpuru refused to sign away his property to Pancho Villa, who had him executed. His widow and three children had to flee; they fled to Parral to hide in the mines, where Barnabe Jurado stayed hidden for four years. Pancho Villa took the estate 'La Hacied de Canutillo' to use as his home, this where Pancho Villa spent the last years of his life. Barnabe Jurado character was formed in the unrest of the Mexican revolution.

Barnabe Jurado diced to study law as his father had not recognized him as a son. His father had had many children out of wedlock was named as one of the reasons for his execution by Pancho Villa.

Barnabe Jurado was present at the bullfights in the 'Monument Plaza Mexico' where he met Jorge Negrete. (Katy Jurado's Godfather; Jorge Negrete also helped found the Union of Film Production in Mexico, and the National Association of Actors.)

Barnabe Jurado also met the actress Maria Felix who had a marriage with Jorge Negrete and Aguistn Lara and was a lover of the Mexican president Miguel Aleman.

Mario Moreno 'Cantinflas, (Heard that name before?) also was there, at the bullfights along with the governor of Puebla, Maximino Camacho the Minister of Communications and Public Works.

The public investment had increased by tenfold in Pueble with money gained by the sale of oil to the Americans made Maximino Avila Camacho the Minister of Communications and Public Works a valuable contact. At the ministers parties Barnabe Jurado met the Mexican elite like Frida Kaho, business filmmaker 'Indio' Fernandez.

Mario Moreno 'Cantinflas' as union leader for the workers in the film industry. Broadcasting industry's Emilio Aracarraga Vidaurreta- XEW-radio. Jorge Negrete and Pedro Armendariz also attended the parties. (Another of Katy Jurado's godfather!)

(Maximino Camacho the' Minister of Communications and Public Works' through Barnabe Jurado into prison because he took the minister's wife to bed, Maximino Camacho the Minister of Communications and Public Works' brother was President Avila Camacho. In this prison Barnabe Jurado made contact with Mafia and their dealings with the corrupted government. The Second World War was under way. The Nazis had sunk Mexican vessels.

Sinaloa Mexico was the main hotbed of the opium worldwide. As American troops faced the Nazis and the Japanese hundreds of thousands of Sinaloa farmers were engaged in planting and harvesting the drug. Mexican Justice saw millions of dollars went to those supposedly guarding the region from Nazi or Japanese attack, what they really did was to guard the truckloads of drugs bound for the United States. Barnabe Jurado had contacts concluding judicial police and the military.)

Mario Moreno 'Cantinflas' (Remembering he was used as a double for Che Guevara.) asked Barnabe Jurado to intervene between him and Susan Cora an actress of the time. At this time Barnabe Jurado met his third wife the daughter of Ambassador of Mexico in Brazil, Don Chema Davila.

Barnabe Jurado stood out as the best lawyer around Mexico as his contacts with the Federal Security Directorate and their secret police guarding the enemies of their regime gave him daily axes to president German Miguel Valdez. (Fernando Barrios Gutierrez).

Barnabe Jurado is living and working in an environment earning him the name of devil's advocate. From corruption cases to seeing assassins did not receive sentences. And seeing the entrepreneurs such as Emilio Azcarrage Vidaurreta's empires could expand.

Having explained that this man has connections in all the interesting parties from the Mexican nobility to drug lords and the entertainment business etc, etc.

Barnabe Jurado was Rosita Fornes' representative in the divorce from Manuel Madel, his lawyer was Victor Velasquez. *(This would not be worth mentioning if he had not been Katy Jurado's first husband.)*

MANUEL MEDEL contra ROSITA FORNÉS

tonypisani1.tripod.com/id129.html
"*Bernabé Jurado*, asesino prófugo de la justicia mexicana, fue quien gestionó la ... ante quien Manuel Medel, por conducto de su abogado *Víctor Velazquez*, ...
Ninon Sevilla, Meche Barba, Rosita Fornes, Rosa Carmina and Maria Antonieta Pons.

Note- Paco Ignacio Toibo 11 was writer and close friend of Gabriel Garcia Marquez. Paco Ignacio Toibo 11 wrote about Che Guevara and Pancho Villa. His name appears in the next address.- Fonfo de Cultur Economica. Information on the culture of the economy.

Revive El libro rojo - Fondo de Cultura Económica

www.fondodeculturaeconomica.com/.../Detalle.aspx.
..

02.03.2009 - ... a *Paco Ignacio Taibo* ii, Eduardo Monteverde, Eduardo Antonio Parra, ... que va de 1980, con la muerte y asesinato de *Bernabé Jurado* (un ...

Elegí la música, luego la historia y después los tragos - El País

elpais.com/diario/2009/.../1247263203_850215.ht...
11.07.2009 - ... el sargento Quintero; el abogado de los bajo fondos *Bernabé Jurado*, ... y se empapó del detective Belascoarán, de *Paco Ignacio Taibo* II.

William Seward Burroughs-
William S. Burroughs - Wikipedia, the free encyclopedia

*https://en.wikipedia.org/wiki/**William_S._Burrough**
s*

William Seward Burroughs II (/ˈbʌroʊz/; also known by his pen name William Lee; February 5, 1914 – August 2, 1997) was an American novelist, short story ...

   What has William Seward Burroughs got to do with it? To start with Barnabe Jurado was his lawyer. William Seward Burroughs needed his services with a drug charge, but when he was playing 'William Tell' with his wife he managed to shoot his wife in the forehead!
   William Seward Burroughs and his lawyer names were all over the newspapers! With the cleaver words of Barnabe Jurado, William Seward

Burroughs walked out of the court. Barnabe Jurado's named as the best lawyer in all the papers. Where did this happen? Palacio de Bellas Artes.

Palacio de Bellas Artes-
**<u>Hotel where Hemingway stayed in Mexico City -
Lonely ...</u>**
www.lonelyplanet.com › ... › Mexico
110 Monterrey, where William S. Burroughs shot Joan Vollmer. And, of course, Palacio de Bellas Artes, where Mario Varga Llosa punched out Garcia Marquez, in what has to be the only recorded ...
http://www.cnn.com/2014/04/17/world/americas/gab riel-garcia-marquez-dies/ ... I met him once, at a function in Ottawa.

*(Palacio de Bellas Arts, 110 Monterrey,was where William S. Burroughs shot Joan Vollmer. And, of course, **Palacio de Bellas Artes was where Mario Varga Llosa punched out Garcia Marquez.** The recorded fist fight between future Nobel Literature laureate.)*

Barnabe Jurado's attorney's status must have got to him as he felt the need for bulletproof car; this car meant so much to him when a driver drove into it Barnabe Jurado shot him. The young man died not from the built but from blood pinioning. As the young man's uncle was the Head of Press for the

Chambers of Deputies, Barnabe Jurado felt the need to get on an airplane to New York.

After a meeting with John Baker an American lawyer he became adviser to John Baker's office. With his knowledge of Mexican law he could assist their American counterparts.

Barnabe Jurado states he is Katy Jurado's Sister!
Palacio de Bellas Artes, where Mario Varga Llosa punched out Garcia Marquez. This is where Gabriel Garcia Marquez lived.

Where Gabriel Garcia Marquez lived-
From DEVON VAN HOUTEN MALDONADO
The News

Gabriel García Márquez, originally from Colombia, called Mexico City home until he died, raising his family here and becoming integrated into the community of painters, poets and novelists working in the capital during the 20th century. In 1949, beat writer William S. Burroughs came to Mexico City on the run from the law and ended up staying for five years. When fellow Beat and friend Jack Kerouac came to visit Burroughs, he also stayed for a time. And Englishman Damien Hirst, the current king of contemporary art, maintains a studio on Mexico's Pacific coast and is represented by Galería Hilario Galguera in Mexico City.
Gabriel Garcia Marquez lived in the Palacio de Bellas Artes, and had a home around the corner.

Barnabe Jurado states he is Katy Jurado's brother!
This statement can be found in- esquivel-zubiri.blogspot.com

And in the address below- look at who he told this to, 'a lie of not' he told General Francisco Franco. The leader and veteran of the Spanish Civil War, the strongest Man in Spain.

<u>Literary Outlaw: The Life and Times of William S. Burroughs</u>
https://books.google.de/books?isbn=0393343243
<u>Ted Morgan</u> - 2012 - Biography & Autobiography
Burroughs went to see Jurado, a tall handsome, flamboyant hidalgo who held court at the Opera ... His sister was the actress *Katy Jurado*. ... out of jail in their native lands thanks to the efforts of *Bernabé Jurado*—American numbers racketeers, ...

<u>Mexico City a refuge for persecuted writers - trivalleycentral ...</u>
*www.trivalleycentral.com/.../**mexico**.../article_c96d7*
05.03.2008 - *Mexico* City had just opened a safe house for persecuted writers, one ... Prize winner *Gabriel Garcia Marquez* to American Beat writer *William S.* ... "The sense of possibilities, whether *met* or not, are generally much ... just down the street from the former home of *Burroughs*, the author of "The Naked Lunch.

They're part of a long tradition of writers who have found refuge in Mexico City, from Colombian Nobel Prize winner Gabriel Garcia Marquez to American Beat writer William S. Burroughs, a fugitive from U.S. drug charges.

EL ABOGANSTER: LA NOVELA SOBRE BERNABE ...

*www.gandhi.com.mx/el-**aboganster**-la-novela-sobre...*

EL *ABOGANSTER*: LA NOVELA SOBRE BERNABE JURADO, EL PERSONAJE REAL QUE INSPIRO EL POPULAR APODO QUE ...
Autor: *EUGENIO AGUIRRE*.

Acercarce a Susana Cora, implicaba también, llegar al hombre del poder.
esquivel-zubiri.blogspot.com

Vigésima Séptima lección e vida. "En determinadas situaciones que te pueden ... esquivel-zubiri.blogspot.com

Returning to Katy Jurado, her cousin was Emilio Portes Gill. He was Mexico's president between 1928 and 1930.
In 1929-
*es.thefreedictionary.com/**Emilio+Portes+Gil-***
This tells us that he was associated with Bugsy Siegel. He was sent or his government sent men to study aviation and industry for the most up to date methods.
The Emilio Portes Gil Dicccionario de espanol/Spanish Dictionary states.

Drugs were legal in Mexico in 1940, one of the reasons were was so they could be exported to the USA. An Italian is supposed to have taught the peasants how to grow the plant.
(chapter 26. Palacio de Bellas Artes- Mafia roots. Gabriel Garcia Marquez creator of Che Guevara.)

During World War Two, Barnabe Jurado saw the poppy fields increase, he states that while thousands of American troops faced the Nazis and the Japanese in the war, hundreds if not thousands of Mexican farmers in the Sinaloa region were engaged in planting and harvesting the drug. From 1929

Mexico's governments were more interested in airplanes than building roads.

Barnabe Jurado was also a lawyer to Bugsy Siegel!

Francisco Rodriguez - El Heraldo de San Luis Potosi

elheraldoslp.com.mx/.../prensa-rosa-amarilla-de-rojillos-y-rojetes...
26.06.2015 - Salvó al astuto penalista *Bernabé Jurado* acusado de posesión de ... del Hotel Flamingo's?, propiedad de *Bugsy Siegel*, uno de los mafiosos ...

The address show, the connection between the said Che Guevara, *Emilio Portes Gil*, and Barnabe Jurado. Fidel Castro. Katy Jurado. And-

BANDERA ROJA: marzo 2014
banderaroja.blogspot.com
Was kind enough to give me a link to Che- I add the translation-

   "Ernesto began working in the Central Hospital of the Federal District, in the department of allergy. With friends occupational physicians, they decided to organize a football match, singles against married. At the end to celebrate a good roast, which would pave the Ernesto himself would cook. The Argentine doctor had earned among his colleagues, the fame of good steakhouse. The gastronomic event was held in the fifth house of *former Mexican President Emilio Portes Gil,* who did kill a bull to make grilled. In the residence of former President on the outskirts of the city, suddenly in the park, a football field to the dispute. Emilio Portes had invited to this fun activity, other personal friends to enjoy football with friends and a good barbecue Argentinean style. After eating began the toasts and congratulations to Ernesto for the roast he had done. With several live for the carvery, Ernesto that noon had become the figure of the gay and toned meeting. Among those present a Chilean singer who had come to Mexico, in order to make themselves known was. His name was Luis Enrique Gatica Silva, "Lucho Gatica," knowing that Dr. Guevara likes tangos, he devotes several of them. In that afternoon where wine and tequila flooded all that atmosphere, Lucho Gatica premiered the songs then triumph in Mexico: "I do not platiques" and "You got used to me"

Amiga y enemiga de presidentes, líderes, militares y artistas - Proceso

www.proceso.com.mx › Archivo

25.07.1987 - ... sus amigos de renombre, a Plutarco Elías Calles, *Emilio Portes Gil*, ... Guzmán, Carlos Serrano, *Bernabé Jurado*, Fernando López Arias, ...

This sight informs me that *Emilio Portes Gil, Bernabé Jurado* enjoyed the Bandits music, together!

:The Bandits had, among his friends renowned Plutarco Elias Calles, ***Emilio Portes Gil,*** Miguel Aleman, Adolfo Ruiz Cortines, Adolfo Lopez Mateos, Agustin Lara, Maria Felix, Marco Antonio Muniz, Alejo Peralta, Rogelio de la Selva, Luis N Morones, Fidel Velazquez, Rafael Camacho Guzmán, Carlos Serrano, ***Bernabé Jurado,*** Fernando Lopez Arias, Jose Garcia Valseca, Pedro Armendáriz, José Gómez Huerta, Alfredo Kawage, Antonio Diaz Lombardo, Pepe Jara, Alvaro Carrillo and many deputies, senators and governors, for whom she was a confidante and sometimes adviser.:

The same address add another useful remark-

:Bernabe Jurado, a friend of my aunt, once brought home four Cubans who, we later learned, were fellow **Dr. Fidel Castro** And soon after, one of those Cubans came to Dr. Castro, who was a very open man, very outgoing He told us he was in Mexico to study for a master Months later, Fidel Castro returned to the house with the newcomers, the friends of Cuba will be exceeded Castro's costs, there was not enough money to pay, but there was no problem : Fidel signed my aunt a voucher for 3,000 pesos.:

Emilio Portes Gil was Katy Jurado's cousin.
Bernabé Jurado said he was Katy Jurado's brother.
(Frank Sinatra said he wanted to have Katy Jurado as his lover, where as Pablo Escobar said he was a better drug dealer than a singer, we find Frank Sinatra and Marilyn Munroe close to the Kennedys!)

Frank Sinatra was 'a good drug dealer' says drug lord Pablo Escobar's ...

*www.dailymail.co.uk/.../**Frank-Sinatra**-better-**drug-dealer**-singer-...*
07.11.2015 - *Frank Sinatra* was 'a better *cocaine dealer* than singer': Pablo Escobar's son makes extraordinary claim that the crooner was his drug lord ...

Chapter thirty.
Katy Jurado's First husband.

Katy Jurado's first husband was Victor Velazquez, her film star's information says she wanted to be an actress, as her parents or grandmother, depending which version you are reading; did not wish she appear in films. She evaded their control by marring a fellow film actor Victor Velazquez; he it is said was some years older than her.

Victor Velazquez had a law firm! He was a prominent lawyer, in the scandalous divorce of Rosita Fornes and Manuel Medel; he was Manuel Medel's lawyer. Rosita Fornes' lawyer was Barnabe Jurado. (Who has stated he was Katy Jurado's brother.)

MANUEL MEDEL contra ROSITA FORNÉS

tonypisani1.tripod.com/id129.html
"*Bernabé Jurado*, asesino prófugo de la justicia mexicana, fue quien gestionó la ... ante quien Manuel Medel, por conducto de su abogado *Víctor Velazquez*, ...

Rosita Fornes and Mario Moreno were married by Jose Ruben Romero; he in his turn was Mexico's ambassador in Cuba, and his novel 'Pito Perez' was turned into a film: in this film acted his young relation Cesar Romero next to Katy Jurado; they played opposite Mario Moreno. Barnabe Jurado was playing opposite Katy Jurado's first husband Victor Velazquez in the device of Rosita Fornes and Mario Moreno.

A side note to Jose Ruben Romero; he was Mexico's consular general in Spain. As an active member of the League of Revolutionary Writers; he paid a tribute to Manuel M Ponce. From whom Alfredo Guevara learned the trade of film producer. (see 'Hotel Nacional de Cuba.) He produced the film 'Torerro' with Katy Jurado.

Rosita Fornes can be seen with Mario Moreno. (Who acted as Che Guevara's double.)

Rosita y Mario Moreno, "Cantinflas"
gumucio.blogspot.com

This address suggests that Barnabe Jurado worked
at the law firm of Victor Velazquez.
 Jurado Barnabe needed help , it is not clear if he has
made an attempt on the life of Pancho Villa or
Pancho Villa's own bullet hit the ceiling of Cantina
La Opera. The result of this encounter saw him on
his way to Buenos Aires, into exile.

The address below also mentions the association
between Barnabe Jurado and Victor Velazquez. Katy
Jurado's first husband.

The Palaico Ballas Artes- the Jurado connection
starts with Francisco Field Jurado.

Francisco Field Jurado es asesinado: Se oponía a los
...
www.memoriapoliticademexico.org/.../23011924.ht..
.

Francisco *Field Jurado* es asesinado: Se oponía a los
Tratados de Bucareli. Enero 23 de 1924. En las
calles de la colonia Roma de la ciudad de México,
es ...

Francisco Field Jurado was born on April 1, 1881,
in Palisade Campeche. He earned a law degree on 28
December 1907 at the Hearty Institute. From 1910 to
1911 he served first as District Judge and later Civil.
During the government of Colonel Joaquin Mucel,

he was Chief Clerk and Secretary General of Government in 1915. Three years later he served as Acting Governor in 1918. He was later senator for Campeche.

Continuara el señor licenciado Vasconcelos en la secretaria ...

icaadocs.mfah.org/icaadocs/.../88/.../Default.aspx
Francisco Field Jurado was murdered on January 23, 1924, on the corner of ... The changes wrought by *José Vasconcelos'* resignation from the Ministry of .

This article conveys the opinions expressed by a variety of institutions in response to José Vasconcelos' resignation in late 1923 as a result of the crimes committed a few days earlier, particularly the death of Francisco Field Jurado, the senator from Campeche. President Álvaro Obregón refused to accept Jose Vasconcelos' resignation and promised that measures had been taken that would solve the cases and clear his administration of any involvement in the killings. In turn, the president of the University was pleased that Jose Vasconcelos would remain on the faculty until the end of Obregón's presidential term. The Students' Federation applauded Jose Vasconcelos' decision to resign over the murder of Field Jurado.

This article or others do not make it clear, if Jose Vasconcelos was responsible for the assassination of Francisco Field Jurado. The Bucareli agreement was with the United States of America. Francisco Field

Jurado was not in agreement that Mexican land should be given in to other hands.

Jose Vasconcelos- Jose Eduardo Vasconcelos was a prominent politician and Mexican lawyer born in Oaxaca, a member of the Institutional Revolution Party; he occupied several positions of importance. He was a supporter of the Mexican Revolution since its inception, as it participated in the Maderista movement as one of the four secretaries of Antirreeleccionista Center Mexico. He was appointed co-director of the newspaper El Antirreeleccionista by Felix F. Palavicini. A patron of the arts.

No wonder he was to be found in the Palaico Ballas Artes- But this where he worked with Barnabe Jurado! They were renowned lawyers to the Mafia.

Frank Jurado- Claire Sterling tell us about him, in 'Thieves World' as Jose Franklin Jurado Rodriguez he looks harmless; he had a Master Degree in Economics, studded at the Columbia University. He worked as a researcher at Harvard Kennedy School. And! He ran the Columbian Mafia. (See chapter- Why have their identities been mixed.)

General Jurado- (See chapter-Why have their identities been mixed.)

Enrique Jurado Barrio fits the profile used when stating he was a guest in the Guevara house hold, inspired the little boy with stories of warfare. But he resembles General Bayo! The trainer use to prepare for the Granma invasion.

Carlos Delmar Jurado-(See chapter-What a circle to find.)
Active in the Mexican labor movement representing actors and production workers. He was a founding members of the STPC (Union of Cinema Production Workers) and a national director of ANDA (National Association of Actors).
Carlos Delmar Jurado was involved with both lawyers Barnabe Jurado and Jose Vasconcelos in political matters in and around the Palaico Ballas Artes.

Katy Jurado-Claire Sterling-Celia de la Serna-Anna Magnani-

   Gabriel Garcia Marquez is the man that brings them all together. He lived and worked in and around the Palaico Ballas Artes, as they did. He needed them to creat a new order.

'Palicio de Bell Arts' where Barnabe Jurado had his offices, as did *Emilio Portes Gil.*

Gabriel Garcia Marquez was friends with President Francois Mitterrand, who also had an interest in the Kennedys demise.
   And then there is-Riges Debray, he was with Fidel Castro in early 60s. Riges Debray and Ciro/Che

were being tried in Bolivia at the time of the death party Francois Mitterrand was concerned about the court case. Riges Debray became Francois Mitterrand official adviser. His wife Elizabeth Burgos-Debray was involved with Rigoberta Mencha, Guatemala. This story has also been proven to be a lie, by David Stoll.
She is a translator Gabriel Garcia Marquez and a close friend of Fidel Castro. Relationship is better explained in 'CIA-Lies-Terrorist-Che Guevara.'

   Not to forget Mario Vargas Llosa, Gabriel Garcia Marquez's close friend and his wife the Bolivan Julia Urquidi. She was born in Cochabamba (Bolivia) in 1926, Julia Urquidi, political writer and was the first wife of Vargas Llosa. The marriage lasted from 1955 to 1964.

After divorcing Vargas Llosa, Julia Urquidi returned to Cochabamba, his hometown, where she worked as a private secretary of the wife of General Rene Barrientos, *then vice president of Bolivia*. He was president at the time of the death party!?
 (Funny how close the reashenships are.) (Funny to think they were supposed to have looked after Che's mother in Paries.)

El escritor junto a Julia Urquidi en París, 1960
latercera.com

The whole cast involved in the making of the Che Guevara myth are in 'Gabriel Garcia Marquez creator of Che Guevara' the death in Bolivia was start the global cocaine surge. Set up a new world order, Gabriel Garcia Marquez, Fidel Castro, William Ayers, Gorge Bush style; with the best of the best actors and film producers the best propaganda machine.

To understand Gabriel Garcia Marquez remarks to Bill Clinton in Justin Webster's film about Gabriel Garcia Marquez.

"César Gaviria - 01:21:45

"He didn't seek out just any president or political figure
It had to be some like-minded"

Bill Clinton - 01:21:55

"We were talking once about Castro and when he knew that I might lift the embargo. And he said "Castro only want two things. I said "What are these things?" He wants you to promise that if the embargo is lifted nobody will try to take away the universal healthcare, the universal education. I said, that's easy. I agree with him. And he said he wants you to promise that you will not permit any Cuban-Americans to weaken his stands against the narco-traffickers."

Chapter thirtytwo-
The real reasons behind the faked death party of Che Guevara.

This is an outline of who were behind the propaganda cover up. I hope you will see how important the words of Bill Clinton were. To find out your father was not a tee-shirt hero but someone involved in the dark side of the drug world is a strange twist of fate.

It is difficult to know where to begin unrolling the ins and outs of what was going on at the time, publically and morally. The Second World War had ended; there was a real fear against communism. President Truman in May 1947 created 'The Loyalty Program' for federal employees.

Artists were accused of disloyalty; Senator Joseph McCarthy conducted a witch hunt, those who did not comply were condemned to spend one year in jail and pay $1,000 fine.

In this atmosphere the film 'High Noon' a 1952film was judged to be in favor of communism. As it has among it stars Katy Jurado; interesting if you believe she played Che's mother. It also makes the point America was oppressing its film artists and producers script writers; this let the film industry fall into the hands of people like Gabriel Garcia Marquez. It has already been stated that Cuba took control of the film industry.

J. M. Caparros-Lera Sergio Alegre- Cinematic Contextural History of High Noon (1952, Dire Fred Zinnemann)

This article explains the atmosphere of the times. I talk about this not to explain the CIA's fear of communist in Bolivia but to point out how the Cuban film industry took a firm hold in world events.

Why holed Che's death party in Bolivia? If you wanted him killed he could have been shot anywhere. Bolivia is in the heart of the drug productizing continent. The death party was a signal to centralize the Drug War.

Did you know Drug distribution increased after this event?

Did you know that that Klaus Barbie contact was Pablo Escobar; he sent letters to Gabriel Garcia Marquez for Fidel Castro.

Did you know Fidel Castro holds the record for the most attempts made to assonate him? The CIA just misted getting him!?

Did you know Klaus Barbie's busyness associate was William Ayers? They owned the shipping company Tranmaritima.

Deckname Adler: Klaus Barbie und die westlichen Geheimdienste

https://books.google.de/books?isbn=310401826X
<u>Peter Hammerschmidt</u> - 2014 - History

Klaus Barbie und die westlichen Geheimdienste
Peter Hammerschmidt ... Kapitän *William Ayers*,
damals Präsident der Ayers Steamship Company
und mit ...

   Did you know that William Ayers', wife's father,
Leonard Boulin was a registered Cuban agent?
Kathy Boudin.

   Did you know William Ayers wanted to use the
tee-shirt hero as his banner? His book 'Prairie Fire.'
Is a communist manifesto.

In ***'The Truth about the Weather Underground' by
Larry Grarthwohl*** you can confirm William Ayers'
connection to Cuba; William Ayers and his girl
friend Bernardine had close contacts with Castro's
intelligence service.
William Ayers at one of his Weathermen meetings
stated the Kennedy murders a good thing-
William Ayers knew the Communist defector Ion
Mihai Pacepa (chapter twenty-one Gabriel Garcia
Marquez creator of Che Guevara.) both men
understood the Lee Harvey Oswald role in the
killing of FJK.

Now we have more connections-   The CIA Events

Placing the Castro's on Cuba's throne-
The Bay of Pigs invasion-
Kennedy's assassination-
Placing Klaus Barbie in Bolivia-
Che's Death party-

Getting Salvador Allende off his throne-
Operation 40-
Watergate-
Contras-

The same names coming up again and again-
Oliver North, Klaus Barbie, Gabriel Garcia
Marquez. William Ayers, The Castro brothers, Felix
Rodriguez, Georg W Bush.

The CIA were involved in these events. Che
Guevara had the same code name as Oliver North
and Felix Rodriguez, *and Ciro Bustos had a code
name to match with Felix Rodriguez (Felix Ramos)*

*(Who is Ciro Bustos- one of the names Che
Guevara usesd.)*

(Che used over twenty different names.)
George Bush- (he was Vice-President and
coordinator of the Drug Task Force in 1984)

This explains Michael Levine's frustration when
the CIA blocked his work for DEA-Drug
Enforcement Administration. 'The Big White Lie'
the deep cover operation that exposed the CIA
sabotage of the Drug war.'

There are many cases of drug traffickers being
protected by the then government.
'Inside the Octopus: the Barry Seal Story by Preston
Peet' has a good example, there is a list of people
known to us under the Barry Seal's Boss Hogs.

How Nazi butcher Klaus Barbie helped kill Che Guevara and unleash ...

www.mirror.co.uk › News › World news › World War 2

13.11.2015 - Getty German SS officer and Nazi *war* criminal Klaus Barbie (1913 - 1991) ... him into *Bolivia* where he helped hunt and kill the revolutionary *Che Guevara* . It was a ... Barbie was the ultimate partner in crime for the *drug* lords.

Yes! The CIA SABOTAGED the Drug war. Why they wanted to control it.

(Don't forget who put Klaus Barbie in Bolivia, the CIA.)

(Don't forget who was running the CIA- Gorge H W Bush)

(Don't forget that Gabriel Garcia Marquez wrote a book 'the CIA in Latin America.')

(I tried to get a copy but this book is not available)

Now you can see a different picture emerging. Gabriel Garcia Marquez would have a great interest in seeing drugs from Colombia were moving in these circles, without hindrance. William Ayers was trying to build a Democrat doctrine on the basis of the Weatherman Underground, No wander Giangiacomo Feltrinelli was drawn in; they both wanted to use a hero!

Bolivia is a land with vast estates to produce cocaine as has Columba. Che did not need to disrupt the government, they where happily changing them,

sometimes three times a day. The people did not
need help as they were employed in the production
of the drugs; Bolivia's presidents owned the estates.
Bolivia needed the drug busyness to survive.

Klaus Barbie and William Ayers provide
transport, weapons were exchanged and the drug
shipped to the USA; ton after ton after ton.

Gabriel Garcia Marquez would not want to
increase a drug war in Columba; the main power
struggle had to be outside Columba, away from their
drug poising laboratories.

Was the death party was planned as propaganda
cover to draw attention from the drug war?

The reasons for having made this research are in
'Spies-CIA-Lies-Terrorist-Che Guevara.'

I reject any complaints as I have repeatedly tried to
contact by email, letter or telephone to ask for help
and advice; to use material or photos to present this
study. I was met with a wall of silence.
A true and honest history is every man's right, not a
cloud of propaganda!

In 'Anti-Castro and Cuba 109-12-210 part 1—60'
there is among the very interesting observation. To
explain I will go back the time where my mother
was with members of the said planers of the Granma
trip. (Spies-CIA-Lies-Terrorist-Che Guevara)
The understanding has been to start a revolution
in Cuba. Turn this idea around, to say take over

Cuba; what better place, what better island to use for the trafficking of drugs?

I point out that the Camp Santa Rosa was owned by the president of Mexico wife's family! The members at the camp were preparing a takeover not a revolution; planning a government.

In 'Anti-Castro and Cuba 109-12-210 part 1—60' the documents show that Che Guevara was given Cuban citizenship. The document also points out that all members involved in the 'Granma' production were also given citizenship- they all served in the new Cuban government.

Gabriel Garcia Marquez was behind this extravagant plan from the beginning. He was a leading member of the Colombian government, had very close connections to the Mexican government. Ran film and TV productions, owned the largest news media's. Gabriel Garcia Marquez was always standing close to Fidel Castro.

It may seem strange to add references to an introduction but there are more connections coming up to prove how Che Guevara was created.

Aída Sullivan - Wikipedia, la enciclopedia libre

https://es.wikipedia.org/wiki/Aída_Sullivan Aída *Sullivan Coya* (23 de abril de 1904 – 17 de agosto de 1975) fue la esposa del presidente *Abelardo L. Rodríguez* y primera dama de *México* entre 1932 y ...

Aida Sullivan Coya was wife of Abelardo L Rodrigue, an Mexcan president that sent Emilo

Portes Gil to study aviation; his cousin was Katy Jurado, for whom Gabriel Garcia Marquez wrote parts for; such as Che Guevara's Mother.